W9-AQN-655

CHARITY ON TRIAL

CHARITY
ON TRIAL

DOUG WHITE

BARRICADE
BOOKS

Published by Barricade Books Inc.

185 Bridge Plaza North

Suite 308-A

Fort Lee, NJ 07024

www.barricadebooks.com

Copyright ©2007 by Doug White

All Rights Reserved.

Library of Congress Cataloging-in-Publication Data

A copy of this title's Library of Congress Cataloging-in-Publication Data is
available on request from the Library of Congress.

ISBN 1–56980–301–3

First Printing

Manufactured in the United States of America

IN MEMORIAM

LYLE STUART

The publishing world will never fill the void you have left. You were an intellectual giant, a courageous man who lived what you believed.

PAM BRICKER

The jazz-loving community in Washington, D.C., will forever miss you.

DEDICATION

TAL ROBERTS
Tal fought the good fight—and won—on behalf of all charities.

and

SANDY SCHULTZ
Every day, for far too few but precious years, Sandy showed our small,
diverse Logan Circle neighborhood near 14th and Rhode Island
what compassion is all about.

CONTENTS

ACKNOWLEDGMENTS

WHILE WRITING IS a necessarily solitary experience, no book is completely the product of one person. I am grateful to the following people for their help, insights, and support:

RANDI ABRAMS, who introduced me to *Tzedakah* and the marvelous Jewish philosophy relating to charity;

MARLA BOBOWICK, my first editor and coach, who took time to review this manuscript when I needed her;

JOE BULL, the planned giving director at the Ohio State University Foundation who provided me with much to show that he and Ohio State are first rate;

RICK CAREY, a friend and colleague from our days at Holderness School in the early 1990s, and a gifted writer whose books are filled with passion and compassion;

ROBERTA D'EUSTACHIO, who, upon reading the first draft of a completed manuscript, wisely and gently suggested several conceptual improvements;

STEPHEN Z. GOLDBERG, a professor at Adelphi University, whose honesty permitted me to write with a better understanding of what really went on at this divided campus,

SUSAN KASTAN, a fellow instructor at New York University who provided context for the history of charities as organized entities in the United States;

MARY MISCALLY, who read and corrected the first drafts of the manuscript, ensuring that a publisher would notice it;

JERRY McCOY, one of the finest attorneys in the United States and an expert on all things charitable, who read the manuscript with an eye to ensuring that I wrote as accurately as possible about the way charities are organized and operated;

CAROL NOBLITT, a fundraising colleague who suggested several technical improvements;

LYLE STUART, my editor, who, along with the others at Barricade Books, knew charity to be a compelling and important topic;

ERIC SWERDLIN, who provided invaluable help during the difficult days;

JANIS TOMLINSON, whose suggestions for structure made the narrative much better than it would have been otherwise;

DALE WILLMAN, who, even as he pursued his own dreams of a nonprofit to help save the environment, was a constant source of support during the research and writing of this book.

Of course, no one named above or anyone else is responsible for any factual errors, which are the sole responsibility of the author.

INTRODUCTION

THERE'S A GOOD chance that you are one of the eighty million Americans who make gifts to one or more charities each year. If you are, you'll find this book useful.

Despite an increasing level of scrutiny in the daily press, not much is written about charities for donors and volunteers. Professionals who deal with charities have their resources, but much of that is arcane and of little help to the average donor. Newspaper stories vary in quality. While some are accurate and helpful, others are poorly researched and misleading. Part of the problem is that often the media outlets don't do much of their own research, which means that far too much of the information in the news about one charity or another is furnished by the very people who run the place.

Even though I think they should be accorded a special place in the scheme of human endeavor, charities aren't exempt from human foibles and folly. They are as vulnerable as any business trying to survive and show a profit—or any person who tries, but sometimes fails, to be good.

In these pages, I'll explore some charities that have not done such a good job and others that have been marvelously effective. I'll take you into the charity world and its struggle as seen by Congress and the public. Through it all, I ask that you consider your own relationship with charity—the money and the time you spend on causes that are close to your heart.

Knowledge will make you a better donor.

Doug White
September 2006

PROLOGUE: AN ANXIOUS ALLIANCE

"In Faith and Hope the world will disagree,
But all mankind's concern is Charity."
ALEXANDER POPE "ESSAY ON MAN"

THE WORD CHARITY has a benign sound.

Charity: a way to help our fellow human beings and feel pretty good about ourselves

Think of it. You . . .

give to the poor through the Salvation Army bell-ringers at Christmas;

mail a check to your college or university at the end of the year, so the place will always remain the way you remember it, even though you know it won't;

contribute generously to the hospital where that great doctor and her staff saved your child's life;

intensely need to show gratitude, however insufficient, for that moment your breath was stolen by a Degas painting or a piece of iron sculpted beautifully by someone you'd never heard of;

have a strong impulse, born of upbringing and spirit, to drop a little something each week in the basket during an hour with God.

Actually, with its unfettered connotation of helping others, charity lets us act just a little bit like God.

Charity is vaguely understood by most of us to be neither government nor business. It undertakes work that corporations cannot perform profitably. In fact, in the everyday lexicon of the professionals who work at charities, charitable organizations *are* nonprofits. Many people believe that charities don't earn any money at all. They certainly can't make a profit. Right? They're charities, after all. Charities exist to help poor people, the disadvantaged. As a result, in the public imagination they are themselves poor.

Charity is that other world where good deeds are performed and capable, well-intentioned people run the organization. It is an article of faith that those who are expected to perform the work of angels know what they are doing. And by the way, bless their souls, they surely do it for very little recompense.

This image of poverty, however, is at odds with an oxymoron: what some think of as rich charities—elite Harvard University in Cambridge, Massachusetts, for example, with its huge endowment and wealthy alumni and alumnae; or the tony Getty Museum in Los Angeles, whose major contributors frequently appear in the society pages, where, certainly, nobody looks poor. That image—and add to it the idea of paying people high salaries, as many charities do, or maintaining state-of-the-art communications centers, as many charities also do—does not fit into the widely accepted notion of charity.

But even at charities charged with helping rich people, such as elite universities and art museums—places that aren't even thought of by most people as charities—the money is somehow expected to be spent only for charitable purposes, on furthering the mission of the charity. Charities might pay their employees well—although not as well as the corporate world compensates its people—but the money they spend, whether the charity is rich or poor, is meant for the public's benefit. Even a charity that you might characterize as wealthy is still a charity, and a charity exists to serve the public.

The people in those society-page photographs aren't themselves the sole beneficiaries of the museum's work, are they? Those museum pieces are for anyone to enjoy. And the education offered up at Harvard, for that matter, is for anyone who can get through the rigorous admissions process; it's not just for children of the rich.

Charities are supposed to benefit the public. The dollars they receive are, in a very real way, provided by the public. Not just by the people who donate to charities, but by everybody.

The concept, however, of where their money comes from—the money required to pay salaries and bills, small or otherwise—is usually a fog-laden mystery.

All charities must balance their checkbooks. In that sense, the realities of business are also the realities of charity. The difference is that a charity's product is so much more difficult to understand. Charities ask for support on the basis of an intangible idea. A mission or goal, after all, is much more difficult to sell than a refrigerator or an automobile. What's more, charities usually don't charge market prices for their services. Providing an education, for example, even at an expensive university, requires more expenditure from the school than is exacted in the form of tuition payments.

To make up some or all of the difference, most charities depend on the success of their annual fundraising drives. If the person who gave $10,000 last year does not give the same, or more, this year, cuts may have to be made. If the foundation that regularly contributes $100,000 is unable to match that gift this year, because of a change in its program priorities or a decline in its stock portfolio, people might have to be let go.

Surviving as a charity is not always easy, but somehow, with their never-ending efforts to generate income—some or all from the public's largesse—most charities stay alive to do their good work. Think not of Harvard, with its goal of producing influential graduates. Think rather of the Trappist monk, who, with his quiet prayer and modest lifestyle, embodies the quintessential idea of charity, dedicated as he is to a peaceful world, to the betterment and happiness of all humankind.

In a way, that's not an inaccurate image, for most charities are not large and do not have much in the bank, and yet most perform well in their efforts to make the world a better place. Their absence would hurt the communities they serve.

Chances are good that you've been asked to give to a charity recently. You may have received a phone call early last night from a solicitor asking you to support what sounds like a worthy cause. Your mailbox today may contain several appeals. Perhaps you saw an ad in a newspaper or a magazine promoting a deserving organization.

Even though the media—sensing the growth of charities and their impact on everyone's life—regularly report bad behavior, people continue to give. Despite sexual abuse scandals in the Catholic Church, despite stories of donations used for purposes unrelated to a charity's work, and even despite news of charity officials running off with the treasury—despite all this and more, people continue to give.

So the appeals must do some good. And even though the bad news about charities seems to grow only more plentiful each year, it is also true that if a list of scandals that violate the public trust were to be compiled on the activities of either government or business, that list would be far longer than anything compiled on the activities of charities.

Charities, in fact, do good work, and it is the exception that doesn't do it pretty well. Most are managed by caring and dedicated people who take their responsibilities seriously. Charity—the hundreds of thousands of organizations that collectively perform the work that government agencies cannot and businesses will not—affects the lives of millions of people every day in a positive way. Based on the giving totals, the donating public seems to be okay with charity.

In fact, charity is big business in the United States. Americans donate hundreds of *billions* of dollars to charity every year.

Everybody, it seems, wants to be associated with charity. Corporations go out of their way to make sure people know they are in the good-cause business, not just the profit-making business.

And it's not unusual for elected officials who have received political donations from questionable sources—or at least from sources that have publicly become questionable—to dispose of that tainted money by giving it to charity. They do this, despite how close they were to the disgraced source, so they can be seen as doing the Right Thing.

The Right Thing and Charity are almost synonymous.

DO YOU KNOW If your gift advances the charity's noble mission? Have you ever asked a charity how it spends its money? Where, exactly, does that ten–dollar- or one–hundred–dollar donation go? More specifically, what result can be attributed to your donation?

You won't find the answer to your question, logical though it may be, in the sparse information the larger nonreligious charities file annually with the IRS. Besides, who is inclined to read through IRS forms? And you probably won't find it anywhere else either. The obligation, as it is meant here, goes far beyond a paltry legal requirement; it is an ethical understanding that charities need to be—and should *want* to be—fully open with the public.

Too few charities take seriously their obligation to inform contributors about how the dollars are spent. The amazing thing is that an astonishing number of donors don't seem to care. Newspaper headlines often turn a harsh spotlight on the shameful way some charities operate, but rarely do donors generate groundswells of protest.

The need for a better understanding of how charities operate and raise their money has been growing for many years. Even Congress is taking a stern look. The House Ways and Means Oversight Subcommittee has reported that several charities may be "operating beyond the scope of their tax-exempt charitable status." Such groups, it noted, "are required by law to engage primarily in activities that meet their charitable or stated purpose, and the IRS is charged with reviewing the activities of tax-preferred groups."

What once was a benignly neglected group of organizations is now slowly coming under the kind of scrutiny that few charities either welcome or enjoy. Yet, apart from the charities with which we are intimately familiar, most of us know almost nothing about charities. We don't know if they do what they say they do or if they do it very well. We don't know who sits on the board of directors or even what the board is supposed to do. We have no idea what the board discusses and votes on. Who knows the name or the background of the organization's executive director or who the senior staff people are? Certainly we don't know the ethnic make-up of the charity's leadership, either at the board or the staff level.

We generally don't know what lawsuits the hospital is fighting or if what you're admiring at the local museum is actually stolen art from another country. We don't know what the charity's ethics policies are, or even if it has an ethics policy.

We don't know how financially viable charities are. We don't know how much a charity collected in donations last year; not really, given the accounting tricks the IRS and auditing guidelines permit. And except for what is reported so broadly as to be rendered almost meaningless, we don't know how charities raise their money or how they spend it.

In short, we know nothing, and people have no way of knowing if their charities of choice are performing well. We may *feel* good, but we *know* nothing, and that's not good. And by the way, what does "performing well" mean?

True, the IRS says that a charity needs to meet certain requirements before it is granted tax-exempt status but, with bigger problems to address—the people and organizations that are actually supposed to pay taxes—the IRS almost never follows up to see that the charity stays its course. Some in Congress have complained that the IRS doesn't do a very good job with charities.

Real oversight is left to the attorney general of the state where the charity is located. But except for scandals reported in the press, the public is not likely to be informed about much. In fact, one important source for the attorney general's office *is* the press.

The public should be informed of more than just illegal activities; we ought to know more. And we don't.

Although charities celebrate the growing amount of support each year, that headline may be hiding a more important trend: in recent years donors have become suspicious of how charities perform.

One study, *The 21st Century Donor*, conducted in 2002 by Epsilon, a public relations firm, found that while tens of millions of people still donate to charity each year, the size of the American donor population has fallen to an historic low. The study showed that confidence in nonprofits has declined substantially. In fact, the idea that seems to give rise to our warm-hearted feelings about nonprofits fades away almost entirely under the examination of matters other than mere numbers, matters that may very well have an impact on the amount of money donated in the future. The study examined five attributes—integrity, problem solving, financial efficiency, responsiveness, and effective leaders—and found that nonprofits led the list on none of them.

Paul Light, formerly of the Brookings Institution, in a column for the *Christian Science Monitor* in May 2002, wrote that "public trust in charitable organizations continues to sour. Since September [2001], the number of Americans expressing no confidence in charitable organizations has more than doubled . . . roughly 1 in 5 Americans says they have no confidence in charitable organizations." He further asserted that "trust in charitable organizations did not improve after September 11, unlike the public opinion bounce experienced by virtually every other organization and institution."

Light went on to say that charities can no longer count on positive media coverage or an absence of government scrutiny. He noted that "newspapers have created new charity beats, state attorneys general have taken their lead from New York's Eliot Spitzer, who made a national reputation from beating up on the Red Cross and United Way, and watchdog groups have seized upon the disbursement crisis as proof that the sector needs stricter oversight."

Dampened by concerns over the Red Cross and United Way disbursement delays, public confidence in the charitable sector began declining and continued to drop even after the September 11 funds began flowing.

Can it get worse? Can the public's confidence, the fuel for donations, get to so low a point that charities, dependent on annual gifts, will be forced to close their doors?

And if some did, would that be so bad?

Before we go there, though, perhaps another question should be asked: "Does charity work?" Donors should care about that because, after all, they should feel confident about a charity before they give to it.

The answer is elusive. The self-appointed charity watchdogs would have you believe that the answer is derived solely by measuring and comparing the amounts spent on fundraising and programming as well as other financial data provided to the IRS. But these numbers are too often misleading and irrelevant. Despite the advertised usefulness of its results, the methodology of the watchdogs is crude, and their reports don't help the average person know if a charity is performing well.

Then there is the criticism that many charities aren't charities at all, if you think that real charities are limited to those that assist the poor and the homeless and that the others are just outlets for the rich and intellectual—the elite. Studies have noted that only a small percentage of donations are annually devoted to groups that support human service programs, and that an even smaller percentage go to those that support social change.

Most charitable giving, it is true, funds educational institutions and religious organizations. Should we therefore conclude that higher education and faith-based institutions, as well as all the others—the arts groups, hospitals, and others—are false charities, not worthy of consideration when taking into account society's ills and charities' efforts at trying to cure them? After all, don't these types of charities, particularly many of the faith-based organizations, do a lot to help the poor and disadvantaged? Don't universities provide financial aid for students of poor families? Don't hospitals often provide free or reduced-cost medical care for the poor?

While it is proper to ask, for example, how a homeless shelter contributes not only to the feeding of the homeless but also to their permanent well-being, it is probably going too far to ask charities to solve all of society's woes. Society's woes are ongoing and few are going away. In the 1930s, President Franklin D. Roosevelt found one-third of the nation's citizens ill-housed and ill-fed. That picture hasn't improved much in the more than seventy years since he said it. The poor are better hidden today, but poverty, especially in this rich country, is still a national disgrace.

Brian O'Connell, in his book *Philanthropy in Action*, said that the importance of charity lies not in the performance of any particular set of tasks, but in "the extra dimension it provides for seeing and doing things differently." So, in examining the question of whether charity works, maybe our expectations of charity should be less than that of changing the world altogether. It could be argued that, even collectively, charities are not and cannot be as directly influential in solving social problems as the government ought to be.

Even so, if our goal is to improve society, we need a stronger, more responsive charitable sector.

With all that money pouring into charities every year—an amount that represents a not insignificant slice of our country's gross domestic product—it might seem that society ought to be improved more than it is. That extra dimension, if indeed that is what charity provides, should be visible on some level.

What then does the money buy?

IT SHOULD SURPRISE no one that in America so many people donate so much to those in need at their most dire time. But while the September 11 attacks, the devastating tsunami in East Asia, and the ruin caused by Katrina's wrath in New Orleans and Mississippi—the high-profile crises—have generated the most publicity in recent memory about the generosity of Americans, the idea of philanthropy in this country is expressed every single day.

Perhaps our structure of government makes the difference. No, not the tax code. While the charitable deduction helps people make larger donations, and is the only way for federal and state governments to make a positive statement about the role of charitable giving, the potential for reduced taxation does not instill a personal sense of philanthropy. Instead, just as religious activity is the root of all philanthropy, so it may be that by separating the church—and therefore all future philanthropic organizations—from the government, the founders of our country created a way of looking at helping others that had not been developed before.

Since charities and the public exist in an awkward relationship of dependency—an anxious alliance—the questions remain: What, exactly, is a charity? What about those rich entities that dare to be called charities? Are there really any bad charities, or does the press, as with so many other things, overreact just to sell a juicy story? Do some donors try to control charities too much? Where does all the money go? Would it truly be terrible if so much weren't raised? What's the IRS got to do with it all? What about those upstart watchdogs that claim to tell you just which charities are good and which are bad? Are charities doing what they should with your money? What should you know about how your money is spent? How can you—alone, but with the power of your checking account and your other assets—evaluate charities for yourself? Does charity matter *to you*? And if it does, then just what is it that excites you about a charity?

Let's find out.

PART I
SEVERED TRUST

1

THE UNITED WAY

"Bill Aramony did more to harm local communities than can be easily measured."
UNITED WAY OF CENTRAL NEW MEXICO ON ITS WEB SITE

WILLIAM ARAMONY USHERED in the modern era of charity scrutiny.

In February 1992, Aramony, in response to a public groundswell of criticism and allegations of misconduct, resigned in disgrace as head of the United Way of America. Two weeks later the United Way stopped paying his annual salary and benefits package of $463,000.

After a tenure of twenty-two years, the man who had brought the United Way to unparalleled national prominence and recognition had designed his own downfall. This was a remarkable chapter in the history of a venerable charity, the more so because of where it all started.

IF YOU'VE EVER watched a professional football game on television, you've seen the public service announcements—the ones where a player, almost always a member of one of the two teams in the game being televised, and almost always with his wife and children at his side, promotes the United Way. The message is straightforward: the local United Way does a great deal for the community, helping its citizens by providing financial support to various charities.

Through these ads, we see a gentle side of the football icon, who, minutes before the commercial break, might have used his 300-plus–pound body to brutally mangle the opposing team's quarterback. The message says: football players are real people too, with families and real concerns about their neighbors.

Illustrating social problems that include needy kids with severe medical difficulties and the elderly in need of food or shelter, the sixty-second, made-for-television spots are effective human dramas. The objective is to increase awareness of the United Way's impact on your community.

In return, you, the viewer, may be transformed into a donor. No one in the spots actually asks for any money, but by showing you how much good the United Way does, the charity hopes to persuade you to give. Would that all charities had access to so many millions of potential donors on such a regular basis.

The brand name in football and the brand name in charity made their deal in 1972, and it survives and thrives today. Pete Rozelle, elected in 1960 as the commissioner of the National Football League and looking for a way to improve ratings, and Aramony, who was named head of the United Way in 1970, were visionaries: each was able to see into the future, each was able to take the difficult but concrete steps to make tomorrow better.

A PRIEST, TWO ministers, and a rabbi established the first United Way, in Denver in 1887. Today, the United Way of America is an umbrella organization that coordinates the efforts of 1,330 independent, separately incorporated, local member groups in the United States. Its mission is "to improve lives by mobilizing the caring power of communities."

The local groups in turn work with community partners—schools, businesses, neighborhood associations, and others—to determine the best ways to distribute money to local charities, which, presumably, would not be able to raise as much or raise it as efficiently without the help.

The first United Way raised $21,700 for ten impoverished but important local health and welfare charities in Denver. In 2004–2005, according the national group's Web site, "the United Way system raised $3.6 billion . . . making it the nation's single largest private charity."

The United Way has long been identified with the practice of raising funds from a business's employees, who are asked to donate a portion of each paycheck to the cause. They often don't know exactly how they are helping their community, although they have a sense that the money is going to a good cause.

We can also find on the Web site an outstanding, comprehensive report entitled "Standards of Excellence," which addresses every conceivable aspect of the programs and operations at United Way of America. The public is able not only to scrutinize many of the charity's activities, but also to read the aspirational document that informs those activities.

The United Way of America is doing what it can to be a good public servant.

It has learned the hard way. The lessons are those of scandal, and memories of scandal do not fade fast.

WILLIAM ARAMONY HAD already established himself as an "innovative, creative thinker" as head of the United Way of Dade County in Miami, so when he took the top job at United Way of America in 1970, he insisted that he alone would fill what had been proposed as two top staff positions. His supreme sense of confidence—even the power grab—not only didn't alarm board members, it seems to have impressed them.

Although some saw him as a maverick, Aramony was highly successful throughout his career as United Way's chief executive officer. He is credited with dramatically increasing fundraising, creating many new programs, improving existing programs while making them more efficient, and demonstrating a keen sense of leadership.

After a detailed review of Aramony's accomplishments, John Glaser, in his book *The United Way Scandal*, says that "Bill Aramony's contributions . . . were prodigious by any standard."

Things rapidly began to fall apart in late 1991. Between Thanksgiving and the end of the following February, the *Washington Post* ran articles that were highly critical of Aramony and the United Way. By the time Aramony resigned on February 28, 1992, the public was just beginning to learn how corrupt he was.

After the initial *Post* stories, a flood of damaging articles and editorials appeared in several national and local newspapers that detailed the wrongdoing and gross mismanagement. The charges included accountability problems, coercion, improper for-profit spin-offs, an immense budget to maintain headquarters, a salary that was too high, inappropriate personal perks, and questionable expenses.

Some of those questionable expenses were for a trip—yes, to the Super Bowl.

It is true that national charities with large budgets are complex organizations that require sophisticated accounting systems. Legitimate expenses can sometimes seem questionable, especially to the untrained or jaded eye.

As Bruce Hopkins, one of the nation's premier attorneys in charitable law, wrote in the foreword to *The United Way Scandal*, people tend to be suspicious of charities that employ sophisticated structures.

> This suspicion is grounded in ignorance of contemporary management and fiscal practices and a yearning for simpler days when charities were operating in the red with the assistance of volunteers or staff paid at bare subsistence levels. The benefits of these practices to the charities involved and their beneficiaries are usually overlooked.

True enough—and something to bear in mind whenever the subject of accounting arises. But William Aramony landed on the front pages of the nation's newspapers not because of legitimate, although confusing, modern-day management and accounting practices, but because he almost destroyed the United Way of America.

In fact, part of the damage was due to the way he spent money.

A *Washington Post* article on February 16, 1992, wrote that Aramony hired chauffeured cars that one year cost $20,000. Whether that was excessive depends on the circumstances, but Aramony didn't help himself when he responded with "I can't afford to be waiting for cabs."

In addition, the article reported that Aramony also flew on the now-defunct Concorde to Europe on several occasions. A seat on the Concorde cost more than twice the price of a first-class ticket on any normal airplane.

With news of the Concorde travel and other revelations, more than thirty United Way chapters decided to withhold their dues. A major donor in the National Capital Area chapter, in Washington, D.C., was quoted as saying, "It is particularly profane to have someone in the good work that the United Way has done all across the country be sullied, by finding out the kind of perks and personal leadership that has been revealed."

Another donor lamented the allegations by implying that Aramony had lost touch and really didn't care what America was thinking.

ARAMONY'S DEPARTURE FOLLOWED weeks of elaborate denials of any wrongdoing. In fact, as John Glaser wrote, in early February, just a little over two weeks before Aramony's resignation, Dr. Lasalle Leffall, Jr., the chairman of the executive committee of the United Way, took pains to respond point by point to a syndicated column headed "Charity Begins at Home for United Way," a scathing critique written by Jack Anderson and Michael Binstein.

An early probe—prompted by the allegations in the *Post*—didn't produce much. Berl Bernhard, a partner whose Washington, D.C., law firm did work for the United Way, reported that "there was no misappropriation, no embezzlement, no fraud, no malfeasance in office. There was no finding of diversion for personal enrichment by Mr. Aramony. Period."

He added, however, that "the investigators had found a number of areas that needed improvement, such as sloppy record-keeping, inattention to certain detail and documentation, and certain issues raised about slowness in accounting and expenditures." One result of that initial inquiry was that the travel policies were changed to prohibit supersonic travel. Some United Way staffers might have wondered how many other charities felt the need to point that out.

Because that investigation was less a search for truth than an attempt to cover up and deny serious wrongdoing, the United Way later commissioned another investigation. It was conducted by the same law firm where Berl Bernhard was a partner. Because that firm had such close ties to the United Way, some people thought the resulting report might be a whitewash, as the earlier investigation had been. *The Chronicle of Philanthropy* quoted Walter Annenberg, a major United Way benefactor, as saying that asking that particular firm to investigate allegations of wrongdoing was "like asking a cashier to audit his own books."

Although some people criticized the report for being rushed, it was hardly a whitewash. Released on April 2, 1992, the report revealed that, in the years prior to Aramony's resignation, the United Way improperly spent the following:

- More than $40,000 for airfares on the Concorde;
- More than $92,000 for limousine services;
- More than $33,000 for journeys to or through Gainesville, Florida, although there were no records of any United Way of America business in that area;
- At least $20,000 on meals, entertainment, gifts, clothes, and golf equipment;
- Almost $38,000 on twenty-nine trips to Las Vegas;
- Almost $60,000 on hotel bills in England, France, Norway, Turkey, Germany, Russia, and Italy;
- More than $72,000 on other airfare, sometimes first-class;
- Over $6,000 in December 1989 for first-class airfare for a personal vacation in Egypt.

Prior to the release of the report, the United Way board voted unanimously that, until the legal questions were settled, it would not pay any of Aramony's pension, worth over $4.4 million at the time.

ONE CAN IMAGINE how local chapters around the country were feeling. Employees have their grassroots job of raising money from their communities, they work out of modest offices, they talk to businesses and individuals about the social needs of a particular area—and then the Aramony scandal surfaces.

The Central New Mexico United Way, as of 2006, still felt the need to distance itself from the national organization by answering the following two questions on its Web site:

Q: Is this United Way part of United Way of America?

A: United Way of Central New Mexico is, and always has been, a local organization. In fact, all local United Ways across the US are local organizations run by local volunteers. For each of those 1,400 United Ways, United Way of America serves as a trade association. It is similar to a teachers' association, plumbers' association, or a doctors association. We affiliated with United Way of America in 1972.

United Way of America provides us with training opportunities, research information and national advertising. For these services we pay them a membership fee. United Way of America has no influence or control over United Way of Central New Mexico, nor do we have control over what they do.

Q: What happened a while back with the United Way guy who took money, Bill Aramony?

A: Bill Aramony did more to harm local communities than can be easily measured. He was fired and later convicted of misusing funds for his personal benefit. He was sent to prison for 7 years and was released in September 2001.

Many people still mistakenly believe that local United Ways are chapters of United Way of America. That is not true nor has it ever been true. Each local United Way is, and has always been, run by local volunteers.

Unfortunately, local United Ways continue to suffer because of Aramony's illegal activity with United Way of America. One of the positive things that came out of that negative experience was that local United Ways were given more representation on the UWA Board of Governors. In 1999, for the very first time ever, United Way of Central New Mexico has a representative on the UWA Board of Governors.

Central New Mexico wasn't the only chapter to make clear how far away it was from the national group.

RESPONDING TO THE second report, Aramony said, "I categorically reject any suggestion of misappropriation or breach of trust during my tenure at United Way of America." He then branded the inquiry "a modern day Salem witch trial-by-press release."

When asked whether he would have done anything differently, Aramony said, "I didn't pay enough attention to detail, or the way some of my actions or my personal style could have been perceived by people. I'm a mover and I get things done, but the price I paid for that was not enough attention to detail."

He also didn't tell the truth. He said that he flew the Concorde only two or three times, when in fact he had taken at least nine flights.

Aramony was an arrogant man who gave the impression that he

believed he was a god unto himself. Of course, anyone is entitled to a full airing of the facts. Aramony's problem was that when he got the airing the facts nailed him.

Aramony wanted to resign quietly, with the relatively modest charge that he was merely unwise in the way he conducted himself in office.

That wasn't to be, however. He would be convicted of embezzlement and other crimes so serious that he would spend seven years in jail.

In April 1995, three and a half years after the initial, damaging *Washington Post* article was published, a federal jury found that Aramony and two other top executives at United Way of America were guilty, as *The Chronicle of Philanthropy* put it, of "systematically looting $1.2 million from the organization's coffers." Aramony was convicted of twenty-five counts, including conspiracy to defraud, mail fraud, wire fraud, transportation of fraudulently acquired property, engaging in monetary transactions in unlawful activity, filing false tax returns, and aiding in the filing of false tax returns.

The most serious and comprehensive conviction was for an eleven-part conspiracy charge that had mostly to do with using United Way money for his personal benefit.

The bulk of the convictions involved the interstate transportation of fraudulently obtained money, including over $67,000 charged to United Way of America for personal driving services in New York City.

In addition, Aramony was convicted for charging to the charity over $6,000 for first-class airfare for a vacation to London and Cairo with a woman—a very young woman. He was fifty-nine and she was seventeen at the time. The woman, whose affair with Aramony lasted four years—into her adulthood—testified that during the two years she was employed at the United Way she did "virtually no real work."

In September 1995, he began his time behind bars. The sentence was tough for a white collar crime, but the assistant US Attorney handling the case said it "sends a message to every person responsible for stewardship of charitable funds." Aramony, he said, "engaged in criminal conduct that was catastrophic to charitable giving in the United States."

Shortly after his conviction, Aramony sued to retrieve his $4.4 million pension. The District Court for the Southern District of New York ruled that he could receive a little over $2 million, but later the United

States Court of Appeals reversed that decision and cut Aramony's retirement award to about $7,800.

In June 1999, the United States Supreme Court let stand a lower court ruling that Aramony's seven-year prison term did not exceed federal guidelines.

IN THE SUMMER of 2003, an audit of the United Way of the National Capital Area in Washington, D.C.—one of the 1,330 local chapters—showed that the United Way apparently had learned little from the problems encountered by the national group.

An audit found that Oral Suer, the local United Way's recently retired chief executive officer, invaded a variety of employee benefits through questionable means, took premature payments from his pension plan, and drew advances on his salary that he never repaid. In essence, according to the report, Suer used the organization as his personal bank account.

He took, for example, almost $700,000 of unused sick leave and vacation time, even though he was often away on personal business. He also took $400,000 in cash advances and $180,000 in deferred compensation payments to which he was not entitled.

He charged his United Way credit card to take trips to cities where, although no United Way business was being conducted, his children were attending college. He also used the charity's money to travel to Tampa, Florida, when the Super Bowl was being played there.

The audit named five other top officials spending almost $70,000 in undocumented credit card charges.

Suer also misplayed his beneficence. He personally pledged as much as $9,000 a year to the United Way as charitable gifts, but according to the audit, he made his payments by taking extra money from the organization.

On March 4, 2004, Suer pleaded guilty to stealing almost $500,000 from the organization that he headed for twenty-seven years.

Two years later, in May 2006, Kim Tran, the chief financial officer at the same United Way chapter, resigned. She said that the group exaggerated how much money it raised and didn't manage its accounting books properly.

She told the *Washington Post* that chief executive Charles Anderson—who had been criticized for taking generous salary increases and more than $50,000 in deferred compensation that year—told her, "I want that total as high as possible." The total in question was the amount raised. Tran said, "I don't like being told what to include [in fundraising totals], especially when I don't see the basis for booking it."

The *Washington Post* also reported that the chapter's auditing firm cited "sloppy bookkeeping, lax cash handling procedures, and failure to monitor employee credit card use."

In the spring of 2003, people were surprised when Ralph Dickerson, the head of the United Way of New York City, announced his resignation after thirty-three years in the service of United Ways in St. Louis, Pittsburgh, and other cities. Joseph Calabrese, a leader within the United Way system, said, "He's looked up to by many of his colleagues. We're going to miss him." Dickerson said he had no plans, that it was time, that "it's really straightforward."

It turned out not to be straightforward. Two years later, in the spring of 2006, *The New York Times* reported that "an internal investigation had determined that Dickerson had diverted $227,000 of charitable assets for his personal use" in the two years just prior to his departure.

2

ADELPHI UNIVERSITY

"This is the story of a university that tore itself apart."
THE NEW YORK TIMES FEBRUARY 5, 1997

IN THE FOR-PROFIT world, the chief executive officer's performance is measured almost exclusively by market-driven forces. Shareholders—as well as the public—forgive obnoxious CEOs so long as the value of the stock rises.

Charities don't issue stock and thus don't work that way. As a result, the success of their CEOs—or presidents or executive directors, as they are called—is not measured by profit. Instead, success at charities is measured almost solely by the good work the organization performs. Even then, the measures are so intangible—"good work" is not an objective term—that a charity's board often fails to assign responsibility to the executive director for failing programs.

Even the finances, which are quantifiable (although not always objectively so), are often either outside the executive director's immediate control—nothing like at a for-profit company—or the board takes the view that immediate changes aren't the solution. Change at charities is often slow in coming.

In fact, not acting obnoxiously is a good strategy for incompetent managers to keep their job. Woe to charity executives—even good ones—who do not heed that advice.

FOUNDED IN 1896, Adelphi University is a commuter college located in Garden City, Long Island, not far from New York City. The school enrolls approximately 6,000 undergraduate and graduate students. A quarter of them are over twenty-five years old, and less than half are graduated in under six years.

About 70 percent of those who apply are admitted (the acceptance rate) and about 25 percent of those then decide to enroll (the yield rate). Harvard, by contrast, admits about 10 percent of those who apply, of whom approximately 80 percent decide to enroll.

Even when Harvard isn't the barometer, however, Adelphi is not a highly selective university.

This is not to say that Adelphi is not a good place. Commuter schools around the country educate tens of thousands of students who might not otherwise attend college because of their finances, poor marks in high school, or other life circumstances. Most of the students at Adelphi are taking advantage of an opportunity they would not otherwise be granted.

DR. PETER DIAMANDOPOULOS, an accomplished scholar, was appointed president of Adelphi in 1985. A descendent of an ancient landholding family in Crete, he trained at Harvard and earned a bachelor's degree in the classics, a master's in philosophy, and a doctorate in the history of science. He wrote his dissertation on the subject of morals.

Later, he was dean of the faculty at Brandeis University, near Boston. Associates say that he was greatly influenced by Abram Sachar, the founding president of Brandeis. Sachar created a liberal arts college from scratch that became known for its academic excellence.

Diamandopoulos was then appointed president of California State College at Sonoma before accepting his post at Adelphi in 1985. At the time, Adelphi was in such bad financial shape that many people thought it would soon be out of business.

Diamandopoulos was ambitious, determined to transform Adelphi's reputation from that of a commuter school to one of a solid liberal arts university, perhaps taking a page from the development of Brandeis. To accomplish this he planned to adopt a much more demanding curriculum to attract better students. He decided he wanted to more than double the enrollment from 7,000 to 15,000 students within five years.

Adelphi's marketing campaign included advertisements, reportedly written by Diamandopoulos himself, that began with the catchy, even cocky, headline: "Harvard is the Adelphi of Massachusetts." Considering Diamandopoulos's determination and experience, Adelphi's future looked bright.

But it was not to be. Ten years later, when the university was celebrating its centennial, the place was falling apart.

IT MIGHT HAVE been the living accommodations.

In 1993, Adelphi bought a luxury condominium for just under $1.2 million on New York City's Upper East Side for its president. Presumably, its purpose was to help him raise money when he was in the city. A few years later, as no fundraising had been conducted there, the trustees agreed to grant an option to Diamandopoulos to buy the condominium, as well as its furnishings and its artwork, for $905,000.

When questioned why the university would take a 25 percent loss in a city where real estate prices were rising by the hour, Diamandopoulos scoffed, insisting the investment was sound.

In addition to the New York City property, Adelphi also bought a condominium in Garden City—where Adelphi is located—at a cost of more than $400,000, although it remained unoccupied for much of the time.

The university purchased the properties even though it maintained a Tudor-style mansion, just a few minutes' walk from the president's office, as the official residence for the president. Diamandopoulos explained the two additional properties: "We bought five or six houses as an investment," he said. "I am a businessman and I invest money in stocks and bonds. I invest money in buying houses."

OR IT MIGHT have been the artwork.

University documents would later leave unanswered the obvious question of who paid for the president's personal collection of original art— appraised at over $700,000. The collection included works by Picasso, Calder, and Miró. About this, Diamandopoulos said, "I invest money buying art for the university and other things that enhance the elegance of the institution."The president's spacious office, official residence, and New York apartment displayed the art, but in written statements to investigators, Adelphi officials maintained that the art belonged to the president. They contended that since 1985 the university had bought only one painting, which hung in the Garden City condominium.

OR IT MIGHT have been the salary.

In 1994, Diamandopoulos was paid $523,636 in salary, benefits, and deferred compensation. According to a survey of 477 private colleges conducted that year by *The Chronicle of Philanthropy*, he was at the time the second-highest-paid college or university president in the United States.

Although many charities rely on detailed salary surveys of comparable organizations to provide them with guidelines for determining the compensation of their top people, Adelphi apparently didn't do that back then. Or maybe it did.

The highest paid university president at the time was John Silber, president of Boston University. Silber, as it happens, was a close friend of Diamandopoulos. He was also on Adelphi's board of trustees, as well as a member of the small group within the trustees that approved the president's salary and benefits package. Silber's salary at Boston University that year was $564,000.

ACTUALLY, ALL THREE items—the apartment, the artwork, and the salary—were contentious issues within the Adelphi family. But even they might not have mattered so much if it hadn't been for how lousy things had become.

While the president's housing and compensation were more than generous, Adelphi was tanking. Instead of increasing enrollment, the university was losing students. By 1995, a decade after Diamandopoulos had arrived, enrollment declined from just under 7,000 students to 4,600, a stark contrast to his announced goal of doubling the number of students in half that time.

Worse, Adelphi was accepting nine out of ten applicants; that is, the university's admissions acceptance rate went from 70 percent to an even more dismal 90 percent. As tuition continued to rise, and enrollment dropped, budget troubles forced layoffs and program cuts.

What was left of the school's academic reputation had declined. *The New York Times* used the term "bottom feeder" when describing Adelphi's level of selectivity.

Diamandopoulos's defenders insisted that he deserved every penny of his salary. They painted a different picture, claiming that he was a brilliant, dedicated administrator who straightened out Adelphi's finances, built a $40 million surplus, and renovated the buildings and grounds. As an academic, they said, he advanced Adelphi's mission with a new core curriculum and honors college, all the while raising standards for students.

"They ought to pay him more, and they're going to, if they're given the opportunity." Those were the words of Adelphi's vice president, Igor Webb, in an interview that he later undoubtedly regretted.

Whatever accomplishment Diamandopoulos's supporters cited, feelings of angst and anger were brewing among the faculty. The president of a small, unremarkable commuter college was making more than twice the salary of the President of the United States, and living like a king to boot.

In October 1995, the faculty voted overwhelmingly—131 to 14—to ask for Diamandopoulos's resignation.

Perhaps during his pre-hiring interviewing process, more attention should have been paid to Diamandopoulos's challenges as president of California State College at Sonoma. There the faculty voted three times to censure him and once to convey no confidence, actions that eventually led to his resignation.

The feeling among the Adelphi faculty was that Diamandopoulos was acting like a dictator. It was not that he was headstrong or too narrowly focused or made unpopular decisions—all true in the minds of the faculty, yet also run-of-the-mill complaints about a president from almost any faculty. Instead, the biggest problem was that he punished at whim those who disagreed with him. According to the faculty, if otherwise deserving teachers criticized him, he would make certain that they did not receive tenure.

That's a level beyond obnoxious.

* * *

WHILE THE EXECUTIVE salaries at some charities may seem high, they are certainly not high by a commercial market standard. When we examine the president's salary at Adelphi, we are looking at the issue within the confines of other nonprofit organizations, particularly universities.

The trustees at Adelphi rewarded Diamandopoulos with the kind of salary and benefits that even the presidents of Harvard, Yale, and Stanford did not receive at the time. In what must have been seen as hypocrisy, John Silber—the Boston University president and Adelphi trustee who helped decide the salary of his friend—said of Diamandopoulos's pay, "It doesn't take nearly as much effort to run Harvard as it does to direct an institution like Adelphi."

That, of course, is simply not true. But let's compare for a moment the fundraising picture at Adelphi to, say, Stanford, another university in that elite group that Diamandopoulos desperately wanted his school to join.

In 2003, Stanford raised $1.2 billion while spending slightly more than $45 million to attract and collect it. That's a little under four cents spent to raise each dollar.

Adelphi in that same year raised a total of just under $6.5 million while spending $740,000 on fundraising. That's about eleven cents to raise each dollar. While the cost falls well within an acceptable range for those who care about such things, Adelphi's effort was, in fact, three times less efficient than Stanford's.

Adelphi was no Stanford and undoubtedly never can be. The problem isn't that Adelphi struggles and, even though it provides a valuable service, probably always will. The problem is that its president and trustees treated the place as their playground. They were oblivious to the realities of the university's finances, as well as to the growing resentment on campus among both students and faculty.

AFTER THE HIGH salary and the luxury condominium became public knowledge, the newly formed Committee to Save Adelphi began its effort to oust Diamandopoulos. The group included faculty, students, parents, alumni, former trustees, and former administrators. (Perhaps current administrators feared for their jobs.)

In the spring of 1995, the committee asked the State Board of Regents to fire Diamandopoulos, as well as the trustees, for mismanagement and conflicts of interest. The Committee to Save Adelphi called Diamandopoulos's benefits excessive, accused the trustees of "conflicts of interest for doing business with Adelphi," and contended that "Adelphi is not carrying out its mission." Ousting the president would be a difficult task, but, as one member of the committee later said, "We were inspired by the William Aramony story at the United Way of America a few years earlier."

The Committee to Save Adelphi held a news conference and presented university documents to show just how bad things had gotten. But in spite of mounting evidence that serious problems infested Adelphi, the oblivious trustees were satisfied there were none. The trustees firmly and publicly rejected the faculty's claims, and, ignoring reality, backed the administration. The only misconduct apparent to the trustees, it seems, was on the part of a handful of misguided agitators.

Long Island's *Newsday* admonished the trustees for their lack of candor in a commentary entitled "Let the Public Know What's Going on at Adelphi."

Adelphi University's overpaid president and underworked trustees got what they asked for when the state Education Department started looking into their performance . . . But they've also still got a parallel investigation by the state attorney general's office that they were trying to cut off.

Serves 'em right. The way these people have been stonewalling, the state may need more than one probe to get to the bottom of the charges raised by the Committee to Save Adelphi.

The issue is whether the Adelphi board has exercised proper control over its own members' business dealings with the Garden City university or the salary and perks of President Peter Diamandopoulos. . . .

The unresolved questions are hurting Adelphi, its students and its faculty. The Olin Foundation, which has given the university $700,000 to hire professors, says it will give no more.

In February 1997, after twenty-seven days of hearings, and in a truly rare action, New York State's Board of Regents fired the Adelphi board.

Eighteen of nineteen trustees—one member had only recently joined and was untainted—were gone, dismissed for neglect of duty and misconduct.

The Regents condemned the trustees for granting excessive compensation to Diamandopoulos, failing to review his performance, and allowing some trustees to engage in private business with the university.

The Regents appointed a new board, which then immediately fired Diamandopoulos. (Only trustees have the authority to remove a university president in New York.)

Diamandopoulos fought to stay on as a tenured professor, but the new board went to court to oppose him. Diamandopoulos countersued; the state attorney general sued the former trustees to recover misspent money; they then sued the Board of Regents.

It was a mess.

In November 1998, Adelphi agreed to a settlement with the Regents. The agreement recovered $3.5 million for Adelphi. This included $1.45 million from the insurance company that indemnified the former trustees and officers, and payments of $1.23 million from the former trustees themselves.

The trustees also had to pay more than $400,000 in legal bills. Diamandopoulos was forced to refund nearly $650,000 to Adelphi and to pay more than $100,000 in rent on the Manhattan apartment, which he also agreed to vacate.

Diamandopoulos, who sued for more than $4.5 million, was permitted to keep $1.8 million in deferred compensation and interest, and received nearly $400,000 more in settlement of his counterclaim against Adelphi for breach of contract. After his reimbursements to Adelphi, he received approximately $1.4 million—about $650,000 after taxes—according to the new board chair.

The settlement ended all the litigation. Neither Diamandopoulos nor the former trustees admitted any wrongdoing.

But it was clear that the good guys had won.

A new president was named, and enrollment surged, after having declined more than 60 percent during the Diamandopoulos administration. The freshman class for the following academic year was twice the size of the previous year, and total enrollment was up 5 percent.

After leaving Adelphi in disgrace, Diamandopoulos went to Boston

University, where his supporter John Silber had been president, to teach philosophy.

A FEW DECADES ago, there was a young woman who did not attend college right after her high school graduation, because she had to get a job and earn money. She then married and had a child. After some years she attended Adelphi, was graduated, and then worked in the New York State educational system as a high school principal, a dream she had nourished since her childhood.

She didn't want to be President of the United States and she didn't want to head up a large corporation. She wanted to teach. She wanted to be an administrator at a school where the students are young and their minds are growing. She also wanted to be a good mother and wife.

When the person who told me this story recounted it originally, to the then newly appointed Diamandopoulos, it was intended as a tribute to the value of Adelphi, but Diamandopoulos's response went this way: "Adelphi is not for losers."

Think about that.

Is a person who struggles a "loser"? Besides, can't a loser become a winner through hard work? Or is the judgment, even granting that it might be accurate, permanently damning? How much more distant from a university's purpose can a president be?

What of the loser in Diamandopoulos's mirror?

Diamandopoulos spent ten years at Harvard obtaining three academic degrees. His doctoral thesis was on the subject of ethics.

Diamandopoulos, who was fond of quoting Plato, said once that the job of an educational institution "is to reorient the souls of the students." Wouldn't a student conducting research for a thesis on morals stumble across the positive role of humility in the ethical development of the soul?

Perhaps an equally lofty goal during the Adelphi crisis would have been for Diamandopoulos to reorient his ego.

On his seventy-fifth birthday, in 2003, he looked back on his years on Long Island and said that he was not emotionally involved any longer and that he enjoyed his teaching.

He also spoke proudly about how his students appreciate the complex nature of ethics.

THE BAPTIST FOUNDATION OF ARIZONA

*"State officials have determined that the Baptist Foundation of America . . .
is thought to have perpetrated the largest charity scam in United States history."*
PHOENIX NEW TIMES, OCTOBER 21, 1999

AT THE END of 1997 the Baptist Foundation of Arizona claimed that over the years it had raised more than $450 million. In that year alone, according to the foundation's literature, $31 million was established that would "someday help more than 130 Southern Baptist and non-Southern Baptist charities."

When somebody asked what all that meant, whether the Foundation was really doing all that well, William Crotts, the foundation's president, replied with this non-answer: "We welcome every opportunity to share our 50-year history of growing an endowment that helps house, clothe, educate and feed children, the elderly and the needy."

That was just before the charity went bankrupt, shut down and awash in scandal, lies, and enormous financial losses.

THE BAPTIST FOUNDATION of Arizona—BFA—was started in 1948 by the Arizona Southern Baptist Convention. Its mission was to raise money to support Southern Baptist charities.

The Foundation's focus broadened over time, so that fifty years later its purpose also called for providing resources and expertise to Arizona Southern Baptist charities. Those resources and that expertise included providing estate planning and financial services for people who had a high probability of leaving some of their assets to Baptist charities.

BFA took in gifts that would be placed directly into its endowment or into trusts. Gifts made directly and put into the endowment would immediately help charities since BFA had the machinery to distribute money to its Baptist charities.

Benefits from the gifts made in trust would normally be delayed until the donor's death. At that point, the money in the trusts would be transferred to BFA's endowment, at which time the benefit to the other charities—payments from BFA—would begin. During the time the money was in trust, as is the case with most charitable trusts, the income it threw off was paid to individuals, usually the donors who provided the money to establish the trust.

In either case, however—outright gifts or gifts in trust—once the money was in the endowment, only the investment income or a pre-determined percentage of the endowment would be paid out to the charities.

In addition to raising money for Christian causes, BFA operated the Baptist Senior Life Ministries, retirement centers in three states with more than 1,200 residents. According to BFA literature, it was the largest non-profit retirement system in Arizona. BFA also owned the Foundation Housing Corporation, which operated low-income housing projects.

Its literature informed prospective donors that through its fifty-year history BFA provided more than $1.3 million in gifts to the Arizona Southern Baptist Convention for church work and other endeavors, and that in 1997 it loaned approximately $6 million to Grand Canyon University and $150,000 to Arizona Baptist Children's Services.

A brochure explained to potential donors the sorts of charities to which BFA would distribute money:

> We are a ministry dedicated to serving the Lord and furthering Southern Baptist and other Christian ministries.
>
> We reinvest your money, and the profit we earn goes to further such ministries as Christian education, care for children and senior adults, missions and new church starts.

Your investment actually touches the lives of countless numbers, while you earn a very attractive interest rate.

In that last sentence are some of the concepts that illustrate the language of planned giving. This is when donors make gifts that pay an income to the donor with the principal going to a charity after the donor dies. During the life of the donor the principal is *invested* and the donor gets the *attractive interest rate*.

An important concept here, often confusing to the public: although it sought donations from the public, BFA was not an "end charity"—it didn't actually help people directly. Instead, it accepted donations on behalf of other, usually small, charities—schools, churches, and other groups—that lacked the sophistication and technical expertise that BFA could provide.

BFA charged fees for its services. It tracked, in what it called "Ministry Investments," the time, talent and services rendered by BFA staff, and calculated these costs to be $2.7 million in 1997.

CHARITIES TEND TO be expansive when talking about how much money they raise, and there's no real way to check up on them. A lot goes into fundraising numbers and too many charities do a poor job of explaining them. Most people get a different and inflated impression from the reality the numbers are supposed to represent. (This is the problem that the chief financial officer of the United Way in Washington, D.C., cited when she resigned.)

Acquiring the gifts, recording them, and accounting for them can get complicated. Nothing's wrong with any of it, as long as all of the work is done properly, but, with enough guile, the numbers can often be made to seem something that they're not.

Donors deserve accurate, easy-to-understand reports on income and expenses. Although the entire picture can be complex, it is not all that difficult for a charity to say what it actually raised—the amount it actually received—over the period of a year. Yet, many times the picture is anything but clear—or accurate. Considering what was going on in other parts of BFA's books, it would have been especially valuable to have the details of the endowment picture.

While some of the $450 million BFA had claimed to raise was money actually in the bank or transferred into BFA-managed trusts, the number also included a lot of *revocable* promises—money from people who said they intended to leave something for the foundation in their will. Charities call these promises "bequest intentions."

People can change their minds on a whim. Or their financial circumstances can change and force them to remove the charitable designation from their will. Most don't, but, when a charity adds up bequest intentions as if they were money in the bank—and they were included in BFA's $450 million total—the number is nothing more than a deceptive ruse. Good charities don't do this. They may let the public know what people have promised will arrive in the future, but good charities make sure they distinguish between now money and later money.

Furthermore, of what was actually invested, a large portion generated interest for donors during their lifetimes. Only the income from a fraction—less than one-fifth—was actually helping charities.

There were essentially three categories of money that added up to the $450 million:

- Money in the endowment where its income was available for charities;
- Money in trust where the income was paid to individuals and was not available for charitable purposes;
- Money that could not be counted as real assets, but which had been promised, usually as a bequest intention.

The sum of the first two categories seems to have been $84 million—less than one-fifth—which BFA said it was "managing." This meant that the far vaster sum, $366 million, was in the third category—the vapor category. Not only did it not exist, unlike money in trusts with concrete terms, there was no assurance it would ever arrive.

Given the overall picture here, one imagines that income from only a tiny portion of the $84 million was actually available to help charities.

Basically, 80 percent of the highly touted $450 million—and probably more—was helping no one except individual donors.

* * *

WERE IT NOT for the muckraking of the *Phoenix New Times*, the alternative newspaper in Phoenix, the public—and the Arizona attorney general—might have discovered the fraudulent schemes much later than they did.

The *New Times* began asking questions in early 1998 and never let up. In an article in its April 16 issue, the paper published a several-part report packed with scathing allegations.

- The Baptist Foundation of Arizona was chartered to raise money for religious charities but instead favored financing real-estate empires for insiders, invested in speculative land deals, and squandered money on lavish offices, inflated salaries, and fancy automobiles for its staff.
- At the same time, its philanthropic donations to Southern Baptist causes were a pittance.
- The Foundation made loans of nearly $140 million to companies controlled by one sitting director and two former directors. The directors converted these loans into highly speculative real estate deals.
- BFA records are clouded by a complex web of 63 interlocking companies—a maze that allowed BFA to insulate the transactions even from members of its own board of directors. Despite the veil of secrecy, records examined by *New Times* during the past six months show that BFA ledgers have been inflated by improbable stock transactions and blue-sky real-estate appraisals.
- While BFA claims it has never missed a payment to its religious investors, its current liabilities suggest a day of reckoning is at hand.

The *New Times* asked for answers to written questions about BFA's financial transactions. In response the paper received an unhelpful and less-than-candid letter from BFA explaining its policies.

BFA said it worked through several for-profit and nonprofit corporations, a structure "dictated by regulatory, tax, and liability considerations."

The letter explained, "In America today, nonprofit organizations commonly form for-profit companies to capture unrelated business income, which is then taxed by the IRS. This national model is followed by BFA. Each for-profit and nonprofit entity complies with applicable laws and regulations."

In its printed materials, BFA insisted that its books were kept in accordance with Generally Accepted Accounting Principles (GAAP), the ultimate accounting reference. The foundation also said it delivered its audited financial statements and budgets annually to the convention. The financial statements were audited by—yes—Arthur Andersen, and had been for fourteen years. The auditors, it was said, followed all of the cash that came into the foundation.

"They know where it is invested and with whom it is invested," BFA said. "To the extent there are related-party transactions, they are disclosed in accordance with GAAP in the notes to the financial statements."

And then, "All of BFA's assets are recorded on the books at the 'lower of cost or market value,' which ensures a conservative value for the listed assets." BFA cited, as an example, a residential community it owned. In 1998, it was believed to be worth $19 million. Years before it had been purchased for $12 million. As far as BFA was concerned, however, the property was on the books at the more conservative $12 million.

Another example showed that stock the group owned at New Century Financial Corporation, worth $29 million, was carried on the books as only a $7 million asset.

As for its investment policies, BFA said its overhead was covered by a return on its investments, that it could not rely on current gifts to fund all its operating needs. With that comment, BFA was responding to growing general criticism of charities that spent too much of what they raised on administrative costs rather than programming. It asserted that it did not "conduct any fund drives to raise operational resources."

It then contended that it invested in "arenas in which our staff, and particularly our Board, has experience and expertise." This meant a lot of real estate. But BFA also had "diversified into operating properties and venture capital companies." The board was "unwilling to invest large sums of money in the stock market because of the potential for extreme losses in short periods of time that could adversely affect the funding of our mission." BFA characterized itself as an "opportunistic investor seeking investments that offer significant returns without inordinate risk," saying it sought, like all investors, undervalued assets.

Further, even though it wasn't a bank, BFA acted like one. It loaned money on assets that it thought—or said that it thought—were undervalued. This approach, the public was told, was conservative and prudent, and allowed the group to meet its "investment objectives needs."

The board also said in its response to the *New Times*, "We take very seriously our service" and "our responsibility to BFA's mission and constituency."

IN OTHER WORDS, the money wasn't safe. Nowhere near.

That entire last section is filled with nothing except BFA's nonsensical corporate-speak balderdash. Nothing more than gibberish meant to stave off—or impress—the casual reader

Note, for example, the questionable explanation of its affinity for venture capital funds. BFA claimed that it was "unwilling to invest large sums of money in the stock market because of the potential for extreme losses in short periods of time."

While all markets have the potential for losses, venture capital funds are, in fact, more likely to incur them, at least more dramatically. Venture funds are positioned to post phenomenal gains, but the swings there are much wider than in the traditional markets—and that makes investing in venture funds a risky business. Only a small portion, if any, of a prudently invested portfolio, should include them. Preferring venture funds over stocks in Standard and Poor's Index is a strategy that contradicted BFA's stated objective: to be conservative and avoid inordinate risk. When the stock market tanks, the first sector of the market to collapse—even though the funds aren't publicly traded—is venture capital.

What was worse, although no one could have known this at the time, BFA was slyly attempting to hide egregious crimes.

You can imagine the reaction at BFA when, as it was actively promoting itself as an instrument of God, its veneer was being pulled back by reporters whose publication—the *alternative* newspaper in Phoenix, after all—could be identified with liberal and ungodly views about sex, gambling, and other so-called sins strongly condemned by BFA. But hypocrisy works that way.

FIRST AMONG THE hypocrites was the BFA executive director, William Crotts, who had inherited the job from his father. Although the Baptists are strictly opposed to gambling, the *New Times* reported what could best be described as a mammoth gambling scheme by Crotts.

BFA claimed it was a $368 million organization that borrowed money and invested it in real estate, with profits returned to Southern Baptist causes. The loan markers were held by churches and the public. All were promised high rates of return.

In an effort to disguise what, in a for-profit company, would be called insider trading, the foundation created no fewer than sixty-three for-profit and nonprofit companies to borrow that money—approximately $265 million as of early 1998.

The insiders did well with their advantages. One BFA director and two former directors, as the *New Times* reported, "received nearly $140 million worth of loans in complicated real estate and stock transactions with BFA." Incredibly, most of the board members were not informed of these transactions. Crotts learned how easy it is to keep a board ignorant when financial reports lack detail and board members don't ask questions.

THE TERM "SELF–DEALING" is important in the world of charities: it's important to avoid. It means a charity must not benefit the people closest to it, such as the executive director or board members.

For example, if the executive director wants to borrow $100 from the charity, is it permissible for the charity to make the loan? What if the charity agrees to a repayment plan that is inconsistent with good business practices? What if it makes that loan with either a lower-than-market interest rate or a long period of time to repay the loan? What if the charity is in fact completely controlled by the person requesting the loan?

Self–dealing violates the law, and in the case of BFA self–dealing was in the millions of dollars. These transactions were unknown to the public in part because BFA was not required to, and did not, file its financial position with the IRS, and because Arizona did not require many of the BFA affiliates to file annual reports with the Arizona Corporation Commission (ACC).

That meant BFA was accountable only to its board of directors—which should have been a high authority, but, perhaps out of deference to its scheming executive director, did not seem interested in knowing very much.

The *New Times* investigation found that nonprofit and for-profit companies controlled by a former BFA board member, Jalma Hunsinger, owed BFA $125 million, or about one-third of the foundation's total assets. Of that amount, the for-profit companies that he controlled owed BFA $67 million. But at the end of 1996, Hunsinger told the ACC that his for-profit umbrella corporation had a *negative* net worth of $116 million.

Meanwhile, Hunsinger's nonprofits owed BFA almost $60 million. In documents filed with the state in 1996, those nonprofits reported a net worth of $11 million. That meant that entities with a net worth of negative $105 million dollars owed BFA $125 million, and, despite the certainty that no one would ever see a dime of it, BFA had the $125 million on its books as a legitimate asset.

Many of Hunsinger's Arizona corporations were managed by BFA. In fact they shared BFA's Phoenix address and designated a BFA staff attorney as statutory agent. The attorney represented Hunsinger on real estate transactions involving both BFA and Hunsinger.

Another former board member, Harold Friend, had borrowed $2 million from BFA.

THE RESEARCH CONDUCTED by the *New Times* revealed that board member L. Dwain Hoover made a gift of real estate in 1996 that the foundation recorded for $3.1 million. Yet a few years later the market value of the land, which was near a ski resort, was only $151,990, according to Mesa County Assessor documents.

Hoover was involved in at least four other real estate transactions with the foundation. By December 1996, BFA held notes totaling almost $12 million from Hoover.

When the *New Times* asked BFA to explain why it allowed a sitting director to borrow the money, the response was: "Director A [as Hoover was identified in the documents] did not borrow from BFA, but rather purchased assets for approximately $11.8 million in 1996. He paid $2,974,937 as a cash down payment and gave a carryback note of $8,825,063. That note has been paid down to $3,259,310 as scheduled under the terms of the note. This produced to BFA a profit of $4.4 million."

The *New Times* then noted that "the foundation did not provide any documentation to support the claim, did not say what the 'purchased assets' were and did not say whether Hoover paid down his note with cash, stock or land."

Arizona law prohibits directors from borrowing from nonprofit organizations. Yet BFA asserted in its letter to the *New Times*, "No laws were violated because Hoover did the deals with BFA's for-profit subsidiary companies."

BFA BORROWED MONEY from people who were told the foundation was doing God's work and then loaned the money to insiders—and did a bad job of it. Interest-bearing liabilities totaled $335 million, while interest-bearing assets totaled $173 million. BFA's liabilities were twice as much as its assets.

Even when payments were made against the loans, the asset wasn't real money. The insiders paid off large loans with stock in their own companies and with real estate. BFA then re-sold some of those non-cash assets to other insiders for huge paper profits.

The foundation spent about half its $69 million operating budget on salaries and administrative expenses. The *New Times* investigation found that:

> In 50 years, BFA itself has given only about $1.3 million to the Southern Baptist community—for new churches and other good works. This may be because its expenses are high. In 1995 alone, BFA spent about $329,000 on staff automobiles. It spent $16 million on staff salaries in 1996. High-profile causes such as Arizona Baptist Children's Services, which cares for children in crises, and Rio Vista Mission, which helps feed the hungry, have struggled financially and suffered cutbacks in services. BFA has not provided either any direct aid, although it has loaned about $150,000 to the children's agency.

BFA reported that it returned $1.7 million to Southern Baptist causes in 1997, but did not disclose how much of that $1.7 million it returned to itself, since BFA was itself a charitable cause.

Clearly the insiders benefited from their bogus loan deals, pumping up the balance sheet with assets that didn't exist while enriching insiders close to the foundation.

Over 10,000 people contributed to BFA. Their money, swishing into thin air, had been given as an act of faith by those who believed in the Baptist Foundation of Arizona and the people who led it. But the charity, taking advantage of its own supporters, took the seductive step that good organizations with an ethical backbone don't: it turned the merely complicated into the deeply and devastatingly devious.

ON APRIL 15, 1996—two years and one day *before* the *New Times* published the first of its many scathing articles—W. Kyle Tresson, executive vice president of Foundation Housing Corporation, one of BFA's subsidiaries, resigned. His letter was long, filled with apologia and grief. In the excerpts that follow, "Bill" is William Crotts, BFA's president, and "Tom" is Thomas Grabinski, BFA's vice president and general council. Both were recipients of the letter.

> Over the last several weeks I have become aware and increasingly concerned . . . about the large debt owed . . . to BFA, and that the relationship between these entities had not been fully disclosed to either the Foundation Board of Directors or the . . . auditors.
>
> During those meetings, Tom and Bill provided their rationale for deciding against a full disclosure to the Board or the auditors. With regard to the Board, you reasoned that telling them would, in your words, "cause the BFA to hit the wall."
>
> Indeed, Tom, you even admitted that perhaps you were "playing God to the Board"—believing that telling them would result in a collapse of the BFA.
>
> Tom and Bill . . . you . . . refuse to make full disclosure to the Board. Non-disclosure was and continues to be wrong.
>
> I am convinced that you honestly fail to appreciate the moral, economic and legal gravity of your actions.
>
> You have indicated that you do not question your ten-year silence. You recognize that full disclosure to the full board would in all likelihood bring the ministry of BFA to an end and cause the many investors at BFA to lose substantial millions of dollars. However, when the end (the ministry) requires the compromise of honesty and integrity the means is never justified, regardless of the magnitude of the ministry.
>
> I know you believe that given time, a work-out of this situation is

achievable. In the absence of Board oversight and involvement, I do not share your optimism. Indeed . . . time is your enemy.

Legally, the current situation is fraught with liability. Beginning with the first transfer of bad assets nearly ten years ago to a so called "bad bank" which would not be audited but which you controlled through an outside party, there was actionable fraud.

Not only have you placed yourselves in a position of civil and criminal liability for your actions, but you have likewise placed the auditors, directors and even innocent officers in positions of civil liability.

In my opinion this situation is tragic.

In the summer of 1999, the Arizona Corporation Commission told the Baptist Foundation to stop selling investments because it was violating the Arizona Securities Act.

BFA filed for bankruptcy later that year.

On October 21, 1999, the *New Times* reported that the state "determined that the Baptist Foundation of America . . . owes about $540 million to investors and is thought to have perpetrated the largest charity scam in United States history."

In January 2001, the ACC filed a civil lawsuit against Arthur Andersen, claiming that the company misrepresented the foundation's financial condition. The Arizona State Board of Accountancy filed a lawsuit against Arthur Andersen seeking $600 million in restitution for victims. It charged that the company's failure to reveal the true nature of BFA's financial status cost investors millions of dollars.

BFA stayed afloat by getting new investors to help meet its financial obligations and hiding bad investments, while, according to the attorney general, "most of the foundation's upper management were paid six-figure salaries and received generous benefits." Janet Napolitano, the Arizona attorney general (later governor), declared that "the BFA case is one of the largest affinity fraud cases in U. S. history" and noted that investors lived in all fifty states and ten foreign countries.

On March 1, 2002, the attorney general announced an agreement with Arthur Andersen for $217 million, an amount that settled all civil and administrative claims against Andersen involving the Baptist Foundation of Arizona. This canceled the class-action lawsuit against the firm over its failure to warn investors about the foundation's financial difficulties. This meant that, combined with BFA's $220 million in assets, victims, many of whom had invested their life savings, were able, according to the attorney general's news release, "to recover up to 83% of the money they invested."

The settlement was the largest victim-restitution award ever obtained by the state of Arizona. In addition to the financial payment, Andersen partner Jay Ozer and audit engagement manager Ann McGrath, both of whom had primary responsibility for Andersen's audits at BFA, lost their Certified Public Accountant's licenses.

"These investors, many of whom are elderly, trusted the misleading financial statements audited by Andersen," said Napolitano. "This agreement will allow Baptist Foundation victims to recover most of their investment."

Yet, as if some force were at work trying to make this story just as bad as it could be, Andersen tried to renege on its agreement, saying its insurance carrier would not make the payment. At the end of March, when she heard of Andersen's decision, Napolitano said, "This is an absolute outrage. This shows that Andersen and its representatives pretended to negotiate in good faith, but in fact never had any intention of making good on their part of the settlement. Here we see that Andersen chose to victimize BFA's victims yet again."

After several punitive measures were called for against Anderson, the firm changed its mind. On June 5, 2002, Anderson made good on its promise—with zero days to spare, since its agreement called for full payment on or before June 4, 2002. Arthur Andersen, once a venerable giant in the accounting world, no longer exists, a victim of its own widespread fraud. The Baptist Foundation of Arizona, however, was small potatoes: Andersen also cooked the books for Enron and WorldCom.

On May 4, 2001, Napolitano announced that five of the top people at BFA had been indicted by a grand jury on thirty-two counts of fraud, theft, and conducting an illegal enterprise. The indictment said that $550 million had been stolen.

Napolitano accused the defendants of playing key roles in "defrauding thousands of investors who put money into BFA investments." Investors were misled by being told that the accounts paid interest greater than most banks would pay and that the profits would benefit Baptist causes.

Why did those "leaders" do it? A professor at Grand Canyon University, a Southern Baptist school, said, "Evil can be very present even under people with a religious façade." Paul Nelson, the director of the Evangelical Council for Financial Accountability, which monitors religious foundations and charities, was quoted as saying of William Crotts and the others, "I don't know what's in the hearts of these people. Whether they set out to do something right and have done it the wrong way or whether this really is something they set out to do so they could perpetrate a fraud on the public. God alone knows their hearts."

NEW ERA

"The collapse of a double-your-money fundraising scheme may have seriously damaged the credibility of many American charities."
THE CHRONICLE OF PHILANTHROPY, JUNE 1, 1995

WOULD YOU BELIEVE someone who told you that he or she could guarantee to double your money in six months? Unless you were the world's prime lollypop, you'd decline the generous offer.

Yet many educated and seemingly smart people once said yes to just such a sucker offer. They were responding to a man who couldn't run a successful business, was always in imminent danger of bouncing his checks, and who seemed to lie every time he opened his mouth.

John G. Bennett, Jr., made Charles Ponzi who promised to double people's money in ninety days seem like an insignificant panhandler. A failure as a businessman, and seeking to replenish his emaciated checking account, Bennett managed to defraud more than 1,000 charitable organizations from 1989 to 1995. Had he succeeded, his take would have exceeded $350 million.

But then, sure as gravity, there was no way he could have succeeded.

Bennett created the "Foundation for New Era Philanthropy," and a program called "New Concepts," to cheat people and organizations who wanted to be do-gooders to the world.

It's amazing how gullible humans can be. The scandal involving New Era epitomizes what's wrong with using all heart and no brain to make charitable donations. Worse, the vast majority of giving decisions were made not by individuals representing themselves but by people who worked at charities, people who worked in the treasurer's office, people paid to be fiscally responsible and for whom skepticism was not a foreign concept.

But, these are the people who were victims of a shallow con game.

Greed is the hunger to possess beyond one's needs. It is the notion that you can get something for nothing or for very little—an insatiable longing for something that, without earning it, becomes yours.

Yes, to get richer quicker is part of the everyday American dream, but most people work hard and are realistic enough to discern the times when wanting is good or bad. History is, of course, littered with examples of excessive desire; it is, after all, one of the ugly sides of the human condition. Unchecked, it invites disaster.

The most common of all schemes that involved playing on investor greed was the Ponzi scheme, the quintessential example of crowd gullibility. But in the annals of charity, the term "New Era" may very well replace the Ponzi scheme.

THE FOLLOWING MATERIAL was filtered from two sources: *You Can't Cheat an Honest Man* by James Walsh and the Web site of Thayer Watkins, professor of economics at San José State University.

Charles Ponzi was a loser—a failed and unhappy man. Named Carlos when he was born in Italy, he arrived in New York City at the age of fifteen. Almost immediately he set out to acquire money.

He didn't do well in this quest and spent time in various prisons throughout the country for mail fraud, passing bad checks, and conducting an illegal immigration scam. Then he migrated to Boston, where he stumbled on what he would later refer to as his "Great Idea."

The vehicle that he believed would make him rich was something called the postal coupon. The idea was to arbitrage the different values of postal coupons from various countries. He would make profits by taking advantage of the currency price differences in various countries. In this age of the Internet and the Euro it may be hard to imagine what went on, but this is how it went down—and how the term "Ponzi scheme" became a part of our vernacular.

AT THE BEGINNING of the twentieth century people in many parts of the world would include a coupon in their letter to someone in another country, and the recipient could exchange the coupon for postage stamps.

In August 1919, Ponzi received an international postal reply coupon from Italy. The coupon could be exchanged in the United States for postage stamps.

Poor countries sold their postal reply coupons for less than rich countries did, and Ponzi figured out that these could be redeemed in the United States for a profit. Ponzi also noticed that the coupon sent to him from Italy had been bought in Spain. This, he realized, was because the price in Spain was lower than it was in Italy. Also, because of the exchange rate between the dollar and the peseta, the cost was lower than in the United States.

In that discrepancy Ponzi saw his golden opportunity. Dollars could be converted into pesetas, which would be used to buy postal coupons in Spain, which would be sent to the United States to be converted to American stamps, which would then, for a dramatic profit, be sold for dollars. The company he formed when he began to exploit the coupons was called the Security and Exchange Company—his own SEC more than a decade before the federal government's Security and Exchange Commission was created.

His great idea didn't succeed, however, because the red tape at postal organizations ate up any profits. What's more, the discrepancy would self-correct, and the profits would disappear when enough people figured out what was going on.

But Ponzi wasn't the kind of guy to ponder long about that last problem. Besides, "long-term" didn't fit into his profit-making lexicon. Even though he was discouraged, he realized that people had been interested in his activity. To him, the investment made sense, and even though he knew it didn't work, it gave birth to what people now know as the Ponzi scheme.

In December 1919, Ponzi began borrowing money with promises to repay as collateral. He called it the "Ponzi Plan." As he alone did not have enough money to exploit postal rate differentials in a big way, he announced that he would allow others to participate.

He explained to anyone who would listen that "he had received a letter that contained a reply coupon that cost the equivalent of one cent in Spain but could be exchanged for a six-cent stamp in the United States." He would say, "I will buy hundreds, thousands, millions of these coupons!" He would make money on them all, he claimed, his talk smooth and his pitch persuasive.

Investment income was modest during that first month of January 1920, when he asked his family members, the people at his church, and personal friends to take part.

But the business rapidly increased when Ponzi promised to pay a fifty–percent return on forty-five-day notes. Soon he was quite busy and hired a small staff to take in the money, which he deposited in the bank. Within eight months he'd taken in $9 million, for which he'd signed promissory notes totaling $14 million.

Although he was cash rich, he was, obviously, poor. He always owed millions more than he brought in—and of course there was no way out.

When there was a dip in investors, he boldly offered a one-hundred percent return in ninety days. Knowing nothing of the process—only the results—people lined up at Ponzi's door. Police had to be summoned to maintain order. It seems that people couldn't wait to turn over their life savings.

Ponzi investors redeemed their notes in the back office of the building. Once the investors had their cash, they had to walk past the line of waiting investors. Upon seeing the mobs of people eager to invest, many who had just redeemed their loan notes couldn't resist the opportunity to reinvest. By early July 1920, eight months after he began, Ponzi was taking in $1 million each week. But that meant, of course, that he was increasing his obligations by $2 million each week.

THAT SAME MONTH, the *Boston Post* published an article saying that the scheme may not be financially feasible because Ponzi did not sell enough international postal coupons to pay the returns he promised to his investors.

When investors began demanding their money, Ponzi paid them with checks from the Hanover Trust Bank, a bank that Ponzi now controlled.

Ponzi then convinced many people that the *Boston Post* article was irrelevant, because he had a new, secret scheme for making money that was even better than the International Postal Reply Coupon scheme. But rumors were flying, and so the Boston district attorney ordered an audit of Ponzi's books. This sparked another run on the firm's assets.

Then the *Boston Post* published an article based on the revelations of a former Ponzi employee who claimed that Ponzi was millions of dollars in debt. The former employee also asked why, if Ponzi claimed the ability to make profits of fifty percent in forty-five days, he was putting his company's money in the bank to earn an annual interest rate of only five percent, one-tenth of what he was supposedly able to return to others. He owned the company, but he wasn't a customer.

The newspaper then uncovered Ponzi's sordid past. He was born in Italy but raised in Montreal, Canada. As a young man he had been involved with arranging money transfers from Italian immigrants to their families back in Italy. There were charges that many of the remittances never arrived. In Montreal, Ponzi had spent time in prison for forging signatures to checks.

The newspaper articles and the audit of Ponzi's Security and Exchange Company burst the balloon. The Massachusetts State Banking Commission closed down Hanover Trust, the mutual savings bank where Ponzi was president, but not before Ponzi took one million dollars to a Boston racetrack to bet on some long–shot horses, hoping to win enough to make his company solvent.

He was charged with grand larceny and using the mails to defraud. He contended that his troubles came from "men of wealth" who were trying to punish him for giving "little guys" the opportunity to make a high rate of return.

Ponzi was sent to prison, but he was released on parole after three-and-a-half years.

A PONZI SCHEME is a scam where old investors are paid off, not with earnings or legitimate profits, but with money received from new investors. When obligations pyramid so that not enough new money comes in to cover payments to old investors, the house of cards collapses.

It was all about greed—not only on the part of Ponzi, but also on the part of the real fools, those who denied truth and reality in search of the easy dollar.

Substitute New Era for Ponzi, and "educated, well-paid finance gurus at some of the top U.S. charities" for the mobs in Ponzi's Boston office, and you have the essence of our modern-day story: the biggest financial scandal in the history of American charity.

NEW ERA, LOCATED in the Philadelphia suburb of Radnor, Pennsylvania, promised that in six months it would double the money put up by donors and charities. John G. Bennett Jr., told charity officials that he had a group of anonymous philanthropists who would provide the matching funds. Operating costs for New Era would be paid not by donations, but by investment interest from the accumulated funds.

In Bennett's scheme, he would approach a charity's development office, which is in charge of fundraising, and its treasurer's office, which is in charge of taking care of the money, and tell the people who worked there that he knew of philanthropists who would match the amount the charity gave to New Era. That is, the charity would give Bennett a sum of money, and Bennett promised that the original money plus an equal amount would be returned to the charity.

Bennett's slick pitch went something like this: "If you give me $100,000 today, I guarantee that you will receive $200,000 in six months. I can do this because I know anonymous donors who care about your cause."

In this, Bennett learned from Ponzi. The only real difference was that, instead of offering a mere fifty–percent return, he right away promised a one-hundred–percent return.

Bennett spoke the language of the charity development office. Instead of using the postal system, as Ponzi did, Bennett used the matching gift, a well-understood concept at charities. Many companies match, to a limit, the charitable contributions of their employees. If a person makes a $100 donation to a charity, it is not uncommon for his or her company to make a similar gift of $100 to that same charity in that employee's name.

But it's not just companies. Imagine, if you will, an individual donor to a charity who says, "I'll match gifts up to $500,000." She means that every $10, $100, or $1,000 from other people will be matched one-for-one out of her pocket. Usually the promise is conditioned on something, such as a period of time or a specific purpose. But it is a way to provide an incentive for donors, who can be told, quite honestly and correctly, that their gift will really mean "double the money." The matching donor is telling the charity that although she can make a gift of $500,000, she'd rather see a broader participation in the process.

Bennett also deftly played the anonymous card. Charities are eager to respect a person's privacy and so would understand Bennett's condition.

Exclusivity is always a come-on and it worked for New Era. Bennett would entice charities by saying, "There are far more candidates choosing to enter the program than there are available slots. It gives me great joy in providing this opportunity to you. May God bless you as you enable needs to be met, challenges to be pursued, and for truly participating in giving that 'makes a world of difference.'"

Bennett arrived on the scene with a veneer of gilt-edged credentials. As a smooth talker, he worked wonders. A former drug program administrator who advised nonprofits on management and fundraising techniques, he was widely known in Philadelphia's philanthropic community. He also knew the people who made the financial decisions at charities.

Indeed, Bennett was soft-spoken, and seemed honest and sincere. He was charming and exhibited a deep religious dedication, and impressed wealthy and influential people with a quiet confidence and understated charisma.

Charities understand the value of references. As with many professions, the circle of familiar names among charities is knit tightly. Names are easily checked. This, Bennett anticipated.

Bennett knew many reputable people. Among New Era's early supporters were Laurance Rockefeller, the mutual fund guru John Templeton, the financier John Whitehead, and Vivian Weyerhaeuser Piasecki, of the timber and paper company family. Bennett's acquaintances included Pat Boone, Philadelphia Mayor Edward Rendell, and former Treasury Secretary William Simon.

An impressive chorus of supporters.

Piasecki, a trustee at the time of the University of Pennsylvania, and an acquaintance of Bennett's for more than fifteen years, said she had great respect for the man. She was quoted in *The Chronicle of Philanthropy* in June 1995 as saying, "He's sincere, dynamic. He appeared to be such a caring person." She also said that she thought Bennett's actions were well-intentioned: "I think he became intoxicated by doing good."

Cathryn Coate, the executive director of the Greater Philadelphia Cultural Alliance, was quoted as saying, "The word on the street was that Bennett was a super credible man, impeccable. You'd hear things like, 'Oh, I've known Bennett for 15 years.' It's not like a bunch of quick-fix guys duped a bunch of bozos."

Actually, that's exactly what it was like.

The bankruptcy court showed that Lancaster Bible College in Pennsylvania was the leading organizational creditor. It gave $16.9 million. Young Life International Service Center in Colorado Springs gave $11 million, and Gordon-Conwell Theological Seminary in South Hamilton, Massachusetts, gave $9.8 million.

Many religious-based organizations each gave more than $1 million. In fact, scores of faith-based charities would be found among the 1,290 organizations that received money from New Era and were later asked to give some of the money back.

The bankruptcy trustee created a list of those charities asked to surrender their profits. Most of them were asked to repay small amounts of money, ranging from a few hundred to a few thousand dollars. But others, including many religious organizations, were asked to refund substantial sums. CB International (the CB stands for Conservative Baptist), an evangelical group in Littleton, Colorado, tops the list with almost $4.2 million; Gordon-Conwell Theological Seminary in Massachusetts, an educational organization with a religious curriculum, was asked to return just over $4 million; Mercy Ships, a Christian organization in Texas, a little over $4 million; Chelten Baptist Church in Philadelphia, slightly more than $3.4 million; the Moody Bible Institute in Chicago, a little more than $2.3 million; and Christian Men, a group from Texas, was asked to repay $2 million.

Even the Salvation Army, one of the most admired charities in the country and one of the nation's wealthiest—and a religious organization—was asked to return $1.3 million.

Although religious-oriented organizations were generously sprinkled throughout the list, a variety of charities participated. The American Red Cross was asked to return a little more than $362,000; Whitworth College in Spokane, Washington, $3.9 million; and Duke University owed $131,000.

Not many environmental groups could be found, but the list showed the Nature Conservancy owed $276,500, the National Audubon Society $25,000, and Defenders of Wildlife $250. Not many hospitals or arts organizations were on the list, either. But the Stanford University School of Medicine showed up with a debt of $50,000 and the Phillips Collection, one of Washington, D.C.'s most famous galleries, was asked to return $25,000.

Many of the charities were Pennsylvania-based, which isn't surprising, since New Era was located near Philadelphia. Examples with geographic proximity to New Era included the Academy of Natural Sciences, with almost $3.5 million; Menno Haven Penn Hall, the human service organization, almost $2.2 million; the Philadelphia Orchestra, almost $2.7 million; and Drexel University, almost $2.6 million.

Then there was the Harvard Business School, which shapes our future business leaders and where business ethics is a required course. Loss: $502,500.

Indeed, other than CB International, the biggest debtor of all was a member of the Ivy League: the University of Pennsylvania, which had received $4,032,118. When Penn first cashed out, it then went in for more. One can only wonder if Bennett thought of having Penn's treasurer walk to the back of the New Era office so that the treasurer could see others cashing out. Apparently that wasn't necessary; Penn, even without that visual incentive, was in for more anyway.

By the time the organization was exposed, New Era's liabilities totaled more than $550 million. Its assets were a mere $80 million.

The scheme began to collapse in March 1995, when Albert Meyer, an accounting professor at Spring Arbor College in Michigan, blew the whistle. An early critic of New Era, he tried to make sense of his colleagues' gullibility. "If you are doing business with your brother," he said, "you don't ask him for his financial statements, especially if he is giving you a deal that is going to benefit you tremendously." He was the one who warned Pennsylvania authorities about New Era's missing financial audit. He also alerted the IRS, the SEC and the *Wall Street Journal*.

On May 11 of that year, Prudential Securities sued New Era and Bennett for approximately $45 million, the amount outstanding on a loan from Prudential. Prudential itself paid $18 million in 1996 to settle lawsuits filed by the bankruptcy trustee for New Era. Then in 2001, Prudential was fined $800,000 by the SEC for failing to properly supervise one of its brokers involved in the scam. The SEC said that the Prudential broker "willfully aided and abetted" New Era in misleading donors and charities about the nature of their investments.

In October 1997, Bennett pleaded no contest to eighty-two charges of fraud. Before he was sentenced to twelve years in prison, he read a statement in court accepting full blame for his actions. He repeated the argument that he had been mentally ill and had not intentionally sought to defraud anyone. "I'm a disaster financially. I'm just very, very bad at handling details, handling money, handling the record-keeping of it." Then, almost as if William Aramony were saying the words, he added, "I'm more interested in ideas."

CHARLES PONZI'S NAME is the very definition of swindle. There isn't an investment professional in the universe who hasn't heard of the Ponzi scheme. Yet, regardless of the SEC's efforts to stop them, variations of Ponzi are part of everyday life in the world of money.

Think how far we have yet to go when you ponder the words of William Simon, an educated, cautious man who served Presidents Nixon and Ford as treasury secretary. He was also a generous philanthropist. In the *Wall Street Journal* of October 14, 1999, two years after Bennett was sent to jail, Simon, an early Bennett supporter, said he did not think of himself as the victim of a scam. In fact, while visiting Bennett in jail, he said he would offer him a job when he received parole (Simon died in June 2000).

Simon viewed what had happened as simply a situation where Bennett was not able to raise enough money to meet his commitments. "People have said to me, 'you were fooled,' and I suppose it is true that I was fooled because I don't believe he did anything to defraud me," Simon was quoted as saying. "To this day I believe his intentions were correct."

How can the SEC or the attorney general or a Congressional committee fight that?

It can't. But just as charity cannot survive without a strong—some might say blind—personal connection and commitment, so that very strength means the people who serve charities as employees must take extra care to protect the public's faith. Charity is too important and too fragile a commodity to throw away and expect it to return.

AFTER PONZI SPENT three years in jail, he went to Florida to sell swampland. He ended up in jail again for defrauding buyers of real estate. He promised a two-hundred percent return in sixty days.

5

THE GOOD THEY FAILED TO DO

"Say it ain't so, Joe. Say it ain't so."
"Yes, kid, I'm afraid it is."
"Well, I never would've thought it."

A YOUNG BOY CONFRONTING "SHOELESS" JOE JACKSON

THE CHICAGO HERALD EXAMINER, SEPTEMBER 30, 1920

IN THE 1919 World Series, the Cincinnati Reds defeated the Chicago White Sox five games to three (back then it was a best-of-nine series). What made that year's championship remarkable was that the series was fixed. Some of the Chicago players, either believing they were underpaid or tempted by an under-the-table windfall, joined together in a scheme to deliberately lose the series.

The plot was funded by the notorious gambler Arnold "the Big Bankroll" Rothstein. After he fixed the game, Rothstein bet heavily against the White Sox.

Eight White Sox players pretended to give their all in what looked to spectators as a hard-fought contest between two good teams. But the games were not hard-fought, and the unholy players took their team to deliberate defeat.

The icon who fell the hardest, the person whose name is most associated with the scandal, was Chicago's left fielder, "Shoeless" Joe Jackson. He was very popular with the fans, and many considered him the greatest player of his day. The irony is that Shoeless Joe knew about the scheme but didn't actually participate in it. Unlike the others, he never confessed to taking part in throwing the games.

Although not one of the players was found guilty of criminal charges, the commissioner of baseball, Judge Kenesaw Mountain Landis, banned them all from major league baseball for life. "Regardless of the verdict of juries," he said, "no player that throws a ball game; no player that undertakes or promises to throw a ball game; no player that sits in a conference with a bunch of crooked players and gamblers where the ways and means of throwing games are planned and discussed and does not promptly tell his club about it, will ever play professional baseball."

Baseball, then and now a national pastime, captures an innocence in our hearts in a way that makes people pause when scandal, and not the wonder of masterful plays, is the news—a pause that is quite different from the reaction we have when the latest government or corporate disgrace is revealed. While baseball is and always has been a business, it is—or strives to be—a business of innocence. Baseball scandal is truly shocking, and it confuses us when we learn that people, under the guise of doing good, have done bad.

In this sense, baseball and charity are not dissimilar. If only we had some "Shoeless" Joe Jacksons in the world of charity, people who, upon being asked if the bad news they generated was true, would say, "Yes, kid, I'm afraid it is."

CORRUPTION HAS ALWAYS been with us. The exposures of massive frauds at places like Enron, Arthur Andersen, Qwest Communication, Tyco, and others—companies once believed to be industry giants that lost all standing with the public—are only recent, large-profile examples.

And it is about the money. It's always about the money.

In 2001, *Business Week Magazine* named Dennis Kozlowski, the CEO of Tyco, "America's Most Aggressive CEO." This was meant as a compliment. It honored the man who, less than a year later, would be disgraced and taken from his plush office in handcuffs.

Kozlowski embodied the tough-guy attitude, but he didn't make money the old-fashioned way. He made illusory money—virtual paper profits—with the only real money being the stuff he took for himself. He stuffed his pockets with company assets as though they were falling out of his own little piggy bank. He seemed to believe that he could rob without consequence.

Similar submissions to the temptations of power are found in so many reports about errant CEOs, one shouldn't wonder that fraud is simply inevitable when the stakes are high enough.

THE FINANCIAL TEMPTATIONS for employees at charities are not as high as they are in the corporate world, of course. No one employed at a non-profit organization has a salary, benefits, or perks even close to those provided to the CEOs of large, for-profit corporations.

So, in the relatively benign and quaint world of charities, should we be unconcerned? So what if William Aramony or Peter Diamandopoulos made a few hundred thousand dollars? So what if a college president bullies, threatens, and acts like a dictator? Compared to their for-profit counterparts, they're in the minor leagues. So what if a few charities lie to their supporters? And so what if a few hundred charities are bilked of a few million dollars?

In the context of the economic impact of charities, isn't society able to withstand a little leakage? Less power, after all, means less corruption, right?

An example of this type of thinking was on display when a representative of the Red Cross admitted that most of the hundreds of millions of dollars in charitable contributions it received for the Katrina disaster in New Orleans and nearby areas had not been distributed months later. And yes, although there had been "some" fraud, since it didn't amount to more than 5 percent of what had been donated, what was the problem? Just a little leakage.

What difference can the greed or averted eyes at charities possibly make in a world where the marketing gurus hired by for-profit companies make careers of lying? (The talents of those same marketing gurus, by the way, are being employed by more and more charities.)

A lot. It's not just the size, but the idea. There's an idea—not merely a long-gone innocence—of an ethic, a value, a special place in society that charities, to stay charities, should want desperately to maintain.

Not only did Congress show interest in Enron's troubles, it also showed interest in the troubles of The Nature Conservancy, when the

Washington Post reported in the spring of 2003 that the venerable environmental group had engaged in questionable activities with its finances and donors.

In late 2002, a grand jury indicted Andrew Liersch, for almost twenty years the president of Goodwill Industries of Santa Clara County. On the run, Liersch was brought back from Guatemala, arrested for defrauding the Santa Clara chapter of over $800,000 and sending the proceeds to overseas banks.

In the spring of 2006, Abraham Alexander, an accountant at the Cardiovascular Research Foundation in New York, admitted that he stole $237,000 over a period of eighteen months, using the charity's credit cards and writing checks to himself. He used a chunk of it to pay for trips to Ohio to visit a dominatrix. Although he paid for the travel, it wasn't clear from the court filings and financial records whether he went to her or she came to him.

Heart research, indeed.

Then there's what happened at United Way of America, Adelphi, the Baptist Foundation of Arizona, and New Era.

While the monetary scale of scandal may be heavily weighted against the for-profit world, fraud in the nonprofit world is worse because its role—its very definition—calls for a higher level of ethical conduct.

Ethics is not about uniformly applying a well-defined set of parameters to every situation. The subjective nature of determining an excessive salary or how much disclosure is needed makes it difficult to point fingers.

But sometimes deciding what's wrong isn't very difficult. Sometimes ethical lapses are not dilemmas at all. Some things are obvious.

What Enron did, what Tyco did, what many companies do every day and try to excuse by saying that the law permits it, or that the law isn't clear, are, from an ethical perspective, so obviously wrong that to call them ethical dilemmas insults the concept of intellectual or moral struggle.

Some things are just plain wrong at charities too.

When things go wrong at a charity, the biggest culprit is usually not the executive director. While he or she may be devious, arrogant, greedy, or just plain dishonest, that person has a boss: the board of trustees. Every charity in the United States has a board of directors—usually called trustees—and the board's primary obligation is to protect the public's interest as expressed through the charity's work.

The problem is that boards often perform their jobs casually and sloppily. While many board members take their jobs seriously, far too many approach the job as a way to enhance their personal résumés or their public statures.

When people scrutinize a charity, they should begin by evaluating the board's sense of obligation. Only foundations that grant money to charities seem to bother with this. Most charities are hardly forthcoming about the crucial matters a board must face, and I'm aware of only a handful that would willingly discuss with the public how those matters are addressed. You might find out how often boards meet or even who attended, but for most charities that's the extent of their concept of disclosure.

Of course, the average donor doesn't know what to ask. While the attorney general's office in each state might be able to identify and stop true malfeasance, what of the smaller stuff that may be legal but not quite right?

How would you evaluate a board member's commitment to the cause? Trustees, that group most responsible for a charity's success, are also often the least accessible people at a charity.

Making information available about its governance should be the first step on a charity's road to disclosure and transparency.

The board should be forthright about its values, its diversity, and its commitment to the charity's mission.

It should begin by publishing how often it meets and who attends or doesn't attend the meetings.

It should make the agenda topics of all its meetings easily accessible to the public. It should make available the results of important votes, as well as a summary of the arguments that supported and did not support the various sides of an issue.

It should take seriously its responsibility to communicate to the public.

The board should make clear whether or not its members are paid. Although most states permit board members to be paid for their time, the vast majority are not. In fact, board members are often told when they join the board that they will be expected to make a financial contribution to their organization each year.

Far too typically, the search committee will approach a prospective board member by saying, "It won't take much time, and you don't have to do very much work." Those who agree under those expectations aren't going to do much. What sense of dignity can a charity have when it asks the group of people most responsible for safeguarding its unique compact with society to take less care in addressing its responsibilities than you or I would in crossing the street?

"IT ALL STARTED hundreds of years ago, when out of the common law of England evolved the concept of legal entities separate from human beings." So begins the pamphlet "Legal Responsibilities of Nonprofit Boards," produced by the Washington, D.C., nonprofit organization BoardSource, and written by Bruce Hopkins, the charitable law expert noted earlier. Hopkins outlines the essential legal responsibilities board members undertake and what they should know as they take on their awesome duty.

This pamphlet should be read by every board member of every charity.

"Trustees of charitable trusts are deemed to have the same obligation toward the assets of the trusts as they do toward their own personal assets," Hopkins writes. "Equally, all board members' responsibility is to act prudently in their handling of the nonprofit organization's resources."

If only board members realized how important their job is. There would be no more knitting and there would be no more talk of the golf game in board rooms, at the expense of the serious job at hand and the limited time to accomplish it. One reason you don't waste time when talking with your attorney is that it's your money. Board meetings are more than social occasions. They may be that, too, but they are much more.

Hopkins also talks about the "Three Ds": duty of care, duty of loyalty, and duty of obedience—all legal concepts.

Duty of care requires that directors of a nonprofit organization be reasonably informed about the charity's activities and that they actively take part in decisions. This means that the board cannot look the other way when its executive director buys tickets on the Concorde. The treasurer of the board must ask why such a wasteful expense shows up. Of course, for that to happen, he or she must review the financial reports to begin with.

The board must also exercise its power to protect the interests of the organization—not the interests of any individual on the board. That's a duty, and it means the executive director or president should be treated as just "another entity," not someone extra special who can spend money without justification or accounting. The head of the charity is extra special, of course, but in the sense that his or her actions require the most accountability of any of the charity's employees.

According to Hopkins, the board must comply with applicable laws and remain guardians of the mission. That means, among other things, that the executive director cannot be lying about falsely inflated returns on the charity's investments. A board must make sure that the charity complies with all reporting requirements and that its statements are truthful.

Hopkins also addresses a variety of other matters the board should be aware of, such as ensuring that the organization has a conflict-of-interest policy. Despite the easy rhetoric that there should never be any conflicts, many boards often have conflicts of interest. The local contractor may be sitting on the board when a decision is made to construct a new building, or an insurance agent on the board may be part of a bid to insure the charity's property. In some organizations, board members actually hire themselves to do work for the charity. Because they are leaders in the community, they tend to be around when things happen. A conflict-of-interest policy is a document to ensure that when conflicts of interest arise they are dealt with in an above-board, professional, and ethical manner. The Baptist Foundation of Arizona might still be in business if such a policy had been in place.

Perhaps no one is more responsible for the attention charities pay to ethics than William Aramony. Charles Kolb, who wrote the booklet *Developing an Ethics Program: A Case Study of Nonprofit Organizations*, also published by BoardSource, examined the United Way scandal and then proposed how ethical considerations can be an integral part of the way a charity does its business. Kolb said that for charities, which do not issue stock, "their 'stock' is their reputation for public integrity, and once that reputation is lost or damaged, it becomes extremely difficult to recover the public's trust."

An active, live code of ethics would help many nonprofits avoid problems. Instead of cowering in a shroud of secrecy, charities should be forthright in telling the public what it does.

Board members have oversight responsibilities that far too many ignore. Yet, because of so many social expectations that accompany the request to sit on a board, they enter an arena full of lions and tigers, all the while looking for flowers and incense. Running a charity is a serious and difficult business. In addition to ensuring that the charity addresses its mission, board members must be serious about their legal and ethical issues.

And they have to keep their executive directors honest.

Wouldn't it be nice if, just once, upon being asked if something was true, the culprit at a charity would say, "Yes, I'm afraid it is"?

"Is it true that you did wrong?"

William Aramony at the United Way of America: "Yes, I'm afraid it is."

Peter Diamandopoulos at Adelphi University: "Yes, I'm afraid it is."

William Crotts at the Baptist Foundation of Arizona. "Yes, I'm afraid it is."

John Bennett at New Era. "Yes, I'm afraid it is."

PART II
SOCIETY AND CHARITY

6

WHAT IS A CHARITY?

"Any measure which establishes legal charity on a permanent basis and gives it an administrative form thereby creates an idle and lazy class, living at the expense of the industrial and working class."
ALEXIS DE TOCQUEVILLE, MEMOIR ON PAUPERISM

WHEN WE HEAR or read the word charity, we do so in the context of beneficence. We know down deep that without charities the world would somehow be a more hostile place. But most people don't really know *what* a charity is. It's that place we give money to, but beyond that, most people don't think much about it.

Charity—the greatest of the three important theological virtues (faith and hope are the other two)—is an idea that goes back to the beginnings of civilization, and a word that goes back to about one hundred years after Christ. Its meaning is not unlike the meaning of philanthropy: the love of humankind. The origins of the word "charity" are found deep in religion.

"A Model of Christian Charity"—the sermon delivered by John Winthrop on board the ship *Arbella* as it traveled from England to the new world in 1630—is widely considered to be the first great discourse on American charity. Winthrop characterized charity as a way for people—that is, good Christians—to behave and expect good behavior in the harsh new world: "For we must consider that we shall be as a city upon a hill. The eyes of all people are upon us."

The phrase "Charity begins at home" was first written around 1670 by Sir Thomas Browne in his essay "Religio Medico." In context, Browne wrote: "But how shall we expect charity towards others, when we are uncharitable to ourselves? Charity begins at home, is the voice of the world."

The concept, though, as far as we know, goes back to the Apostle Paul's advice in the first book of Timothy: "But if any widow have children or nephews, let them learn first to show piety at home, and to requite their parents; for that is good and acceptable before God."

God and charity are tightly linked.

As time passed, the idea of charity slowly moved from obedience to God to love and affection, with connotations of generous or spontaneous goodness. The meaning evolved further, as we can see in various dictionaries, to "a disposition to judge leniently and hopefully of the character, to make allowance for apparent faults and shortcomings; large-heartedness."

The idea then evolved to include fair-mindedness toward people disapproved of or disliked. In the context of asking society to be kind to illegal immigrants, Cardinal Roger Mahoney of the Roman Catholic Archdiocese said it this way in 2006: "We are called upon to attend the last, littlest, lowest, and least in society. . . ." Liking the people whom nobody else likes must certainly be a virtue.

Go down this road for a while—being kind to those who are scorned, even thought to be evil—and, unless you have made a profession of caring for the world's neediest, you will travel with many doubts. For while few can quarrel with the value of fighting evil or helping others, most of us find comfort or relief by ignoring the sad plights of others.

Even so, society being full of breadth and surprises, there are many kind deeds performed every day, deeds that are never celebrated, never reported, but go unrequited, except perhaps inside one's own heart. Those individual acts of intended kindness are plentiful enough—or at least generate enough hope—for the optimists among us to celebrate what might be called a pure, charitable spirit.

★ ★ ★

CHARITY INSIDERS REGULARLY trot out Alexis de Tocqueville, the French aristocrat who in 1831, when he was only twenty-five years old, traveled throughout the United States to learn something about how things were going with the experiment in democracy. After his tour, he wrote *Democracy in America*, an insightful collection of his observations on American culture. It is often said today, as if it were an explanation of just how great we all are, that he recognized the charitable spirit as part of American society's uniqueness.

He noted this country's "associations" or charities and thought they comprised one of our greatest assets. Such associations, he observed, were used to "found seminaries . . . construct churches, distribute books, dispatch missionaries to the antipodes." Americans, he said, "establish hospitals, prisons, schools by the same method." (Yes, he felt compelled to make at least a passing reference to prisons; France sponsored his trip so that he could study the prison system in the United States.)

If something good needed to be done, he observed of Americans, it would be done best by charity.

All well and good for those who see in Tocqueville a benign observer of just how merrily the United States, so early in its history, was trying to come to grips with its social ills. But the whole of Tocqueville's story is not the unique benignity of American society. Those who think that miss the most important lesson about charities—one brimming with controversy—that Tocqueville tried to convey.

Democracy in America was actually written in two parts, with an interval of five years between the publication of each. During that time, Tocqueville went to England to observe society there and when he returned to France he wrote *Memoir on Pauperism*, in which he opined on charity far more directly than in his more famous *Democracy in America*.

In *Memoir* he distinguished between *public* charity and *private* charity. Public charity, or what we now know as government welfare, was mostly to be avoided. He argued that "the inevitable result of public charity was to perpetuate idleness among the majority of the poor and to provide for their leisure at the expense of those who work."

In the second half of *Democracy in America*, which was written after he returned from England and after he wrote *Memoir*, Tocqueville critically noted that in France and other wealthy European sovereignties, "The state has undertaken almost exclusively to provide the hungry with bread, the sick with help and shelter, and the idle with work; it has become almost the sole relief against misery." He also said, "I am not afraid to affirm . . . that religion is threatened with falling into the hands of the government."

But while Tocqueville thought it was important to help the needy, it was more important to him that government didn't do most of the helping. The utility of charities is that they provide a way for government to avoid—or lessen—what it shouldn't be doing anyway.

He was celebrating charity much less than he was criticizing public welfare.

Tocqueville wasn't absolute on this point, however. In *Memoir* he wrote that the public charity provided by the government was at times useful, even necessary, in addressing "inevitable evils such as the helplessness of infancy, the decrepitude of old age, sickness, insanity." Sometimes God gets a little angry, and life is, at times, unfair. Still, government aid was best, he argued, when it was temporary.

Not much has changed in two hundred years, either with society's problems or with our government's efforts to deal with them. Tocqueville thought, as many people do today, that the answers to many of our social problems resided in private philanthropy, where aid would be collected voluntarily and, he would argue, distributed on a temporary basis, so that it does not pauperize its recipients.

But he also took a dramatic step further, addressing a notion with which today's donor struggles because of its profound and philosophical implications. Unlike many of his contemporaries, Tocqueville doubted that assistance could or should be distributed on the basis of "character."

Who, he asked, "would dare to let a poor man die of hunger because it's his own fault that he is dying? Who will hear his cries and reason about his vices?"

A complex man, Tocqueville, for those words make him sound like a downright bleeding-heart liberal, and in so sounding, his view presages the guilt or awkwardness—to say nothing of the ambiguity—many of us feel when we see a homeless and hungry beggar on the street.

★ ★ ★

A KEY DEVELOPMENT in the notion of charities over the centuries is that the effort to help others has become much more institutional than individual. Today, charity is almost exclusively seen in the context of institutions: places set up for the purpose of accepting gifts on behalf of those who need them.

Individual people don't qualify as charities unto themselves. The beggar—the last, littlest, lowest, and least—may be needy, but he or she is not a charity.

To obtain charitable status in the United States, an organization must operate exclusively for an approved charitable purpose. The state where the charity is located approves its organizational structure, and the IRS grants a federal tax exemption.

And it's all about benefiting the public. The IRS ensures that the organization does not work to benefit individuals close to the charity, such as the trustees, the executive director, or other key employees.

The primary legal difference between charitable organizations and commercial enterprises is that charities can have no shareholders. They have boards of directors, but no one owns any stock because charities don't issue stock. Some hospitals have been in the news recently, in fact, because they are abandoning their charitable status to become for-profit corporations. On the other hand, some hospitals have been criticized lately by important people in Congress for not doing enough to help the poor. Why do the hospitals have charitable status, the thinking goes, if they're not providing any charity?

Another popular synonym for charity is *nonprofit*, a moniker that derives from the absence of shareholders. A charity is, in fact, permitted to make a profit. Many charities are quite healthy from a financial per-spective. Schools charge tuition, clinics charge for healthcare services, museums charge admission and sell gifts. Charities also earn money on their investments. Except in unusual situations, they don't pay taxes on their income or earnings.

The range of charities is remarkable. To get a macro-organizational handle on the world of nonprofits, the National Center for Charitable Statistics has developed a classification system of charities. Known as the

National Taxonomy of Exempt Entities, the system classifies twenty-six types of charities.

The largest categories are the following:

- Religious organizations
- Educational institutions
- Health charities
- Human services agencies
- Organizations that promote public or societal benefit (such as foundations, United Way, United Jewish Appeal, and others)
- Institutions in the arts, culture, or humanities
- Environment or animal-welfare groups
- Organizations engaged in international affairs or international aid

Despite this well-established and logical way to think about the types of charities, many people remain confused. We often hear lawmakers and other public figures speak, as one did recently, of protecting "charity, as well as hospitals and schools," or "charities and faith-based organizations," as if hospitals and schools and faith-based organizations weren't charities. But they are.

Lots of people work at charities. You probably have heard of some of them because they're well-known, or because the charity's leaders live in your community. Some you may know personally. A charity employee may even be your neighbor. Actually, chances aren't all that small that you work at a charity.

The conductor at the Kennedy Center in Washington, D.C., works for a charity. The curator at the San Francisco Museum of Modern Art works for a charity. The host of public radio's *A Prairie Home Companion with Garrison Keillor* works for a charity. Almost all Nobel laureates work for charities. The doctor who delivers babies in Topeka, Kansas, probably works for a charity, as do college professors and priests and rabbis.

The highly paid, highly skilled surgeon at Massachusetts General Hospital is in the same universe as the driver earning barely a minimum wage who spends his time taking a beat-up old truck around town to give the homeless a bowl of soup before they sleep.

While you probably recognize some organizations, some may not come to mind so quickly.

Have you heard of Doctors Without Borders in New York? It was founded in 1971 by a small group of French doctors who believed that "all people have the right to medical care and that the needs of these people supercede respect for national borders." This concept is intriguing, especially in times of war. Annual revenues for Doctors Without Borders are in the area of $50 million.

How about World Vision, located in the state of Washington? Founded in 1950, World Vision is a "Christian humanitarian organization, serving the world's poorest children and families in nearly 100 countries." It's a big place with more than $500 million of annual income.

Human Life International, headquartered in Virginia, is not at the top of the easy-to-remember, well-known charities list. It exists to "restore respect for the sanctity of life from the moment of conception through natural death, and to restore the preeminence of the traditional family as paramount in God's plan." Its annual revenue is about $3.5 million.

Even the local YMCA and YWCA, the gun club on the edge of town, many day care agencies, battered women's shelters—all of these, and more like them, are charities.

Then there are charities like the Jeremy Bullock Memorial Fund in Butte, Montana. This group maintains a soccer field, a "first class soccer facility" that benefits thousands of players each year. It gets along with about $12,000 of annual contributions.

A charity called 2nd Chance Sanctuary can be found in Sarasota, Florida, with a mission to "restore to health injured wildlife" and then release the poor creatures. Its literature informs the public that, "Severely injured animals are given perpetual care at our facilities." There are far more volunteers here than there are paid employees—another example of a good place doing good work with very little money.

A little larger, with a budget of just over $500,000, is Calvary Women's Services in Washington, D.C., which provides shelter and social services for homeless women.

Hundreds of thousands of charities never attract the attention of the media. This is so even though their work is often magnificent and constitutes the fabric of America's charitable cloth, so rich are they in texture and dimension. But sometimes a good, small charity gets its day in the spotlight.

The *Washington Post* a few years ago ranked Calvary Women's Services as one of the top five charities in the District of Columbia.

By the way, local and state governments and the federal government are also, in a sense, charities. If you make a gift to the government over and above your tax obligation, you are entitled to a deduction. No one does this, however.

THE BROAD DESIGNATION for the nonprofits with which the public is most familiar is found in one part of the complex IRS code: Section 501, subsection (c). That's where they find their legal status. The IRS reports that, as of 2005, more than 1.7 million organizations are tax-exempt, a number that increases by tens of thousands every year.

Section 501(c) is divided into twenty-seven categories. The largest of those is 501(c)(3). This sub-sub-section, "Religious, charitable, and similar organizations," contains a little over one million charities: public charities, public foundations, and private foundations.

When you think of how important a charity is and how much paperwork is involved, the IRS approves a remarkably high percentage of applications each year. In 2005, for example (in a trend that doesn't change much from year to year), over 63,000 new charities were approved, while only 765 applications were denied. That's a 99 percent approval rate.

Not all charities raise money from the public, however. The actual number of organizations that come to mind when the word "charity" is spoken is probably closer to 85 percent of the one million charities described in section 501(c)(3).

Public charities are the ones you hear of: the Red Cross, the Salvation Army, the United Way, your college, the art museum in your town, the homeless shelter. These charities are the ones that do the work of helping society, and they come to you for money.

Public foundations, usually large organizations that must give part of their assets each year to public charities, include places like the Rockefeller Foundation, the Carnegie Foundation, and the Pew Charitable Trust. These are the types of nonprofit organizations that often sponsor public television and radio. They typically don't raise any money.

Private—or family—foundations, like public foundations, also must give a portion of their assets to public charities each year. They are much smaller than public foundations, and their money is almost always controlled by members of the family that established them. Private foundations also don't raise money.

You wouldn't normally want to give to either a public or family foundation because the board—and not you—decides which public charities will get money each year. Besides, most of them already have all they need.

This means that the number of charities the donating public is interested in is actually considerably under one million.

About 600,000 charities file their financial information with the IRS each year, but a lot of small charities that raise money don't have to file. Religious organizations, regardless of their size, don't have to file either. Taking into account the charities that don't ask for money from the public and do file, and those that ask for money but don't file, there are probably around 850,000 charities that solicit funds from individuals.

Regardless of how we estimate it, a lot of organizations in this country are asking for your dollars.

JUST BECAUSE PEOPLE can donate to an organization and deduct what they give doesn't mean that people will—or that they should.

A charity's definition can be parsed in many ways, but the key to success for a charity is what it does for society and what *you* think makes it worthy. That a charity has no stockholders may be why Charles Kolb, who authored the pamphlet *Developing an Ethics Program*, said that the only "stock" a charity has is its reputation.

True enough. And that makes you the final arbiter.

7

CHARITY IN AMERICA

"When we place a value on society that succors the poor, the weak, and the infirm, it is a value that cannot be evaluated in any marketplace."
JAMES DOUGLAS, "WHY CHARITY?"

TAXWISE GIVING, a newsletter for planned giving professionals at charities, reported that in the early 1980s a doctor—we know him only as Dr. Lary—gave blood to the Red Cross and then deducted from his income taxes what he thought the value of the blood was. He claimed that it was a gift of a service. The IRS said no, and so he took his case to court.

The deduction was denied because gifts of "services" are not deductible. If you volunteer your time to a charity, you cannot deduct the value of that time. This is true for everyone, including professionals such as attorneys or accountants who bill by the hour.

Should anyone volunteer anything that he or she actually makes, other than the cost of the materials, the product is not deductible. The example used in tax classes is the artist who paints a piece that becomes valuable. If she donates it to a charity, she is permitted to deduct only the cost of the canvas, the paint, and the paint brushes she used. The time she spent on the project, and the artwork's value, are irrelevant.

Certainly blood is not a service, at least not the way most people understand it to be a service. Blood can be weighed and measured. It's physical. So Dr. Lary, realizing his error, changed his argument. Blood is not a service, he said, but it is something that can be felt and touched and therefore should be deductible as a charitable contribution—of property.

The IRS has rules about gifts of property such as stock, land or, almost anything that's not cash. The asset must be owned by the donor for at least one year (back in the early 1980s it was six months) before a donor may deduct the market value of the gift. If stock purchased for $100 rises to a value of $200 within a year, and the person who bought it makes a gift of that stock to a charity within that time, his deduction is still only $100. He just didn't own it long enough. That $100 value is called the donor's cost basis—the amount he paid for the asset.

So, for Dr. Lary's argument that blood is property to prevail—he claimed a deduction for what he thought the value of the blood to be—he had to prove that he "owned" his blood for longer than six months and, if not, what his cost basis was. The following year, *Taxwise Giving* reported that, in again denying Dr. Lary his deduction, the judge, apparently after a fair amount of research, noted that "red blood cells have an average life of approximately four months, and blood platelets have an average life of approximately ten days." As the good doctor did not go so far as to claim that in some bizarre way he actually paid something for the blood in his body, the deduction would be reduced to zero.

The rules in this area require an advisor who knows her stuff. Generally: a donor can deduct the appreciated value of a charitable gift of personal property—the value when it's more than what he or she paid to acquire the asset—only when the charity is able to use it in furthering its mission. A yacht at a landlocked charity that helps animals, for example, is rather pointless, and so the deduction is limited to what the donor paid. Or, if the asset has gone down in value—as cars, for example, tend to do—the donor can deduct only that value. If, however, the property can be used by the charity—such as rare books that students are permitted to read—and the charity says it will use the gift, the donor may deduct the higher market value. Call a competent advisor.

NOT EVERYONE WHO gives to charity can claim a deduction. Only those who itemize—list and add up—all their deductions are entitled, and then only when the total of that list is more than what the IRS already allows with the standard deduction. About 75 percent of all taxpayers don't itemize and so can't deduct any charitable gifts they make.

Deductions, when they are claimed, are not painless; it's not as though charitable gifts don't cost the donor. That's because the amount of the deduction is subtracted from the donor's income, not from his or her tax bill. For example, say a person makes $100,000 and, after all the accounting gymnastics in figuring out taxes, ends up in the 25 percent tax bracket. Normally that person would pay $25,000 in taxes. But if the person makes a $10,000 gift to charity, he or she then subtracts $10,000 from the $100,000, which makes his or her taxable income $90,000. Assuming the reduced income doesn't change the tax bracket, the donor pays taxes of $22,500—25 percent of $90,000. The tax savings are $2,500, which, as you might have already calculated, equals 25 percent of the $10,000 charitable contribution.

So the donor still pays $7,500 by making the gift. The gift costs something.

The charitable deduction—just like the interest deduction available to homeowners with a mortgage—is the way Congress, which writes the tax code, encourages donors to support charities.

The charitable income tax deduction was born in 1917, but the idea of excluding charities from paying taxes is older. In 1863, Congress exempted charities when it enacted the first federal income tax on businesses to help finance the Civil War. By the time World War I broke out, the charitable deduction was incorporated into the income tax structure we know today, because Congress felt that charitable contributions would otherwise diminish during the war.

Today's tax code is so complicated and vast that some attorneys specialize in just the charitable portion. Despite the simplicity of the deduction example above, a large gift or a gift of an unusual asset usually requires the assistance of a tax attorney or an accountant, to ensure that all is right with the deduction.

Some people claim, despite the passage in 1913 of the Sixteenth Amendment, which is pretty straightforward, that the income tax is illegal and unconstitutional. In 2006, one anti-tax crusader, Irwin Schiff, was sentenced to more than thirteen years in federal prison for making money by telling people that the United States was illegally collecting taxes. The judge disagreed, saying it was a "flimflam operation" that encouraged several thousand people to evade taxes, costing the government billions of dollars.

Most people don't feel that way, and charities certainly don't. Without the tax, charitable deductions would not be possible, and so, when they argue to preserve the charitable deduction, charities are also supporting the income tax. The higher the tax rate, the more valuable the deduction. Charities don't talk much about that; they're a little squeamish about acknowledging how laws that call for higher taxes benefit them.

For a charitable gift to be deductible in any year, it must be made by the end of that calendar year, on or before December 31. When a check is mailed through the United States Postal Service, if it's postmarked by the end of the year, it's deductible, even if the charity doesn't receive it until early January of the following year. If the check bounces, though, it's not. Everything else—things that aren't sent through the mail—must be in the hands of the charity by the end of the year.

For the first time ever, Congress permitted a one-time exception to the by-the-end-of-the-year rule when it extended through January 2005, the time by which a donor could make a tax-deductible contribution of cash to support relief efforts in the aftermath of the tsunami in Southeast Asia at the end of December 2004.

IN 2001, THE Hewlett Foundation gave $400 million to Stanford University. The foundation was funded in large part by William Hewlett, the co-founder of Hewlett Packard, who died that January. He and David Packard, both 1934 graduates of Stanford University, parlayed $538 from their now-famous humble garage in Palo Alto, California, into one of the nation's largest and most successful computer companies. With that success came, apparently, an understanding on the part of both men that repayment was due to what they considered, at least in part, the place that trained and prepared them for their success.

The $400 million foundation gift was in addition to approximately $400 million that had already been given to Stanford by the two families over the years.

That gift was simply the latest and largest in what seems to be a growing line of major gifts to universities.

By 2004, when the stock market had stabilized after its fall from its irrational exuberance of the 1990s, America's sixty largest individual donors gave $10 billion to charity. *The Chronicle of Philanthropy* reported that Bill and Melinda Gates pledged $3.35 billion to the foundation they established, and Susan Buffett, the wife of the investor Warren Buffett, left approximately $2.4 billion to the Buffett Foundation when she died.

The list of big donors is not diverse: obviously each donor is wealthy, and most are not young. One of the few exceptions in 2004 was thirty-eight-year-old David Filo, a co-founder of Yahoo, who pledged $30 million to his alma mater, Tulane University.

Often, large gifts are not as simple as they seem by just reading the numbers—later on, we'll get to the strings some donors attach to their gifts. But an example of how some large gifts are made is the case of T. Boone Pickens, the Texas oilman-turned-investor and one of the nation's most generous philanthropists.

At the end of December 2005, he made a $165 million gift to Oklahoma State University, specifically to one of its supporting charities: OSU Cowboy Golf, which runs the golf program.

The twist here was that Pickens, as a member of the board that governs the golf program, has say over how the charity's money is invested. When he made the gift, it was simply transferred from one fund that he controlled into another. The money was out of hands for all of one hour. Thus he was able to take a huge deduction on his taxes while every dollar of his gift remained under his control. The perceived conflict wasn't that the money continued to be his, but that he would earn management fees from continuing to invest it.

The transaction, according to charitable tax experts, appeared to be legal under IRS regulations. Nevertheless, Marcus Owens, the former head of the charity division of the IRS, was quoted as saying, "Sadly, it's another case of a rich man manipulating charity for his own benefit."

WEALTHY PEOPLE CLEARLY play an important role in charity. Today, more than seven million households have a net worth of over $1 million.

Over 300 people in America today have a net worth of over $1 billion; in 1982, that number was thirteen.

An analysis of IRS data by the Boston College Center on Wealth and Philanthropy shows that the wealthiest five million households account for 28 percent of the value of all reported charitable gifts. The top 5 percent of households, in net worth as well as income, give over 45 percent of the value of all charitable gifts. And charities are well aware that over the next generation, many billions of dollars will be transferred to charity through bequests and other estate gifts.

Paying special attention to the wealthy is a very high priority to charities.

Not all charity, though, is giant-size. In fact, almost all donations are small, of the ten- and twenty-five-dollar sort. But a multitude of small gifts makes a big difference, even if those gifts don't make headlines.

When we think of charity, many people think of the Salvation Army, of tossing their loose change into that pot next to the person shaking the bell at Christmas. To many, that's what charitable giving is all about. It is a far different image from the donor who makes the million–dollar gift. After Jim and Julia Citizen drop their coins onto the mound of other coins in the bucket, they can feel good about themselves and free to shop without guilt.

Even the Salvation Army, however, gets big gifts. In 2003, Joan Kroc, the widow of Ray Kroc, who built the McDonald's empire, left $1.5 billion to the Salvation Army in her will. She also left $200 million to National Public Radio.

The Salvation Army has been known to turn away a big gift. A man named David Rush gave the Salvation Army $100,000 in late 2002, part of the proceeds of a $14 million lump-sum payment he won in the lottery. The Salvation Army refused his gift on the grounds that Rush had acquired the money through illicit means: gambling. Maribeth Shanahan, a spokesperson for the charity, was quoted in the *Naples Daily News* as saying: "The money that Mr. Rush received was from a lottery: We preach against gambling. To accept his money would be to talk out of both sides of our mouth."

Back went the $100,000. It caused Mr. Rush to wonder aloud why winning a lottery was evil but playing the stock market wasn't. Both, after all, are forms of gambling.

Other charities gratefully accepted Mr. Rush's donations.

Some charities take the view that the poisoned tree bears only poisoned fruit, and charities need to follow their consciences. Also important to consider, however, is that the money, if refused, is taken from a deserving cause and returned to the entity that may deserve it far less than the charity and the people it serves. Perhaps with that logic as their guide, few charities ever return a gift, especially when there aren't any strings attached. A more practical maxim, and equally ethical, may be: the devil's had it long enough.

That perspective, however, even for those who agree with it, doesn't provide a guide for all gifts. In the fall of 2004, Hakan Yalincak, an entrepreneurial twenty-one–year-old student at New York University, pledged $21 million to NYU from his family's foundation to establish a professorship and lecture series in Ottoman studies. The following year he paid $1.25 million, which he said would be the first installment of his pledge.

The problem was that the family foundation was bogus. In the summer of 2006, Yalincak pleaded guilty to fraud after being charged with duping investors of more than $7 million in a hedge fund and kiting checks for more than $43 million. In what amounted to a Ponzi scheme, he used the hedge fund to take in money and then paid investors—the ones that started to get antsy—with money from new investors. Prosecutors said that the NYU gift was made to reassure investors that Yalincak could be trusted—nothing like donating to charity to show how good you are.

Once the facts came to light, and well before the guilty plea, NYU decided to return the gift. Not to Yalincak, for the money was never really his, but to those the courts decided really owned it. "True philanthropy requires good faith," said university spokesman John Beckman. "Clearly that was lacking here."

GIVING USA, WHICH records the amount Americans give to charity every year, reported that charities took in over $260 billion in 2005. That was a little more than in the prior year. Much of the increase was earmarked for disaster relief—tsunamis in Indonesia, the earthquake in

Pakistan, and hurricane Katrina.

With few exceptions, the amount rises every year. But the percentages from the four general sources don't change much from year to year. Living individuals account for approximately three-quarters of all giving. Dead people, through their wills and other estate devices, account for between 5 and 10 percent; the percentage varies because, although people can decide when to give when they are alive, they don't tend to know when they will die. Foundations account for a little more than 10 percent of all giving, and corporations are responsible for 5 percent.

That's where it comes from. This is where it went in 2005.

- Religion took in about 35 percent of all gifts, over $93 billion. Yet, while giving to support religious causes is stronger than for other segments of the charitable world, it has declined as a percent of all giving in recent years;
- Education—donations to universities, colleges, and independent schools—received $39 billion, or 15 percent of the total;
- Hospitals and other health-related charities are next with $22 billion, a little under 9 percent of all giving;
- Human services, which include what many people think of as real charities—the soup kitchens, the homeless shelters, the YWCAs, and the disaster–aid charities—received $25 billion, a little under 10 percent;
- The arts received $14 billion, about 3¹/₂ percent of the total;
- Environmental causes such as the Sierra Club, the Ocean Conservancy, the World Wildlife Fund, the Wilderness Society, the National Audubon Society, and the Nature Conservancy, as well as the many small local and regional groups around the country, took in $9 billion, about 3 percent of the total.

The rest was scattered around to a few other categories of charities.

MEASURED BY ITS monetary value, the quarter trillion dollars that Americans donate every year makes them the most generous people on earth. Independent Sector, the Washington, D.C.-based consortium of charities, reports that 89 percent of American households—about one hundred million households—donate money every year.

Also, according to the Corporation for National and Community

Service, a federal agency, almost 30 percent of adults—some sixty million people—volunteer their time. Independent Sector calculated that the value of that time in 2005 was $18.04 per hour, which translates into approximately $280 billion—more, even, than the amount donated outright.

It is true that if philanthropy is measured another way—as a percent of the national Gross Domestic Product—the value of donating money and volunteering in the United States ranks only seventh in the world. The book *Global Civil Society*, written in 2004 by Lester Salamon and S. Wojciech Sokolowski, shows that the Netherlands ranks number one, with Norway and France also ahead of the United States. Measuring donations alone as a percent of GDP, the United States ranks second, behind Israel.

Keep in mind, though, that the GDP of the United States is the largest in the world by far, about three times as large as second place Japan's. The GDP of the Netherlands, ranked sixteenth in the world in 2004, is about 5 percent of that of the United States.

EVEN THOUGH A poor economy has its effect on donor attitudes, and some charities do go out of business or lay off people, charities seem to survive.

Taking a look at the elite of education, for example, in 2002, *The Chronicle of Philanthropy* indicated that the giving trend from 2000 to 2001—a bad time for investments and the economy—did not slow. Harvard University raised more than $680 million in 2001, more than any other college or university in the United States. Harvard was in a capital campaign then and in 2004 was able to muster up only $540 million. Second-place Stanford raised $524 million. Ranked twentieth in 2004, and therefore last in the *Chronicle's* report for that year, was the University of North Carolina at Chapel Hill, which raised $187 million.

As we saw earlier from the *Giving USA* information, some of the money going to charities—a little more than 10 percent—comes from foundations, some of them private, some public. A public foundation's requirement to distribute at least 5 percent of its assets each year to charities means that they, too, are generous benefactors. As foundation endowments swelled during the mid-1990s, so did the foundations' obligation to give money away. Then, after the dramatic collapse of stock prices, the opposite was true. Even charities that convincingly argued their case could not rely on as much income as they had before.

A KEY ASPECT of charity in the United States is that it is not allowed to be political. Charitable missions are expected to transcend politics and political agendas. The tax code says a charity is not allowed to "participate in or intervene in any political campaigning on behalf of (or in opposition to) any candidate for public office."

The IRS distinguishes between political and legislative activity, and so charities have more flexibility when it comes to initiatives before Congress or state legislatures. Charities are allowed to fight for causes that affect them, such as a bill that would retain the income tax deduction for charitable gifts. They are also allowed to sponsor a debate to educate voters, as long as they don't show a preference for either candidate.

Even though charities can lobby, they can't lobby very much. The Sierra Club, AIPAC (the American Israel Public Affairs Committee), the National Rifle Association, and others we commonly know to be packing big guns on Capitol Hill are actually not defying the rules. Even though they seem to spend all their time and money lobbying Congress, the distinction for those groups is that they are not public charities. They fall into one of the other twenty-six categories of tax-exempt organizations, a category that allows them to lobby.

Lobbying groups typically don't solicit you for gifts—at least not for the kind you can deduct. Instead, you might receive an invitation to join the group. Furthermore, when you do receive solicitations for donations, most likely you are receiving them from their foundations, which usually declare their mission as education or research—something that isn't political. Donations to these groups generally are deductible.

Even though charities are aware of the issue, one ongoing controversy, rekindled every presidential campaign, is just how political charities are getting.

As a result of a speech in July 2004 by Julian Bond, the chairman of the NAACP, the IRS sent a letter informing the charity that it was investigating "whether or not your organization has intervened in a political campaign."

The letter charged that Bond "condemned the policies of George W. Bush on education, the economy, and the war in Iraq."

Bond said this: "If whites and blacks vote in the same percentages as they did in 2000, Bush will be re-defeated by three million votes."

The statement could be construed as a call not to vote for Bush, especially as Bond uses the word "re-defeat," which encapsulates what many Democrats are certain happened in the presidential election of 2000.

After the NAACP story was reported, where it was noted that the IRS letter arrived a month before the 2004 presidential election, IRS commissioner Mark Everson said that "any suggestion that the IRS has tilted its audit activities for political purposes is repugnant and groundless." He added, "Law enforcement decisions at the IRS are made without regard to political considerations."

The IRS spent ten years investigating the Christian Coalition, the religious organization founded by the broadcaster Pat Robertson, and denied the group tax-exempt status until it sued and then prevailed. The issue there was how involved Christian Coalition had been in Robertson's 1988 presidential campaign.

In 2006, the IRS issued a report on charities that improperly deal in politics. Of the 132 organizations that were examined, a little less than half were religious. Three-quarters of the charities examined were guilty of some political wrongdoing. Many of them were given warnings of various degrees. Three charities had their tax-exempt status revoked. The bad behavior included: distributing printed materials that specifically endorsed or criticized candidates, religious leaders using the pulpit to direct votes, Web sites that directed viewers to preferred candidates' sites, distributing one-sided voter guides, placing signs on charity property, permitting some candidates to speak while denying others the same opportunity, and even making cash contributions to a campaign directly from the charity.

HARVARD UNIVERSITY COLLECTED more than $2 billion in its recent capital campaign, and its endowment is approximately $25 billion. Yet, as illogical as this may sound, a few years ago the University claimed it could not find the means to pay its service employees a decent enough wage to keep its own students from protesting. Harvard explained that the budget was tight and, even with its big endowment, cited rising costs of tuition and room and board to make a strong case to continue raising money.

The topic of endowments is a philosophical battleground in America's charity world. Critics and some charities contend that all available money should be used for current programs. Help those who need it now, they say. Others take the view that building an endowment is the surest way to guarantee their continued existence.

It's not just Harvard. Many of the larger universities and several select organizations in other sectors of the charity universe measure their endowments in the billions of dollars. Most of the charities we hear about on a regular basis have strong endowments. This does not mean, however, that they are exempt from working within the constraints of a budget. Just because an endowment may seem large, it may not be large enough if the charity's annual operating expenses are high.

But if a charity is able to bank millions of dollars, how does that square with the rules ensuring that they stay on a narrow line defined by their mission and make certain that they do not engage in anything that would actually turn a profit? After all, isn't having a bank account in the millions at least a little like making a profit?

Again, there is no rule that says charities—nonprofits—can't make a profit; they just don't have shareholders for whom to make profits. Even so, if a charity has an abundance of cash, and there is work to do, why not use it? This is where the rubber meets the road of public perception, a perception that is often out of sync with reality.

A charity that may go out of business once its work is done—a charity working to eradicate cancer, for example—probably should keep its endowment very low and devote every resource to its mission. A charity whose work is ongoing—a university or an arts organization, for example—should probably have an endowment.

The author of an article entitled "Why Colleges Cost Too Much," published in *Time* magazine a few years ago, reported that tuition at the University of Pennsylvania had climbed dramatically in the years since he attended the school. After outlining the ingredients of the school's budget, including a disapproving note about the president's large salary, he asked why costs were so high when the endowment was so large. (In 2004, Penn's net assets were approximately $4 billion.)

People may feel that, with tuitions rising so much, more money from an endowment ought to be used each year to keep tuition lower. The article proposed that, instead of spending 5 percent of the university's endowment per year, 7 percent would be much better.

In the short run, more money could be made available from the endowment and maybe, for a while, tuition could be kept constant or even reduced. But in the long run—and endowments, if anything, are intended for the long run—the eventual effect would be to stifle growth and increase economic uncertainty at the university. The cost of providing programs would rise even faster if endowment income were not available.

Charities—at least those that plan to be around for a while—need endowments. In addition to keeping down costs, charities need to make sure resources will be available for projects such as new buildings, as well as for maintenance, repairs, and the growing cost of ongoing programs. Otherwise, there will be trouble down the road: a fast scramble some day in the future to keep things as they should be.

The University of Pennsylvania has been around for more than 200 years. Perhaps a good way to approach the question of endowment is to imagine what the place will be like in the year 2200. Will the university still exist? It is entirely possible, of course, that by then colleges and universities will be extinct, replaced by some other educational mechanism. But if the board of trustees thinks that society will benefit from a University of Pennsylvania, those in charge today need to protect its future.

Every charity should pause on that thought.

8

FIRMLY ESTABLISHED

"I again ask forgiveness for all the harm done to young people by our clergy."
Reverend Sean P. O'Malley At his installation as
Boston's archbishop, July 30, 2003

THE OLD NORTH Church in Boston's historic North End is not a controversial place—unless you're a Tory who believes the British should have won the Revolutionary War.

The church, where in 1775 Paul Revere saw two lanterns hanging, to tell him that the British were coming by sea so he could alert the colonial leaders and militants of the day, was in the news again in the spring of 2003. The Bush Administration announced that it would provide a federal grant of $317,000 to spruce the place up; after all, here was an historic and important building.

The Old North Church is also, however, an active church with a congregation that attends a regular schedule of religious services.

There are those who pay close attention when public money is channeled to any religion. Despite a policy to the contrary, as well as an understanding—vague and inciting as it simultaneously seems to be for a large number of Americans—that religion and public dollars are separate, the Bush Administration said that it would pay federal grant money to this church for renovations, as well as to other religious sites designated as historic landmarks.

Gale Norton, Secretary of the Interior, as reported in *The New York Times* on May 28, 2003, said, "Today we have a new policy that will bring balance to historic preservation and end the discriminatory double standard that has been applied against religious properties."

With a different emphasis, Jim Towey, at the time the director of the White House Office of Faith-Based and Community Initiatives—and once a lawyer for Mother Teresa—said the change in policy applied only to places of worship that qualify as landmarks under the Save America's Treasures program, and that the money would be used to preserve physical structure, not to advance the religious agenda of the church.

The general idea put forth publicly by the Bush administration was that churches, under the right circumstances, need to be helped and should not be deprived of that help just because they house faith-based organizations. After all, the renovations wouldn't require much: just a bunch of nails, some paint, and a few planks of wood to hold together an important piece of our heritage. Nothing terribly religious about that.

At the same time, even though the memories of the American Revolution have wafted through the rafters of the church for more than two centuries, people worship there today. The Old North Church embodies both religion and history.

At first, the Old North Church was denied the grant. Concerns about separation of church and state have historically kept religious organizations from receiving federal money, a policy formalized in a Justice Department legal opinion in 1995. But the Bush administration requested a new ruling from its Justice Department, one that would permit churches to receive federal money for renovations.

But why stop there? If government help doesn't involve proselytization—the act of converting someone from one religious belief to another—why shroud the effort, as Towey did, in historical terms, when the real agenda, obvious to anyone paying the slightest bit of attention to Bush's rhetoric and actions, is to have the federal government help churches and other faith-based organizations? Acknowledging that at least takes us to the real question: does a federal grant from taxpayer dollars tear down the wall separating church and state in a way that violates the Constitution?

In the end Bush got what he wanted, as well as some severe but expected criticism. "This is just one more step in a government-wide drive to fund religion with taxpayer dollars," said Joseph Conn, a spokesman for Americans United for Separation of Church and State. "Literally you're putting public money in the collection plate for the church's building fund."

WHEN YOU DISCUSS religion you often start a quarrel, and the discussion gets stopped in its tracks. Even in a world where ideas matter, and differences of opinion can be freely aired, the topic of religion is often avoided.

While most of its leaders call for peace, religion, not unlike tribalism, is the major cause of human conflict. Most religions are supposed to spread love, but the reality is that many religious differences breed distrust, division, and even hatred. From the beginning of time, it has been the leading cause of war. Religious differences have resulted in more deaths than any plague known to humanity.

Religion stops Congress, the Supreme Court, and many lesser courts, while we as a society try to figure out how to make democracy and religion—both needy and demanding concepts—co-exist.

When the founding fathers took up the matter, a keen sense of history—all the bloodshed and oppression—informed their skepticism about the official role of religion in civic life. Frequently referenced as the "establishment clause"—the word "separation" isn't used—our Constitution's First Amendment deals with religion by saying that the government must stay away from it:

> Congress shall make no law respecting an establishment of religion, or prohibiting the free exercise thereof. . .

The law cannot respect—read *favor*—any religion. The ban on public school prayer is perhaps the most well-known example of the establishment clause in action. Conversely, and just as important, the law also cannot prohibit the free exercise of religion. This basically means that the American government cannot prevent any of us from practicing our faith. This has led to the belief that, as we keep government out of religion, so we must also keep religion out of government. A phrase that captures the sentiment: "Our elected lawmakers swear on the Bible to uphold the Constitution; they don't swear on the Constitution to uphold the Bible."

The quote is attributed to Maryland state senate candidate Jamie Reskin, who testified in March 2006 on the issue of a proposed same-sex marriage discrimination amendment. He had been asked whether "God's law" forbids same-sex marriage.

It's not a new debate. Ever since the ink on the Bill of Rights was dry, Americans have been divided, acutely uncomfortable with the clash of ideals between those who want religion in our civic life and those who don't.

Religion was an important part of government when Britain was still in control. On the eve of the revolution, nine of the thirteen colonies recognized established churches supported by tax dollars. Then came the war, the Articles of Confederation, and in 1787 the Constitution, which finally unified the nation. Soon after, in the first session of Congress, came the Bill of Rights with the First Amendment, the meaning of which we've been arguing about ever since.

After the country got going, in the late 1700s and early 1800s, many people thought that the main principle of the Enlightenment (reason) ought to take priority over that of the Second Awakening (faith). This was, after all, not a faith-based government but a republic, defined and ruled by a written, intellectually rational Constitution. A lot of people in the early years of the republic were unhappy about the continued prominence of religion.

Of course, a lot of others were unhappy with them for feeling that way.

Although the public is divided in much the same way today, this was more than 200 years ago. The problem simmered for a few decades until, in 1819, the Supreme Court heard the *Dartmouth College* case.

As hard as it may be to imagine today, Dartmouth was being taken over by the advocates of religion, and the governor of New Hampshire thought that, since the college was a government-sanctioned corporation, it should reflect the Enlightenment, or republican, ideals as portrayed in the Constitution.

The state legislature took over the college and renamed it Dartmouth University.

The college trustees, as one might predict, would have nothing of that.

They took the case to court, and it eventually wound up at the Supreme Court. After a stunning and persuasive argument on behalf of the college's position by Dartmouth alumnus Daniel Webster, the court decided not only that the state could not simply take over the school and overturn a contract (which is what the case is mostly known for among law students), but also that private, incorporated charities need to be protected from the state.

Chief Justice John Marshall, who wrote the majority opinion, thought that the founders and original donors wanted to forever further the interests of the college, not the state.

Dartmouth would never again be a university. Even though its national prominence leads some people to assume it is a university and even though its peer institutions are all universities, from that day in 1819, when it was a victor at the Supreme Court, it has been a *college*. The school and alumni are very sensitive on that point.

Mark McGarvie, who wrote on this topic in the book *Charity, Philanthropy, and Civility in American History*, says that Marshall's reasoning "clarified the status of charitable institutions in the early republic," and that "Marshall not only distinguishes private charitable corporations from governmental offices and agencies, but also requires legal formalization of those charities in order for them to be legally secure in the pursuit of their purposes."

As the court saw it, without the legal protections that would permit charities to flourish, many of America's social needs would remain unaddressed. In his ruling, Marshall wrote, "These eleemosynary institutions do not fill the place which would otherwise be occupied by government, but that which would otherwise remain vacant."

After the decision, more and more charities in the United States were formed, leading to Tocqueville's observations a little more than a decade later about the vast number of "associations" in this country.

This action significantly pre-dates the time that most people think charities acquired legal protection. Again, McGarvie: "The beginning of philanthropic organizations occurred not with the funding of the large trusts at the turn of the twentieth century, but in the creation of the legal model for philanthropic pursuits during the early republic."

So it is that faith-based organizations, as well as so many other charities with a vast array of social agendas, have their secure place in society, free from government interference.

The *Dartmouth College* case, as the decision that protects charities in an ironclad way, should demonstrate that mixing up government and religion would actually work *against* the interests of those who want to protect the role of religion in society.

Religion in society and religion in government are two entirely different ideas. Except, of course, when they're not—when society and government intersect.

THE FIRST $100 million in grants to faith-based organizations during the Bush administration went to Christian groups. Esther Kaplan, in the November 1, 2004, edition of the *Nation*, wrote, "No direct funding [as of that date] from the faith-based office has gone to a single non-Christian religious organization, whether Jewish, Muslim, Buddhist, or Sikh." Noting that Pat Robertson's Operation Blessing and Chuck Colson's Prison Fellowship Ministries, both of them religious and conservative, were among the first and largest beneficiaries of federal grants, Kaplan then opined, "The Bush administration has effectively turned over tens of millions of public dollars to the Christian right to distribute as it sees fit."

Of course, even absent the criticism that faith-based grants favor Christian groups, many people would still have a problem with public dollars being granted to any religious organization.

In 2002, President Bush signed an executive order to end what he saw as discrimination against faith-based organizations. That led to the federal grant to the Old North Church. But renovation money isn't really the issue. Instead, as the president sees it, the idea is to ensure equal protection under the law. Non-faith-based organizations receive money from the federal and state governments to do their social work, so why shouldn't faith-based groups, which also do a lot of social work, get the same break? That is, why deny them the subsidies they need to do their jobs well when others are getting that same funding? Why penalize them for being faith-based?

President Bush, in the White House pamphlet *Protecting Civil Rights and Religious Liberty of Faith-Based Organizations*, said that he knows that government has no business endorsing a religious creed or directly funding religious worship or teaching. But as he interprets the law, this does not mean that government can't support social services provided by faith-based organizations.

Faith-based organizations are natural conduits for helping the poor and the needy. Of the organizations that provide such assistance, more of them are religious groups than not.

Critics claim that giving money to religious groups wrongly allows them to bar homosexuals and others from employment. "When unemployment is reaching alarming levels, it's especially disgraceful to deny someone a public job on religious grounds," the Reverend Barry W. Lynn, executive director of Americans United for Separation of Church and State, told *The Chronicle of Philanthropy* in 2003. "White House staffers," he added, "can try to dress this up any way they want, but it still smells like government-sponsored bigotry."

The government is interested in addressing social ills and does so through social service programs with several objectives, and many religious organizations run social service programs. In a real way, to deny money to faith-based groups that do this work is to deny the humanity of our society. The poor people lined up at a church-run soup kitchen are more likely to ask how hot the food is than to wonder about the proper application of the First Amendment.

The problem occurs when organizations use federal money to inflict their religious agenda on others. But that's not what is going on. At least not now, not yet. And if that does happen, the offending organization alone ought to suffer by being barred from receiving federal money. We can't deny the role of faith in the lives of so many, and those who have no faith at all need to appreciate the role it plays in others' lives.

Our experiment at separating the government from religious influence, at least partially informed by its more than two hundred years of experience, is in no danger of establishing a national religion or preventing people from worshipping the way their hearts tell them to.

★ ★ ★

GOVERNMENT HAS FOR many years subsidized religious activity—well before anyone uttered the phrase "faith-based initiatives"—and no one has complained.

The charitable tax deduction, not even imagined in 1787 or 1819, is another—and far more important—axis of intersection. In fact, even though Americans energetically debate faith-based initiatives, and keeping the crèche off the front lawn of city hall and the state house, the charitable income tax deduction is far more compelling evidence that, aside from establishing a national religious entity, we have essentially made moot the concept of separation.

Think about the religious chaplains in the armed services. Think about the ministers who bless Congress. No problem. This may be good or it may be bad, depending on your perspective.

But if that's bad for you, it's actually far worse.

We've already seen how the deduction works for donors who itemize their tax returns, but we haven't looked at how it works for society. How is it that the donor's tax savings means he or she pays less than the gift amount, while the charity gets the whole gift? Clearly, someone is making up the difference, and that someone is the government, which means, of course, all the other taxpayers. All of us. Since the charitable deduction is a public subsidy, it is paid for not by one person but by the whole public.

Like the rest of us, your tax dollars support the military and Medicaid budgets and all the other things the government pays for. Except for a few people, we all accept that.

In the same way, it's also true that as a taxpayer, but not necessarily as a donor, in today's United States you also support charitable contributions to all sorts of places: the Methodist church down the street, the Temple on the opposite side of town, the Catholic Church next door, and the mosque on the next block.

You may be an atheist or an agnostic, but your tax dollars, through the deduction structure, provide financial support to these religious entities.

You support a lot of other charities, too.

This may come as a horrid surprise. Despite the everyday news to the contrary, by law and tradition government support of religion is firmly and squarely established in our society. The Bush administration's faith-based initiatives simply made that support more overt.

Since many donors don't itemize their deductions or are in low tax brackets, while others are in the highest tax bracket, let's say for argument's sake that the average donor to religious causes might be in the 15 or 20 percent bracket. This means that, of the $88 billion that religious organizations collected in 2004, a minimum of approximately $13 billion dollars worth of religious support was subsidized by the public that year. By that standard, the current levels of grants through the faith-based initiatives—$2.1 billion in 2005—while they get the headlines and the protests, add up to small potatoes.

The very idea of a charitable deduction works to undermine what many people think is one of our most cherished constitutional principles. With our knowledge as well as our endorsement, religion in the United States is already significantly supported by public money. If you really want to talk about a collection plate piled high with public dollars, look no further than the tax code, the largest collection plate of all, and take note of how much controversy it *doesn't* generate.

IT'S NOT JUST the gifts, either. Religious organizations are a large part of our charitable landscape, and, almost stealthily, religion has gained a front position at the public trough. *The New York Times Magazine* ethics columnist Randy Cohen wrote in an article on July 2, 2000, "Why church property . . . is exempt from tax is a mystery to me."

Depending on the state and town where the charity resides, most charities—not just religious organizations—are exempt from property taxes. This can mean large sums of lost municipal revenue. Think of universities and other charities, the largest of which use acres of land and are often located in the best parts of town.

In addition to the tax deduction and the property tax, the exemption issue for religious organizations has come up in the context of the parsonage allowance, a tax-free amount provided to the nation's clergy, who are less well-paid than others.

All the fuss might be lost on those who work for charities, however, and, in particular, on those employed by faith-based organizations. For most of them, in fact, this is not a question at all; it should seem to everyone perfectly natural and legal to exempt property owned by religious organizations from property taxes. Not to exempt churches would deny them the benefit every other charity enjoys.

Here's something that some people will like even less: of all the categories of charities, faith-based organizations are the only ones that do not have to report to the IRS each year. That's why we know so little about the activities of, say, the Salvation Army. It's not widely known, but the Salvation Army is registered with the IRS as a religious organization. Other than in press releases issued from its headquarters in Alexandria, Virginia, telling us how many people it serves in a given year, we aren't told—and have no way of knowing—anything about the Army's finances.

All other charities, in exchange for accepting and investing dollars that are not taxed, must report to the IRS what they spend on programs and fundraising, how much their key employees are paid, and other matters related to their financial structure. That information is public and available to anyone who's interested. Not so for religious organizations. Not only do faith-based organizations receive the benefits of other charities, they are free of the obligation to publicly report their activities.

While this lack of a reporting requirement, unique among all the classes of charities, is apparently an effort to honor the First Amendment, it shows that faith-based organizations receive tremendous slack when it comes to the issue of transparency.

They use public money, so why shouldn't they be required to post their financial information like everyone else?

THAT SLACK MAY be at least partly responsible for what happened in Boston, where thirty years of buried secrets began to burst out from their pockets of concealment in 2001.

On January 6, 2002, the *Boston Globe* reported that John Geoghan, a former priest, had been accused of fondling or raping more than 130 males over a span of three decades. "Almost always, his victims were grammar school boys," the *Globe* reported.

One was four years old.

Cardinal Bernard Law, the head of the Boston Archdiocese at the time, admitted that he knew all about Geoghan's problems as early as 1984. At that time, in a sort of "out of sight, out of mind" approach, he transferred the priest to another parish. In 1980, according to an archdiocesan record, Geoghan said that his repeated abuse of seven boys in one extended family was not a "serious" problem. *Seven boys. Repeated abuse. Not a serious problem.*

The 1984 assignment to another parish proved disastrous, however, as Geoghan was forced to go on sick leave after his superiors received additional complaints of sexual abuse.

He spent months in two institutions that treat sexually abusive priests. Cardinal Law's attorney said the archdiocese received medical assurances that each of Geoghan's reassignments was "appropriate and safe."

The *Globe* asked, "Why did it take a succession of three cardinals and many bishops thirty-four years to place children out of Geoghan's reach?"

On July 23, 2003, Thomas Reilly, the attorney general of Massachusetts, issued a scathing ninety-one page report in which he said that the magnitude and the duration of the sex-abuse scandal in Boston was staggering. He noted 789 victims and 250 accused church personnel—all but thirteen of whom were clergy—and that more were definitely abused.

Reilly added that he could not criminally prosecute the church's top management. He couldn't, because the law, until recently, had not provided enough clout. As chronicled in the *Globe* the following day, he did not mince his words in assigning blame.

The conduct of the leadership and senior management, while not criminal, was absolutely deplorable. Any claim that the cardinal or senior management didn't know what was going on is simply not credible.

They knew full well that children were being sexually abused. Yet time after time, decision after decision, when they were tested, when they were forced and faced with the choice between protecting children and protecting the reputation of the church and the priest abusers, they chose secrecy, and they chose to protect the church at the expense of children. In effect, they sacrificed children for many, many years.

The report stated that the "staggering magnitude of the problem would have alerted any reasonable, responsible manager that immediate and decisive measures must be taken," and that the "archdiocese has yet to demonstrate an appropriate sense of urgency for attacking the problem of sexual abuse or for changing its culture to remove the risk to children."

The report also said that the archdiocese's response to the "disclosure of the long history of clergy sexual abuse of children demonstrates an insufficient commitment" to find the causes of clergy abuse, removing priests who committed crimes against children, and addressing its failure to prevent sexual abuse of children.

The attorney general's laser then aimed at the person at the center of it all:

> There is overwhelming evidence that for many years Cardinal Law and his senior managers had direct, actual knowledge that substantial numbers of children in the archdiocese had been sexually abused by substantial numbers of its priests.
>
> Members of the cardinal's senior management team received complaints of abuse; determined the archdiocese's response to the complaints; determined the approval for their actions; and conferred with the cardinal and sought his approval of their recommendations.
>
> Any claim by the cardinal or the archdiocese senior managers that they did not know of the abuse suffered by, or the continuing threat to, children in the archdiocese is simply not credible.

Even though many people were disappointed that no criminal charges would be brought, this report, with its stark absence of qualifiers, was anything but a whitewash.

In a year and a half, the world of the Catholic Church was turned upside down, as other parishes around the country, and some in other parts of the world, revealed that they, too, had priests who abused children. The scandal was enormous.

On April 12, 2002, Cardinal Law announced that he would not resign from his post, that he would continue for "as long as God gives me the opportunity." Eight months later, God rescinded the opportunity, and Pope John Paul II accepted Cardinal Law's resignation. In its wake were almost one thousand abused people and, from a financial perspective, a nearly bankrupt archdiocese. From any other perspective, such as the ones that religion promotes—morals and values, for example—the bank had been empty long before.

Over the past decades, donors and the rest of the public have demanded more and more accountability and transparency from charities. But the archdiocese of Boston was doing what it could to hide its shameful secrets.

Because they don't have to report to the public, faith-based organizations are more immune from public examination than other types of charities are. Donors can make their decisions—fundraising fell off, and the church decided to declare victory in a $300–million capital campaign, even though it raised only $200 million—but the victims can't erase the abuse from their memories.

In April 2006, the archdiocese did open its books. Perhaps the pressure was too great, and its leaders felt they needed to come clean with the public. The financial accounting showed that the archdiocese was $46 million in debt, the largest debt of any diocese ever. The church paid out more than $150 million in connection with the sexual abuse scandal, $127 million of which went to settlements with the abused. The difference paid for counseling and legal costs. Ninety-nine percent of the money came from insurance and the sale of assets. The remaining 1 percent—about $2 million—came from donors who requested that their gifts be used to pay for therapy for the victims.

WHAT DID THE men who met in Philadelphia in 1787 really hope to accomplish regarding what was, even back then, a thorny issue?

Although no one in that long, hot summer meeting said one word about charities, the role of religion was ever-present. Many of the delegates supported the Constitution only because a Bill of Rights would immediately be added. They were concerned about how such a powerful and important social force as religion could be kept separate from the workings of government, yet free to flourish at the same time.

Religion was important to the founders. But so was a government independent of religion.

In a real way, religion fits well into our complex social and governmental structures. We intrude neither on a religious organization's ability to raise and invest money nor on its standing as a charity.

But we do this at the same time that we permit a unique degree of financial privacy. Religious groups have it both ways: they receive public money and they maintain their privacy.

Yes, scandals take place at many other charities—we've examined a few so far, and newspapers daily tell us of others. But at least the public can examine what those other charities report to the IRS.

Not so at religious charities; there is, you see, a separation going on.

The many hundreds of boys (and no one knows, really, how many more throughout the country) referred to by the Massachusetts attorney general were abused with public money. We all paid for it.

Denying religious organizations tax-deductible contributions, or taxing property owned by them, would insult their good work and proper status as legal charities. Furthermore, either action would rightly arouse vast opposition, and therefore neither is viable. And Chief Justice John Marshall just might turn over in his grave.

Instead, the solution is to require faith-based organizations to report to the public, just like everybody else. Requiring public reporting won't by itself prevent scandals of course, but if the public is footing a good chunk of the bill, then certainly those who pay for the product ought to know what's going on.

Something else we can do: stop equating the phrase "make no law respecting an establishment of religion"—the words in the First Amendment—with "separation." They are not the same sentiments, and confusing them has led to a heap of trouble. The deduction, while it supports all religions, favors none.

FROM THE ASSOCIATED Press on August 23, 2003: "Former priest John Geoghan, the convicted child molester whose prosecution sparked the sex abuse scandal that shook the Roman Catholic Church nationwide, died Saturday after being attacked in prison. Preliminary indications are that Geoghan, 68, was strangled."

Other than in Boston, his death was scarcely noted.

9

CHARITY AND TERRORISM

"From the beginning of this fight, I have said our enemies are terrorist organizations of global reach, and all who harbor them and support them."
PRESIDENT GEORGE W. BUSH, DECEMBER 4, 2001

YOU ARE THE kind of person who cares about other human beings, not just in the United States but throughout the world. While you realize that many people in this country are homeless, you are also drawn to those who are in abject misery in other parts of the globe. In your view, the hungry people here are relatively well off.

Your ancestors lived in Beirut, and many of your relatives live there today. Your grandfather immigrated to the United States and opened a small restaurant. His son followed in his footsteps. You, the grandson, didn't continue in the restaurant business but entered the teaching profession, and you now teach at a small liberal arts college in California.

You have been to the Middle East three times in your life and maintain contact with your extended family. On every visit you observe for yourself the harsh poverty in the arid regions south of the city. The struggle to survive in the mountains to the north is as awful as it can get. The beggars on the streets of New York and San Francisco seem almost wealthy by comparison.

Some time ago, you received a mass-mailed letter from an organization that called itself the Holy Land Foundation for Relief and Development. Your inherent skepticism of something contained in an envelope without a first class stamp discouraged you from automatically responding to this type of thing. Still, you found yourself intrigued by the short headline on the outside of the envelope, where you read that the group was providing relief to refugees, orphans, and victims of human and natural disasters in the war-torn Middle East.

You thought about it for a while and discussed it with a friend. Then you looked it up on a charity watchdog site, but couldn't find the organization. Interesting, but not alarming, since there are so many charities, and the watchdogs review only a small number of them.

Nothing can take the place of the satisfaction of a donor helping a worthy mission, and this mission tugs at your heart. As you reexamine the literature and stare at the pictures in the brochures, you conjure up mental images of the squalor in the Middle East. You mail the organization a check for $1,000.

The following year you send $1,500. The year after, $1,700.

A few years after you first heard from this group and began to support it, less than two months after the events of September 11, 2001, you learn that the Holy Land Foundation has come under scrutiny for, of all things, the suspicion that it aids terrorists.

The Department of Justice and the Department of the Treasury—even the White House—all have things to say about this organization, and none of them are good.

How can this be? This is a charity. How is it possible that the charity that you determined was doing work that you thought was so important is now the subject of accusing headlines in the national press?

IN DECEMBER 2001, the president blocked the assets of three charitable organizations, one of which was the Holy Land Foundation. The three charities were accused of funneling millions of dollars each year to Hamas, the Mid-East terrorist organization. A Treasury Department news release on that date reported

> Federal agents today locked down the Holy Land Foundation's head-
> quarters in Richardson, Texas, as well as its other offices in Bridgeview, Illi-
> nois, Patterson, New Jersey, and San Diego, California. They seized relevant
> business records.
>
> This action against financiers of Hamas makes good on our promise
> to go after the fundraisers for all terrorists of global reach.

The authority for such action was Executive Order 13224. It was
signed by President Bush on September 23, 2001, and authorized aggressive action against the bankers of international terrorism.

The order was just a few pages long, but its addenda added another
eighty pages and included the names of hundreds of individuals and
organizations throughout the world.

Just a few pages down, in a part added on December 4, was the name
"Holy Land Foundation for Relief and Development," the very name on
those heart-driven checks you have written.

After describing the malfeasance of Hamas, the Treasury Department
outlined the basics of its case.

- The Holy Land Foundation raised millions of dollars annually that was
  used by Hamas. During the prior year it raised more than $13 million.
- Holy Land supported Hamas activities through direct fund transfers to its
  offices in the West Bank and Gaza. These were affiliated with Hamas and
  transferred funds to Islamic charity committees and other charitable
  organizations that are part of Hamas.
- The Holy Land Foundation, originally known as the Occupied Land
  Fund, was established in California in 1989 as a tax-exempt charity, not
  a religious organization. In 1992, the Holy Land Foundation relocated to
  Richardson, Texas.
- Mousa Mohamed Abou Marzook, a political leader of Hamas, provided
  substantial funds to the Holy Land Foundation in the early 1990s. In
  1994, Marzook (who was named a Specially Designated Terrorist by
  the Treasury Department in 1995) designated the Holy Land Foundation as the primary fund-raising entity for Hamas in the United
  States.

That last point stung you to the quick: *the primary fund-raising entity for Hamas in the United States.*

The FBI claimed that the leader of the foundation attended a mid-1990s event where $207,000 was raised for Hamas.

Not only was a group in the United States being used to funnel money to aid terrorists, but it was public money—tax-deductible money—at that.

So much for your good-will giving. The satisfaction you felt when you mailed your check each year has shriveled to feelings of horror and a sickness. If you stretch your imagination, you can connect those checks to the terrorists who flew into the World Trade Center towers and the Pentagon and killed thousands of innocent people.

But you mustn't think that way. It is too awful to contemplate.

IN FEBRUARY 2003, four men were indicted in New York on charges that they sent more than $2.7 million to Iraq through charities based in the United States. The charities were Help the Needy and Help the Needy Endowment.

Neither of the related charities denied sending money to Iraq, even though this was against the law. They insisted that the money was used only to help needy Muslims.

Later that year, a prominent Yemeni cleric was arrested in Germany on charges of financing terrorism by using a Brooklyn mosque to collect millions of dollars—perhaps as much as $20 million—for Osama bin Laden. The cleric, Sheik Muhammad Ali Hassan al-Mouyad, told an FBI informant that he was a "spiritual adviser to Mr. bin Laden and had worked for years to provide money and weapons for a terrorist 'jihad.'"

He claimed that "jihad was his field" and boasted about his "involvement in providing money, recruits, and supplies to al-Qaeda, Hamas and other terrorist groups." New York City's police commissioner, Raymond W. Kelly, said al-Qaeda operatives "did their fundraising right here in our own backyard in Brooklyn."

This is the real thing, or so we are led to believe by the highest authorities of the United States government. The accusations come at a time when terrorism is a true fear and a demonstrated threat, at a time when Americans are jittery even at news of a small plane mistakenly flying off course over the Potomac and into Washington, D.C.'s restricted air-space for a few minutes.

Now, to learn that the most benign sector of our society has been used to feed the most evil force in the world is unthinkably horrible. You supported the Holy Land Foundation and now you can't help but ask yourself, "Was any of my money used to buy box cutters?"

We think of Hamas, officially declared by our government as a terrorist organization, through the eyes of Israel and the ever-present pictures on television and the Internet. This view informs us that the people who run Hamas are the world's evildoers. They blow up adults and children who are guilty only of riding buses, shopping at the open-air market, or eat-ing dinner at a restaurant at the wrong moment.

That's not how they see it in the Middle East, though. Outside of Israel, Hamas is seen as a complicated group. To many Palestinians, Hamas is not an evil organization but a heroic one. One of the group's three foundational pillars is charity, while religion and the fight against Israel are the other two. Hamas's charity to Palestinians is just that: it pays the bills for many families who have lost a wage-earner. It pays for school and clothing and food.

Its counterpart in America might be Second Harvest, the largest domestic hunger relief organization in the United States, or the local shel-ter. The difference is that our food shelter volunteers are not also blow-ing up innocent people who disagree with them. That's not the world we live in.

It is the world of the Middle East, however, and right now there is not enough of a governmental structure in place to make the distinctions that we in the United States have the luxury to make. Poverty is abundant and charity is—from a humanitarian perspective—essential, even though there are no organizations or government sanctions to support it.

People are conflicted about the Middle East. It may be a struggle between right and wrong, but not everyone in America—and certainly not everyone throughout the rest of the world—agrees on which side is right.

In April 2002, Enaam Arnaout was the thirty-nine-year-old Syrian-born director of one of America's largest Muslim charities: Benevolence International Foundation, in Worth, Illinois. He was arrested for his connections to terrorists, and was accused of lying under oath in a federal civil lawsuit. At issue were his denials that the foundation was "engaged in violence, terrorist activities or military operations."

The FBI charged that Arnaout had a relationship with Osama bin Laden and many of his key associates; that these ties dated back more than a decade, during which time the foundation was used by Bin Laden's al-Qaeda terrorists for logistical support; that terrorists attempting to obtain chemical and nuclear weapons on behalf of al-Qaeda had close contacts with the foundation and its office personnel; and that the foundation dealt directly with Chechen rebels, providing them with military support, money, and equipment.

The FBI also said that Arnaout was entrusted to take care of one of bin Laden's wives in 1979.

In 2002, federal agents said that Bin Laden used Benevolence International's ten offices worldwide to transfer money to al-Qaeda operatives. Al-Qaeda would withdraw funds that were purportedly contributed to build schools or provide food for the poor.

The FBI also said that firearms, explosives, and fraudulent passports were found in foundation offices raided in Bosnia-Herzegovina. The foundation sent $685,560 to Chechen rebels.

Arnaout admitted in court that he had made illegal donations to rebel fighters in Bosnia and Chechnya to pay for boots, tents, and other military supplies in the 1990s. In his plea bargain, however, he denied having any ties to al-Qaeda.

The FBI searched the offices of Benevolence International, and agents found documents concerning the use of smallpox as a biological weapon. The FBI also searched Arnaout's office in Palos Hills and his home in Newark, New Jersey. The government blocked the charity's assets.

In 2003, the foundation filed a lawsuit seeking a court order to overturn the government action. In seeking the court order, Arnaout maintained, "I have no idea or understanding as to why the government has taken these actions against BIF."

A review of Benevolence International's filings with the IRS for the year 2000 carried no warning flags. The group reported that it raised $3.6 million and spent $252,000 to raise it. As a percentage of either the total amount raised or the foundation's annual budget of $3.3 million, the cost of raising money was actually quite good, well within the informal guidelines of those who keep track of how much charities spend on fundraising and other things. A prospective donor would also be informed that the group distributed food and medical supplies, and helped orphans.

By traditional standards, Benevolence International was a good charity. Yet, there it was, listed by the Treasury Department in late 2002 as a "Specially Designated Global Terrorist."

TERRORISTS CAN USE charities in a surprising number of ways. In addition to raising money for terrorist groups, as some charities have done, they can use their money to smuggle terrorists into the United States, set up training centers, and launder money for criminals.

While the source of the donation is important for legitimate charities that fear being used by the unsavory, the main focus, as far as American policy and granting charitable status are concerned, should be on what a charity does with the money it receives. Donors need to be vigilant. But if a charity claims a 501(c)(3) charitable status, and a review of its official documents and the IRS Web site confirms that the organization is a legitimate charity, what can donors do to be certain that the charity is not a terrorist front?

The donor's job of due diligence has changed a little since 9/11.

Ensuring that charitable dollars do not finance illicit activities is a worthy goal, and there are many things donors can do to avoid sending money to organizations that are not what they say they are. This is a particularly sensitive issue, because so many charities work in foreign countries, doing good things and helping poor and needy people.

The best way potential donors can make sure their money is not furthering terrorist objectives is to get to know the charity intimately. If the location is convenient, it is worthwhile to visit the charity's office. At least talk by telephone with a senior employee and perhaps some of the board members, to personally ascertain the worthiness of the organization. Another step is to carefully read the charity's annual report.

In addition, potential donors should at least briefly review, despite its limitations, a charity's IRS filings, which show what the charity spends on fundraising, administrative expenses, and programs, as well as information designed to reveal its overall financial health. It is filed annually and is available for public inspection. Its usefulness as an evaluative tool is limited, however, because it contains scant narrative about the real work of the organization, and the financial information is not current.

In its Publication 78, the IRS lists all charities that are eligible to receive tax-deductible contributions, as well as those that have recently been added or removed. Added in the few months after 9/11 were the names of more than 300 charities established specifically to help the victims of the attacks. Listed among the organizations that the IRS has removed or suspended from charitable status were several suspected of being related to terrorism.

Fortunately, this is not a problem of epidemic proportions. Most charities that donors want to help are legitimate and have received donor support for many years. So on one level, nothing about the job of due diligence has changed. A donor needs to decide the type of charity he or she wishes to support. The vast majority of causes that Americans support are furthered by organizations that have been established for many years, and their history and financial activities are immediately and willingly made available

But for people who want to help small or unknown charities that help people in the Middle East—and there's nothing wrong with that—the job of due diligence is not clear; the old rules, to the degree they were ever employed at all, are not enough.

IN OCTOBER 1998, well before 9/11, a longtime Milwaukee businessman, fifty-year old Jamil Sarsour, a Palestinian by birth, found himself in an Israeli jail after being convicted of financing terrorism through a group that supported Osama bin Laden. The military court that convicted him said he gave $40,000 and other aid to Hamas.

Sarsour's relatives said he was jailed only because Israel tortured him into a confession as part of its campaign of repression against Palestinians. His son said that his father did not do anything wrong. "He did something that anybody would be proud of, to help poor people."

American Palestinians complained that the United States would have come to his defense had he been prosecuted in any country but Israel. "There is total hypocrisy," said attorney Othman Atta, a leader of the Palestinian community in Milwaukee. "Americans of Palestinian descent are second-class citizens when it comes to our government."

Before his arrest in Israel, Sarsour had shown no sign of being anything other than a successful immigrant. He owned a number of real estate properties. He had no criminal record.

He had settled in Milwaukee in the 1970s and took courses at the University of Wisconsin-Milwaukee. He earned money by buying, fixing, and reselling properties, and then eventually running a number of grocery and furniture stores in Milwaukee.

Sarsour typically traveled two or more times a year to the West Bank in Israel, where he owned a home, and ran a car dealership and a laundry business. His family said that he regularly brought money for poor Palestinians, many of whom had no means of support after losing breadwinners in the conflict with Israel.

The destination of those donations was at the root of the criminal charges that were brought against him in Israel. In October 1998, on one of his trips to the West Bank from Milwaukee, Sarsour was taken into custody at an Israeli airport. When he telephoned to say he would be late getting to his home in the West Bank, he wasn't concerned, because Palestinians often are detained by Israelis. But Sarsour remained in custody and, according to his family, was not allowed to meet with an attorney or any family member for more than three months.

In December 1998, he was charged by an Israeli military court with having given $40,000 to Hamas in 1997 and 1998.

Despite Sarsour's U.S. citizenship, his family members said, American officials made virtually no effort to investigate the case, even though he had complained of being tortured before making a plea bargain and receiving a nine-year sentence. In bringing its charges, however, the Israeli military court detailed what it said were extensive ties between Sarsour and Hamas. Sarsour was convicted of giving money and information directly to Adel Awadallah, a man from his West Bank hometown who was a Hamas leader.

On October 29, 2001, a *Milwaukee Journal Sentinel* news account said Sarsour denied charges of financing Hamas, saying he had only made "a small contribution" to the Awadallah family.

That small contribution did Sarsour in. He was in jail during the September 11 attacks; when released by the Israelis, Sarsour returned to a changed America.

And what is today's America? It is not, and never has been, a cookie-cutter place. We have always been a multi-layered people, and in at least one of those layers there are people who are glad to be Americans, and at the same time feel the need to help the poor in the Middle East.

There are those of us who embrace the ideals of America but also know that those ideals are not embraced by everyone in the world.

Jedediah Purdy, the young author of *Being American*, spent the months after the attacks traveling to all parts of the world "to understand the attraction and resentment, the imitation and rejection that America inspires everywhere."

Purdy found an Egyptian woman by the name of Ingy to represent many contradictions. Ingy described Osama Bin Laden as a hero, because he attacked the United States. "And of course, people like me," she says, "think that the way Osama did it was criminal. He should have attacked the White House. Then, no one could have said it was murder."

How this young woman could think that killing anyone in the White House (including, presumably, the president) would not be considered murder is impossible to fathom. But she does. Yet Ingy is also an attorney with materialistic ambitions and an upscale lifestyle. While many of us would say that's a hypocritical viewpoint, Purdy thought she was human, embracing an ambivalent and complex perspective, one that predates September 11.

Can it also be true, then, that some American donors are ambivalent and complex as they decide how to help the world's poor? Helping a terrorist organization to kill is one thing, but helping an organization that, by its mission, spills into some of the seamier sides of life abroad is a complex decision.

A dominant characteristic of a terrorist is poverty, and some people feel that addressing that is a good first step toward ridding the world of terrorism—a world that, while despicable, is difficult to identify.

IN JULY 2003, Chicago federal judge Suzanne Conlon declared that Enaam Arnaout, the head of Benevolence International, would not be convicted of terrorism, "nor does the record reflect that he attempted, participated in, or conspired to commit any act of terrorism." Arnaout admitted that he defrauded donors who thought they were giving only to the poor. For this he was sentenced. He also admitted to the accusation that he'd befriended Osama bin Laden in the early 1980s, but denied that he had given money to al-Qaeda and insisted that he was opposed to terrorism.

"The government has not established that the Bosnian and Chechen recipients of BIF aid were engaged in a federal act of terrorism," Judge Conlon said. She added that the boots, blankets, uniforms, and other goods donated to the Muslim fighters by the charity were not shown to fuel terrorism.

By the way, the United States itself supported and funded Bin Laden in the 1980s, when the Soviet Union invaded Afghanistan.

In February 2006, OMB Watch, a nonprofit government watchdog that promotes government transparency, reported on the fate of seven charities, including Holy Land Foundation and Benevolence International Foundation.

After years of back and forth legal maneuvering, the U.S. District Court for the Northern District of Illinois found Holy Land Foundation guilty of aiding and abetting Hamas.

Benevolence International has been shut down permanently. This, even though no terrorism-related charges were proven, and, as the OMB Watch report put it, "BIF never had the chance to challenge Treasury's evidence in open court or present witnesses in its own behalf." In a speech at Pace University, BIF attorney Matthew Piers described the legal action against BIF as the "malevolent destruction of a Muslim charity. It is hard to see how the government's activities with regard to Muslim charities have had any positive effect on the war on terrorism."

The OMB Watch report says that the BIF case, as well as others, shows the problems with the "active disruption" of charities "through criminal prosecution." So far, it says, "The government has officially charged only one organization with supporting terrorism, and secured no convictions. There is an absolute need for the government to reexamine policies that target the nonprofit sector with little prospect of stopping terrorism and at the expense of important humanitarian work and the constitutional rights of U.S.-based charities."

Even some of the people working within the government have their doubts. At the Treasury Department, one high-ranking employee, whose job is to investigate the financial activities of charities suspected of being linked with terrorism, said privately that he is conflicted. "Who are we," he asked me, "to equate providing food and shelter to terrorism? Are we to punish the women and children too, just because a relative joined the crusade against the United States?"

Maybe; maybe not. While the way the government has handled suspected Muslim charities may be open to criticism, something else is clear, and wholly unrelated to the government: We all need to examine closely where our charitable dollars are going.

PART III
WARNINGS AND LESSONS

10

THE TEXAS LAWSUIT

"With the stroke of a pen . . . American philanthropy was thrust into what assuredly is its darkest hour."
<small>CHARITABLE ACCORD, AFTER CHARITIES WERE NAMED IN
A CLASS-ACTION SUIT, OCTOBER 25, 1995</small>

ONE DAY BEFORE the close of 1994, Tal Roberts, executive vice president of the Baptist Foundation of Texas, sat at his desk in Dallas, his thoughts wandering to what was ahead for the coming year.

December 30 was the last business day of the year, and things from the charitable gift-receiving perspective had pretty much come to a close. So that day he may have had his mind on his other job, the job for which he received no remuneration: head of a group known as the American Council on Gift Annuities (ACGA).

An attorney and former FBI agent, Roberts had headed the tiny organization for many years and had recently been named its chairman. By the time he retired a few years later, Roberts would serve the council for almost twenty-five years. His career's accomplishments at the ACGA were solid, and he had much to be proud of. Thanks to his efforts, as well as those of a dedicated board of trustees and many nonprofit organizations around the United States, the number of charitable gift annuities that donors established grew tremendously during his tenure.

Despite his busy schedule, Tal Roberts always had time for others, and made them feel that they and their problems were important. A devout Baptist, a good businessman, and a person who knew the importance of philanthropy, he was the perfect individual to head the organization respected by so many charities.

Although the American Council on Gift Annuities is itself a charity, it's not the kind of place to which many people actually donate gifts. Instead, it's a membership organization, and most of its revenues come from dues and the professional conference it sponsors. It exists to assist other charities to attract gift annuities.

The "gift annuity" is a charitable gift that a donor makes in exchange for regular payments for the rest of his or her life. In the vernacular of charities, a charitable gift annuity is in the family known as "planned gifts." It is also called a "life-income gift," because the donor receives payments for the rest of his or her life.

The idea is to provide the payments while the donor needs them. Because the payments are structured so that the present value of the total paid out over the years will be less than the amount of what a donor parts with, the balance left at the end of the donor's lifetime will be a charitable gift.

The most important service the Council provides to other charities is the recommended payment schedule, the annual amounts charities pay their annuity donors. The schedule is based on a complex actuarial formula that takes into account the ages of those who are to receive payments, and the current and projected economic climate.

Approximately 1,800 charities are sponsors of the Council, and hundreds of thousands of donors throughout the United States and Canada have established charitable gift annuities. Big and small alike, and you've heard of most of the big ones: Harvard, Stanford, Northwestern University, Tulane University, the Red Cross, the Mayo Clinic, the New York Public Library, the Salvation Army, and many more. Then there are the many hundreds of smaller charities that issue gift annuities, such as homeless shelters, local arts centers, and houses of worship, particularly churches. Researchers believe that the first gift annuity in the United States was created for Yale University in 1831. The donor was John Trumbull, a history painter and portraitist, who gave the University over eighty pieces of his work in exchange for

$1,000 per year for the remainder of his life. Four of those paintings now hang in the United States Capitol.

Most donors don't use such rarefied gift assets. Instead, they use plain old money, or take something from their stock portfolio.

The charitable gift annuity is a basic tool of fundraising, and, under Tal Roberts's leadership, the American Council on Gift Annuities became a strong and respected voice in the philanthropic community. Despite its importance, however, the organization remains small. Except for its tiny staff, shared office space with another organization, and rent on a conference hall for biennial meetings, it has few overhead expenses. In the mid-1990s, the Council received remunerated part-time assistance from an employee at the Annuity Board of the Southern Baptist Convention.

In retrospect, Roberts perhaps wishes that he had retired before that day in late December 1994, because on that day he received his life-changing phone call. The person at the other end informed him that the American Council on Gift Annuities was party to a federal lawsuit.

Two and a half months earlier, on October 10, 1994, a state lawsuit had been filed in the District Court of Travis County, Texas, against the Lutheran Foundation of Texas, three other Lutheran charities, and five individuals. The suit had been brought by Dorothy Ozee on behalf of her ninety-six-year-old great-aunt Louise Peter.

Miss Peter had been in the habit of giving money to charity all her long life. Some years earlier, in anticipation of her death, she made several substantial and complicated gifts to Lutheran causes. Because Miss Peter had been declared mentally incompetent shortly after the gifts were made, Ozee was acting on her great-aunt's behalf with a power of attorney.

On December 30, 1994—just one day before the statute of limitations expired—the grand-niece also filed a federal lawsuit. In addition to those named as defendants in the state lawsuit, the federal suit named the American Council on Gift Annuities. The legal action then quickly expanded to a class-action lawsuit. No doubt Ozee was urged on by attorneys, who saw a payoff for themselves in this unique arena; the class-action lawsuit would eventually include almost 2,000 charities around the country.

The fifty-page legal document accused the Council, as well as the other charities, of violating the Sherman Anti-Trust laws and federal investment and disclosure laws, and accused the Lutheran Foundation of

Texas of pressuring Miss Peter into making a charitable gift she should not have made, a gift, it was said, that went against her interests.

The woman's philanthropy, it turns out, also went against the interests of her grand-niece.

Within a few days after the new year of 1995, the battle was joined, and the charitable community would slowly come to realize the importance and danger inherent in the legal action.

Charity representatives and a regiment of their attorneys devoted hundreds of hours of time, most of it unbilled, to combat the lawsuit. A new organization, Charitable Accord, was formed to lobby for charities on Capitol Hill.

Charities were not used to lobbying, at least not intensely. Before it was all over, the Texas legislature, Governor George W. Bush, Congress, the Supreme Court of the United States—Chief Justice William Rehnquist, in particular—and President William J. Clinton would also play major roles. The next four years of Tal Roberts's life became a low-key nightmare.

THOUGH SUMMER IS a month away, a late May day in northern Texas can be hot and muggy. And so it was on May 23, 1988, when Carl Heckman and Gerald Kieschnick visited Louise T. Peter, at her home in Wichita Falls, a rural town fewer than ten miles from the Oklahoma border, to discuss her charitable intentions to support the Lutheran Church.

Miss Peter was eighty-nine years old at the time. She had been born on September 24, 1899.

Carl Heckman was the development director of the Lutheran Church-Missouri Synod in Austin, the state capital. In that capacity he was the chief staff fundraiser for the church and had known Miss Peter (she would not have liked Ms.) for several years. Gerald Kieschnick, who on that day met Miss Peter for the first time, was executive director of the Lutheran Foundation. Note that the foundation and the church are two distinct entities.

The journey to her home was long and tiring. The two men drove from Austin to Wichita Falls, a distance of approximately 500 miles. The purpose of the visit was to discuss how Miss Peter might best accomplish her philanthropic wishes while maintaining enough assets and enough income to sustain her for the remainder of her life.

Miss Peter, a retired secretary who had never married, had been a substantial contributor to the Lutheran church in Texas. Her grandfather, who emigrated from Germany in the 1800s, founded the Lutheran church in Wichita Falls—the equivalent of starting the Lutheran church itself in Texas.

She was not without means, as she had inherited about $2 million from her brother, who owned land on top of oil reserves.

Throughout her life, she had given the church many substantial gifts and was a frequent donor to the Lutheran Foundation of Texas. So it should have come as no surprise that, as she grew older, she had already thought about how she could support Lutheran causes in her estate plan.

Four interconnected charities were discussed that day: the Lutheran Church-Missouri Synod, the Texas Lutheran Church, the Lutheran Foundation, and Concordia University. The Lutheran church has its national headquarters in Missouri, with offices in every state. Its office for the Texas Lutheran Church is in Austin. Then there are the local churches, the actual churches people attend, in many towns and communities across the United States.

The Lutheran Foundation is an organization formed to raise money for the Lutheran church. So when Heckman and Kieschnick visited Louise Peter, their goal was to raise money for the local church as well as for the national church. They also were responding to Miss Peter's desire to help Concordia, a Lutheran University.

The May 23 discussion went well from the fundraisers' point of view. During their two-hour visit, Miss Peter agreed to leave the bulk of her estate, and perhaps all of it, to the Lutheran Church and Concordia. Her philanthropic wishes were not new, as she had often said prior to that time that she wanted to give what she could to Lutheran causes.

On the day after the meeting, Carl Heckman wrote a letter confirming the content of their discussion and thanking Miss Peter for her generous support of Lutheran causes.

On that day, Gerald Kieschnick, independently, also wrote a letter, essentially for the same purpose, thanking Miss Peter for her loyal and generous interest in the Lutheran Foundation. In addition, Kieschnick asked Miss Peter to send him a list of all the property she owned. The idea was to see what would be appropriate to use to fund the gift vehicles she was then considering.

While requesting such personal financial information may seem aggressive, the relationship between Miss Peter and the Lutheran organizations, as well as the complexity of the charitable planning, was such that a follow-up request asking for such personal information was quite routine. In fact, to do a good job of presenting charitable options, it was necessary. Although the three discussed large and complex gifts, that type of visit is not unusual in the world of philanthropic fundraising. Every day, fundraisers from all types of charities throughout the United States visit people who have made known their wishes. Ways to make a planned gift include several vehicles, and every year many millions of dollars are raised by charities through those vehicles.

In the part of the fundraising world where things are complicated, donors employ planned gifts to reduce income taxes, reduce or eliminate estate taxes, increase income, and obtain professional asset management. That's in addition to expressing their charitable intentions. Donors may have various reasons for making large gifts, but one common desire is their interest in the missions of the charities to which they make their gifts. Louise Peter was a lifetime supporter of Lutheran causes.

People who are attracted to the profession of fundraising often care deeply about others. Talking to someone about her personal plans and about how the fundraisers might accommodate those plans is a natural result of the empathy good fundraisers bring to the relationships they form with donors.

As found in court documents (as are all other legal references in this chapter), Kieschnick's May 25 letter said, in part:

After this list [of Peter's assets] has been accumulated, I would recommend, as you and Dr. Heckman have already discussed, the process of transferring these assets to the Lutheran Foundation of Texas, to be held in trust for you.

The trust agreements, which we would prepare, would need to state the amount of income which would be disbursed by the Foundation to you on a monthly basis. The trust agreements would also give you and the Foundation the authority to take money out of the trust, if the principal amount of the trust is needed for your health and welfare.

The purpose of transferring your property and assets into such trust agreements would be:

- To avoid a lengthy and costly probate process at the time when our Heavenly Father calls you to your heavenly home;
- To place responsibility for management of your financial matters in the hands of the foundation;
- To provide the greatest possible degree of security for your property and possessions.

The trust agreements would make provision for accomplishing your wishes as stated in your will.

Unless there is a specific need to keep open your brother Walter's estate, I would suggest that his estate be closed and that the property of Walter's estate also be transferred to the Foundation and held in trust for you.

The letter referred to "agreements." Miss Peter's assets would be divided into more than one trust. At the time, Kieschnick meant that a revocable trust would be established, but a "charitable remainder unitrust" (the name of another type of planned gift) and two gift annuities were also established.

So to what, exactly, did Miss Peter commit herself?

ON JULY 25, 1988, two months after the fundraisers' May visit, Miss Peter transferred $80,000 to a revocable trust, a trust written by the attorneys for the Lutheran Foundation. Later she transferred another $675,000 to that trust. Ultimately, the revocable trust was funded with approximately $800,000 of Miss Peter's assets.

A revocable trust is a trust in which terms can be changed, or revoked. The charity would be the trustee—that is, the Lutheran Foundation would take charge of the trust's management and administration—and whatever remained in it at her death would be transferred to the charity. She would, however, have access to income and principal as needed during her lifetime.

This type of trust is common in the world of estate planning. Because there was no guarantee the charity would ever receive a penny, she received no charitable income tax deduction for establishing it. The charity was, in effect, doing her a favor by acting as the trustee of a trust from which it might never benefit. While this is not an everyday practice, it is not unusual for charities with close relationships to their donors.

On that same day, she put $100,000 in another type of gift—a charitable gift annuity—that would make fixed payments to her for the rest of her life. This was not a trust, but an immediate and direct gift to the Texas Lutheran Foundation in exchange for the payments. Then, in September 1988, she established a second gift annuity for $100,000. For these gifts, she received charitable income tax deductions, because a charity actually received the money. Payments would be made to her for the rest of her life, but, as noted earlier, this is the way gift annuities work; the amount of those payments was calculated to provide a substantial net charitable gift by the end of her life.

The lawsuit contained several charges, but those attacking the gift annuities had the most potential for damage, and threatened charities nationwide. The issue hinged on the amount of the payments, payments that had been calculated by the American Council on Gift Annuities, the small group headed by Tal Roberts.

Later that summer, on July 29, 1988, Kieschnick wrote Miss Peter a letter in which he explained how to add a codicil—an amendment or an addition—to her will. The letter contained the following instructions:

> Enclosed, as promised, are the following: 1) A new page 1 and page 2 for your will. These two pages take care of changes you requested. On page 1 $25,000 is given to each of the people listed, instead of the $35,000 previously mentioned. On page 2, Dorothy Ozee has been added as an Executor of your estate. Please initial the bottom of each page on the line below which are typed your initials. After you have initialed both pages, please put them in the envelope which is also enclosed with this letter and drop it in the mail to me.
>
> After I have received these pages, I will send you a copy of your completed will.

The pages referred to in the letter were revised by attorneys who served on the Lutheran Foundation Board. Also note that the amounts going to individuals had been reduced.

On August 10, 1988, twelve days after sending the revised pages of the will for Miss Peter to sign, Kieschnick wrote her another letter confirming that he had received the initialed revisions, including her own copy, which was "properly signed, sealed, notarized and witnessed."

On February 28, less than two years after she established the revocable trust, Miss Peter established another gift, also in trust, that would pay her an income for the rest of her life. This gift was more restrictive than the revocable trust, as its terms could not be changed. Furthermore, she could not get at any of the principal. This type of trust is known as a "charitable remainder trust" because whatever remained in the trust at her death was destined for the charity.

Although Miss Peter's intentions for the two trusts were identical, the trusts were different: the first trust could be changed and provided no guarantee that any assets would ever get to the charity; the charitable remainder trust did provide that guarantee, and Miss Peter put $400,000 into this trust.

Essentially, Louise Peter decided to leave much of her estate to the charities. She was childless and had no close heirs. Her niece had long been aware of her aunt's intentions, having faithfully assisted in the handling of her affairs for many years. When Miss Peter's grand-niece stepped in, however, and discovered that an inheritance she hoped to receive was now being directed elsewhere, she contacted an attorney.

FOUR CHARITIES AND five individuals were named in the state and federal lawsuits, and the American Council on Gift Annuities was added in the federal suit.

The essence of the state charges was that the charities were up to no good, that they had acted outside of the law by advising Miss Peter on investment matters that they had no business doing. Later, the situation would get even worse. After the federal suit was filed, someone got it into his head that this case could be even more profitable for the plaintiffs' attorneys if many hundreds of charities were named in the suit. With the help of federal district judge Joe Kendall, the lawsuit moved quickly toward certification as a class action.

The plaintiffs' attorneys said that their clients had been harmed by a systematic and pervasive pattern of illegal conduct on the part of the charities. The specific issue at hand was that the charities that offer gift annuities were breaking a federal law: the Sherman Anti-Trust Act. The attorneys claimed that the charities had illegally fixed the rates that they would pay on their gift annuities. Why, they asked, wasn't Miss Peter urged to shop around for the best rate? Surely other charities, to get the business, would offer more.

The problem with this allegation was that, aside from the assertion that to do so was illegal, it was perfectly true.

Charities did not and do not fix the rates. They usually follow rates that are recommended by the American Council on Gift Annuities. To avoid competing on the basis of their payout rates, almost all charities that offer gift annuities have cooperated on this point since 1927.

No one, until 1994, saw anything wrong with that rationale. All the Lutherans wanted to do was raise money to help in God's work. That, not insignificantly, is what Louise Peter wanted as well.

Yet the attorneys for the plaintiffs—who, let's face it, just didn't get it—argued that "rather than be willing to let the forces of fair competition permit the allocation of societal resources to the spectrum of charitable organizations, they have intentionally banded together to insulate themselves from the forces of competition." You'd think the lawyers were talking about fixing prices on refrigerators or automobiles.

This is what the attorneys didn't get: the concept of "donative intent." Does a donor make a gift to make money or to help a charity? This is where the unique language of philanthropy—and planned giving in particular—differs from commercial or political approaches.

Language nuances aside, though, people who make a charitable gift should do so with the understanding that they are parting with their money. If there is any other expectation, a charitable gift should not be made. Even though a gift annuity provides payments to the donor, in the donor's mind the emphasis needs to be not on the annuity aspect of the transaction but on the gift aspect.

Seasoned fundraisers don't like to be told they are doing something wrong when they solicit a gift, especially when they're not doing anything wrong. Think of a high school sophomore who has just completed trigonometry. He reads about Einstein's Theory of Relativity and, as he has not been schooled in the laws of physics and calculus, he can't understand it. Instead of telling himself that he has more to learn, he decides that, because he is unfamiliar with the concept, the concept is flawed.

Einstein, who may have encountered that kind of reasoning from time to time, could simply ignore it, knowing that his real audience knew what he was grappling with. Charities, called before the court, did not enjoy Einstein's luxury, and had to confront and take seriously a plaintiff, her attorneys, and a judge who did not understand—and, worse, mocked—the principles and philosophy of philanthropy.

Using a sophomore-level of comprehension and arrogance, they even denied the existence of those principles. Fundraising is a profession, and it takes study and experience to understand it.

The solution to the phantom problem, as expressed in the lawsuit, was to punish the charities by forcing them to pay triple damages (single damages being the amount of one donor's gift). Assuming that the average donation to establish a gift annuity was $10,000 (it was probably more, but no one knows), and that each charity that offered annuities had an average of twenty agreements, this meant that single damages for that charity would be approximately $200,000. Multiplying that by 1,800—the number of charities that were members of the American Council on Gift Annuities at that time—equaled $360 million. Throw in a multiple of three for triple damages, and the total was slightly more than one billion dollars. This is what the plaintiffs' attorneys were boasting they would get for their clients. Not to be overlooked, of course, was a 40 percent contingency fee for the lawyers.

Tal Roberts, the Council's chairman, insisted that the suit was without merit and pointed out that the hefty legal fees charities would have to pay to defend themselves should be available for far worthier causes.

THE SHERMAN ANTI-TRUST Act was never meant to apply to charities.

According to the Congressional Record from 1890, the year the law was passed, Senator Sherman himself made that clear during a speech on the Senate floor.

But that information did not sway Judge Kendall. Not only did he sympathize with the plaintiffs, he also saw no reason for the lawsuit not to be given class-action status.

Charities began to understand that they could be in big trouble. They could be sued for establishing gift annuities and might have to pay three times the amount of the gifts they had taken in. Even worse, one of the more chilling effects of the lawsuit would be to encourage donors to become legal adversaries against the charities they had been supporting.

The class-action strategy was being used to attract disgruntled donors, and you can bet that, of thousands of donors, some would not understand the principles of the American Council on Gift Annuities. The idea was that donors would testify that, sure, they would have liked more money in return from the charities. That disgruntled donors could be found was probable because charities often seek gifts by highlighting how much donors will receive.

Unfortunately, charitable gifts that provide money to donors are too often marketed as a way to help the donor and not the charity. This approach, especially when it is used in the extreme, is not healthy. It can sometimes help charities, but it doesn't purely promote philanthropy. In the context of the Texas lawsuit, that approach could have been disastrous.

One charity that stood out and did the others a disservice during this time was the United Jewish Appeal (UJA), which has since joined with its counterpart, the Council of Jewish Federations, to become today's United Jewish Communities. The person in charge of the planned giving division, Neal Myerberg, offered donors higher annuity rates than those recommended by the American Council on Gift Annuities, and the UJA budget permitted a large, nationwide marketing campaign, including radio spots and full-page ads in *The New York Times*.

When Myerberg met with his fundraising peers in New York City, they told him they were concerned that he was smothering the spirit of gift annuities, trying to steal donors by offering bigger returns. He told the group that he thought "fixing rates or fixing prices was wrong." This comment by a fundraiser, reported in the *Wall Street Journal*, fueled optimism on the side of the plaintiffs.

Fortunately for the sake of charities, Congress, in tandem with the Texas legislature, didn't see it that way.

THINGS WERE LOOKING grim early in 1995 as the lawsuit crept forward. Charities started to fear their own donors might be called upon to testify against them. The plaintiffs demanded the names of all the donors, and the judge said they must be provided. New concerns arose, this time about donor privacy. By this time, the lawsuit hung like an invisible pall over thousands of fundraisers in the United States.

To make things worse, not all charities were united. Rather than stand up for the entire charitable community, some charities consulted their legal advisors to see if they could escape being part of the lawsuit. One of the more egregious—some might say uncharitable—reactions was "It's not my fight." Trying to hide their heads in the sand, they seem to have missed an important point: no charity had done anything wrong.

On October 25, 1995, despite reasoned and valid objections by the defense's legal team, Judge Kendall certified the lawsuit as a class action. Every one of those 1,800 charities across the United States that issued gift annuities between 1990 and 1995, at rates recommended by the American Council on Gift Annuities, was now a defendant in the lawsuit.

Charitable Accord, the group that lobbies on behalf of charities, said, "With the stroke of a pen . . . American philanthropy was thrust into what assuredly is its darkest hour."

In addition to defending against the lawsuit, charities also went to the Texas legislature and to Congress. The idea was to clarify state and federal laws that were already on the books to protect charities, not only from lawsuits like this one but from any others that might spring up from related issues. The grand strategy, incorporating both legal and political efforts, was to fight the lawsuit in the courts and to fight the ideas behind the lawsuits on the legislative front.

If it weren't for Charitable Accord, charities and donors would today be in a very different and far less friendly fundraising environment.

The Dallas law firm of Thompson & Knight marshaled its resources to go head–to–head with the plaintiffs while Terry Simmons, the chief counsel for the Baptist Foundation of Texas, and the volunteer head of

Charitable Accord, took on the work of going to Capitol Hill on a regular basis to get protective legislation passed. Without Simmons, there would have been no legislation and, since the legislation would eventually have a big impact on the courts, the lawsuit might very well have succeeded.

Each week for a full year, Simmons traveled between Texas and Washington to meet with anyone who would meet with him: representatives and their aides, senators and their aides, the Washington-based lobbying law firm hired to help, representatives of charities who were in town, the press, and sometimes, even members of the unaffiliated public.

The travel back and forth was exhausting by itself, but the time in Washington was packed with meetings during the day, and phone calls and e-mails to people around the country during the evening. To Simmons, midnight always came too soon.

Every Friday, however, he would fly to his home in Dallas to make sure he did not miss any of his children's school or sporting events. This schedule consumed his life for more than a year.

He did the whole thing without pay.

To be sure, Simmons was still on the payroll of the Texas Baptist Foundation and continued to attend to his duties in that capacity, which meant that during some weeks Simmons would make two round trips between Dallas and Washington.

I served on the board of Charitable Accord at the time, along with about thirty other individuals. I also joined Terry when four people were called upon to testify before Congress. While the federal district judge in Texas was eagerly trying to find merit in the allegations that charities were breaking the law, Charitable Accord was trying to put two bills through Congress.

One would immunize charities from the anti-trust laws when it came to offering gift annuities, by explicitly excluding from the Sherman Anti-Trust Act charities that adopt the rate recommended by the American Council on Gift Annuities.

The other bill, running parallel to this one through Congress, was intended to permit charities to act as trustees of trusts and to invest money without having to register with the Securities and Exchange Commission (SEC).

The SEC was in favor of the legislation because it did not want to spend its time regulating charities. Barry Barbash, then the head of the investment management division at the SEC, said, "We have larger problems to deal with." As long as it could be assured that donated money was being used for charitable purposes, and that certain processes were observed, the SEC would be happy to be relieved of this oversight headache.

On October 31, 1995, Barbash and I and three colleagues testified before the House Subcommittee on Telecommunications and Finance in favor of what would be known as the Philanthropy Protection Act of 1995. This bill was intended to permit charities to invest gifts in common funds maintained by the charities for that purpose.

Paul Kling, from the University of Richmond and Katelyn Quynn, from Massachusetts General Hospital, testified with Terry and me. In his opening remarks the Committee's chairman, Jack Fields of Texas, said:

> I have rarely seen a piece of legislation that has enjoyed such strong support from its very introduction. It seems incredible but charities and other nonprofit organizations that seek only to help our fellow Americans are under attack.
>
> Many of these organizations have severely curtailed their planned giving programs. Some have even turned down gifts, afraid that the lawsuit will establish a precedent that will enable Plaintiffs to revoke every gift made through one of these programs. This abuse of our legal system must be stopped.

Here are some highlights from the testimony. The excerpts include questions from Jack Fields, Edward Markey of Massachusetts, Rick White of Washington, and Anna Eshoo of California.

The first section deals with charities acting as trustees of revocable trusts, a common and legal practice that the plaintiffs in the lawsuit said was illegal. Keep in mind that Louise Peter established a revocable trust.

Mr. Fields: The question I asked Mr. Barbash just a moment ago concerning charitable pooled funds that include revocable assets: Is there a need to work in that particular area to perhaps look for more flexibility or is that something that is not that important?

Mr. Douglas White: The vast majority of charitable organizations who act as trustee for revocable trusts do so in a manner that is extraordinarily and extremely responsible.

Mr. Fields: As I understood, what he is really looking at or what the Commission would look at is true donative intent, rather than someone perhaps giving something that they really haven't given.

Mr. Douglas White: The vast majority of charities throughout the United States are reluctant to act as trustee of revocable trusts. Those that do, do so for the donors who are the most close to them, and they act in an exceedingly prudent manner with those assets.

The charities are undertaking an extremely heavy burden and they do so with the greatest care.

The questions then went to how charities are being hurt by the lawsuit.

Mr. Markey: I am very confused, Ms. Quynn, about the potential impact of the cuts in Medicare and Medicaid that have been approved by the House and the Senate. These cuts, if enacted, could have an adverse impact on teaching hospitals such as Massachusetts General. Is that correct?

Ms. Quynn: I am certainly not an expert is this area but I imagine that would be the case.

Mr. Markey: In light of these pending cuts, isn't it true that there will be additional pressure on your office to increase the percentage of the Mass. General's activities; that is, funding through charitable donations?

Ms. Quynn: We are very concerned about future monies, the future of hospitals, the future of money for research, so we are particularly looking to raise money to help cover some of these deficits.

Mr. Markey: How has the pending lawsuit down in Texas affected your fundraising activities?

Ms. Quynn: Right now we have donors who know about this lawsuit, and they call with questions; they are concerned that maybe they shouldn't have made a gift; we are very concerned that other new people will not make a gift; and that those who have made a gift will not make a second one. I think the longer this goes on the worse it will become for us.

Mr. Markey: I know that many charitable givers make their plans toward the end of the year in order to take advantage of the tax benefits. Does that make it important for us to move quickly here legislatively in terms of clarification of what the legal terrain will be for potential givers?

Ms. Quynn: Yes, absolutely. The year-end is a great time for planned gifts, the time many, many people make their gifts. November and December are very important to our development programs.

Mr. Markey: Mr. White, if I may, briefly . . . What impact has the pending Texas lawsuit had on the charities that you advise?

Mr. Douglas White: An enormous impact. As you know, last week, two thousand charities throughout the United States were certified as a class. As a result, my clients fear that they will no longer be able to contact and talk with their donors about this issue.

Mr. Markey: OK, now, you note in your written testimony that the bill would not create any exemptions from the antifraud provisions of the Federal and state securities laws. Do you support assuring that regulators can continue to take action against fraudulent activity in the future?

Mr. Douglas White: Let me be very clear. No one on this panel nor anyone in the 8,000-member organization that I represent on the board would in any way want to support fraudulent activity. I want to emphasize in my response to you that, yes, I do support any anti-fraudulent provisions of the bill.

Mr. Markey: And are you aware of any donors throughout New England, throughout the country, that have cut back.

Mr. Douglas White: Yes, I am.

Mr. Markey: Cut back in terms of the number of contributions?

Mr. Douglas White: Yes.

Mr. Markey: And, finally, how much of a concern is this legislation to charities that are based in Massachusetts and throughout New England?

Mr. Douglas White: It is extremely vital that it pass and pass immediately.

Congressman Rick White then addressed the complexity of the tax code.

Mr. Rick White: And I would like to ask you a question just so I understand the way these charitable donations or charitable investment funds work. I take it that during a person's lifetime, the donor's lifetime, they will make a gift to the charity and then they will ask . . . they will receive the income on that gift during the time they are alive. Do they typically receive the entire income that that gift produces or do they ask for a certain amount or how does that typically work?

Mr. Douglas White: The idea here is that several charitable gifts that we are talking about are in a lump of life income gifts. There are four, and those four have varying ways of being established. Normally, in a pooled income fund, it is the entire net income from the fund.

A charitable remainder trust can be either a percentage of the gift asset or a fixed dollar income. And the gift annuity is not really based on an investment return at all; it is really a payment based on the amount that was given to the charity, and which includes some return of principal as well.

Mr. Rick White: But I take it I could do it a number of different ways. If I wanted to make a contribution, I could give the corpus or the income-producing property to the charity and I could ask for $100,000 back or all the income or half the income. I could do it just about any way I wanted to?

Mr. Douglas White: The tax law says for the charitable remainder trust that a minimum of 5 percent has to be paid back. The $100,000 figure would be really a function of a percentage of the ultimate—of the total asset really, so it wouldn't normally be discussed in those terms on that front anyway.

Mr. Rick White: I take it, do donors get an immediate charitable deduction on their tax return at the time they make this donation to the charity or is there some restriction on that?

Mr. Douglas White: Both.

Mr. Rick White: Sounds like the tax code I know.

The final portion of the testimony underscores the seriousness with which this committee would address this legislation, and their concerns about the effects of the lawsuit on charities.

Mr. Rick White: Just one other question. Is it anticipated that if we pass this legislation, it will have an impact on the existing lawsuit that is filed in Texas or is that suit being already filed immune from what we do or do you know?

Mr. Simmons: Obviously, that is a question that the courts will determine but it is our belief that if legislation, appropriate legislation, is passed on both issues, that it will terminate the lawsuit if not in the District Court then in the appellate courts.

Ms. Eshoo: Mr. White, thank you for representing some of the outstanding institutions in my congressional district and I just want to say that I have a deep and abiding regard for what philanthropy represents. Our institutions in the country really would not be what they are today if it were not for the gifts that are forthcoming. I just have two quick questions. One, what is the average gift or is there one? Do they fall in the small-donor category? I mean, maybe from Massachusetts General you might be able to enlighten us. The other, because I am a fairly new Member of Congress, has there ever been this kind of legal challenge to charitable giving as this lawsuit represents today?

Mr. Kling: One of the real benefits of charitable gift annuities in particular is that folks can create them with smaller gifts.

Ms. Eshoo: I have an appreciation of that. Just my curiosity question was, you know, what does the average donation represent? Is there one or do you know? Maybe Ms. Quynn, since you wrote a book about it.

Ms. Quynn: The minimum for—

Ms. Eshoo: Maybe I need to go out and buy the book to get the numbers.

Ms. Quynn: Maybe I should send you a copy for free. The minimum for pooled income funds and charitable gift annuities at Mass. General is $5,000. Since I have been there, which has been for 3 years, our smallest gift has been $5,000; our largest has been $450,000, in terms of life income gifts, since I have been there. We see many, many for $10,000, $25,000. Maybe in the $25,000 range might be just a guess.

Ms. Eshoo: Thank you. I don't think my other question was answered.

Mr. Simmons: Having dealt with this for some 18 months, I can tell you that looking back and having 17 years of experience, and talking to a lot of people around the country who have been working in this effort to achieve passage, I cannot believe this is happening. It has taken a while for people to believe that it is real. There has been no precedent for it, but it is indeed real and now that charities are being told by the attorneys and the courts that they can't speak to their donors. The plaintiffs are saying, "Your donors are my clients," and charities are really beginning to understand how terrible that is.

Less than a month later, Congress unanimously passed the Antitrust Relief Act of 1995 and the Philanthropy Protection Act of 1995. On December 8, President Clinton signed the two bills into law. Every human, Democrat or Republican, in Texas or in Washington, D.C., who could vote on the legislation relating to the lawsuits voted with one voice.

After the hearing, Congressman Rick White, a Dartmouth alumnus, asked me if this legislation would help Dartmouth. When he was told that it would, he then asked, "Would it help mediocre charities, such as Harvard, as well?" When he was reminded that the tax code doesn't discriminate among charities, he said that he would still consider voting for the bill.

And he did.

THE PLAINTIFFS WOULD still not let go. They argued that the new laws did not apply to their case.

The response to what should have been seen as an administrative closure was not only quick but chilling. Not only would this lawsuit not disappear, but the plaintiffs also thought the new laws added sting to their charges. They argued that the new legislation should be read narrowly, that courts have a duty not to read into the law that which was not specifically intended. This is true and reasonable, but the legislators in Washington left no doubt about their intentions

The New York Times reported in November 1995 that "Charities and Congressional sponsors hope that the legislation will make the lawsuit moot." Representative Henry Hyde, one of the bill's co-sponsors and chair of the House Judiciary Committee, said, "Without this common sense protection, charitable organizations would lose a much-needed and useful tool for raising funds, and that would be a tragedy."

Hyde was also quoted in *The Chronicle of Philanthropy*: "If the plaintiffs in the class action lawsuit prevail, thousands of charities nationwide would be required to refund donations and to pay treble damages. This would mean that virtually every charitable organization in America is threatened with losses which would total billions of dollars."

On January 8, 1996, a month to the day after President Clinton signed the bills into law, the plaintiffs responded to the charities' motion to dismiss the case. They said, "Contrary to defendants' blithe assertions, this case is not over." After all, justice needed to be carried out, to say nothing of the several million dollars in attorneys' fees at stake. The strategy in the wake of legislative defeat—and with what was all along a weak legal position—was not only to fight, but also to attack.

The plaintiffs amended their charges by insisting that the new law did not protect the American Council on Gift Annuities from antitrust charges.

It got worse. They then said that the ACGA, in contrast to its stated mission, was not an educational organization. After the group changed its name and took on its own legal identity, it filed as an educational organization with the IRS. (The gift annuity group, until just prior to the lawsuit, had been part of the American Bible Society.) The plaintiffs said that an activity may be "educational" or "instructional," but that "is not sufficient to make an entity an 'educational organization' if the entity has a single substantial non-educational purpose." Then:

> A terrorist organization might in the course of its activities provide lessons on explosives safety, and might even make those lessons open to the general public. While such lessons are certainly "instructional," they do not make the entity an "educational" one.

Judge Kendall refused to let go. As he set the jury trial date, he had this to say:

> When they were a little younger, I took my children to a children's theme restaurant called Chuck E. Cheese's. Located there was an arcade game called 'Whack-A-Mole.' The player had a large mallet and the object was to strike a number of plastic moles with the mallet on their heads as they popped out of their holes.
>
> The player that hit the most moles in the allotted time won. What made the game challenging, and difficult, was every time you'd hit one mole, two or three others would rear their ugly little heads. That game aptly describes this lawsuit.

That passage was written on a legal document and aptly reflected the judge's mindset on this case: charities are mere moles and ought to be smashed down. In addition to defending themselves on a legal front, the defendants had to fight the judge's strong anti-charity bias.

The lawsuit stretched on even after the law was enacted to end it. When the Court of Appeals for the Fifth Circuit also refused to dismiss the suit, Congress passed another law in 1997, clarifying the first antitrust amendment, to make sure that the lawsuit would die.

After more legal wrangling, on December 8, 1997, two years after President Clinton signed the original bills into law, the United States Supreme Court ordered the Court of Appeals to take the new laws into account when making its ruling.

Six months later, on June 12, 1998, the Appeals Court dismissed the federal antitrust lawsuit against charities.

IN THE SUMMER of 1999, the state lawsuit came to a close. But that took unraveling one of the gifts and giving the money back to the donor.

Something else, though, is important. Do you remember Gerald Kieschnick's May 25, 1988, letter to Miss Peter, in which he said that the Lutheran Foundation would prepare the trusts? He followed that up in July, writing, "Enclosed, as promised are the following . . . a new page 1 and page 2 for your will."

The Foundation, and not her own attorney, wrote the trusts and the codicil to her will. As many donors do, Louise Peter welcomed that help. With complicated gifts, donors often trust the person representing the charity more than they do attorneys and financial planners.

Even though things generally ended up satisfactorily for charities, the Foundation should not have prepared the legal documents on Louise Peter's behalf. Even when you don't account for Miss Peter's state of mind at the time she made the gifts—only a short time later she was declared mentally incompetent—charities should never perform personal financial or estate planning for a donor; that's the job of a professional who represents only the donor's interests.

Both charities and donors should keep that in mind.

11

THE OHIO STATE UNIVERSITY

"It is dangerous in that we must maintain high standards."
MICHAEL FELLOWS, FORMER DIRECTOR OF TRUSTS AND ESTATES
THE OHIO STATE UNIVERSITY FOUNDATION

PERHAPS FOOTBALL, AND the legendary coach Woodie Hayes, come to mind when you think of The Ohio State University. Maybe you watched the national title game on New Year's Day 2003, one of the most exciting in college football history. Or maybe you think of its band, the one the students call "the Best Damn Band in the Land."

Founded in 1870 by the Ohio legislature, the university today enrolls approximately 60,000 students, 50,000 of whom attend classes on the Columbus campus. Those students rank third in population behind Arizona State University and the University of Minnesota. More than 300,000 members of the Ohio State Alumni Association today populate the globe.

Ohio State's 2005 operating budget was almost $3.5 billion, and the combined endowment of the university and its supporting foundation was $1.6 billion. During the prior year, over 100,000 donors contributed more than $210 million to the school.

By any measure, Ohio State University is a big deal. With its storied history, its prominence in American education, its influence on so many thousands of people, and its reputation for providing a good education, nobody should be surprised to learn that Ohio State attracts many people who want to support its educational mission.

Not surprisingly, the university has put together an effective fundraising office that offers a variety of ways for donors to make their gifts.

This is the story of one of those gifts, and how it went wrong.

AS YOU READ in the last chapter, one of the several advanced ways supporters help charities is through charitable trusts that benefit both the donor and the charity. In particular, a "charitable remainder unitrust"—one of Louise Peter's gifts—is a gift where (1) a donor irrevocably transfers money or other assets into a trust, never to be accessed by the donor, (2) the trust pays an income to the donor for life, and (3) at the end of the donor's life, the charity gets what remains in the trust.

And—just a little more detail, important to the story—the donor receives a substantial income tax deduction at the time the trust is established, although it is less than the value of the amount put into trust. In addition, because the trust is set up to help a charity and is tax-exempt, the donor avoids paying any taxes on assets that have grown in value when the trust sells the gift assets. This means the value that determines the donor's income is not reduced by the payment of a capital gains tax. Because it is, in essence, less expensive to give than cash, stock that has grown in value over the years is the most common asset used to fund a charitable trust. As a result, many donors use anything *but* cash to fund a charitable trust.

Even though a planned gift is sophisticated and complex, it is legitimate and is often used to help charity in the future; most of the time the charity actually receives the asset only after the donor dies. A planned gift is not a tax loophole. Congress and the IRS are quite aware of the transaction and, with minor tweaks here and there, have endorsed this way of charitable giving since 1969, when Congress wrote the law.

Ohio State has established planned gifts that are valued at over $100 million, which, over time, will become available to the university. Also, that value may grow over time; remember, other than through the income specified in the gift agreement, the donor cannot withdraw money from the trust. Sometimes the values decrease, but usually, over the years, they increase.

That $100 million, of course, represents only what Ohio State is aware of. Some people prefer not to make their intentions known before their deaths. There's no law that says donors have to tell a charity when they name it to receive money in the future.

Nationwide, thousands of donors make planned gifts every year, and the IRS tracks the number of charitable trusts established and their values. Even though many people don't inform a charity of their intentions, an important point to realize here is that many others do.

Not surprisingly, Ohio State's program to acquire planned gifts is quite aggressive. Not many charities are in a position to know that it will receive $100 million over the next several years. It's kind of like filling a financial pipeline into the future: the money isn't here now, but it will be. That doesn't happen when fundraisers sit around the office waiting for the phone to ring. People are out on the road, visiting prospects constantly,

And when the gifts come in—since the money must be invested and used to pay the donors—they must be taken care of, and someone needs to be in charge of that. A large number of charities around the country act as the trustee of charitable trusts. Sometimes donors act as their own trustee, and other times a bank or law firm will. But so do charities.

Acting as trustee is a weighty role. It is the most important function of any trust, because the trustee guards the assets and must protect both the income beneficiaries and the entity that will receive the trust's assets when they are ultimately distributed. The Ohio State Foundation acts as the trustee whenever it can, and when the donor wants the school to do that.

This is what the Baptist Foundation of Arizona did, too, but the people there were using that sophisticated façade for devious purposes. Ohio State did no such thing.

To help prospective donors deal with the inherent complexities of planned gifts, charities have an obligation to disclose certain information so that there are no misunderstandings. Often, charities work with financial advisors who work on behalf of a charity's donors and are usually part of the planning process when a charitable trust is established. After all, most people don't understand what planned giving is all about. Often, fundraisers encourage potential donors to consult their own advisors about their intentions. The concern is that the lure of tax benefits may entice a person to make a planned gift that is not in his or her best interests.

This was one of the allegations in the Texas lawsuit. Most of the time donors enter into these complex arrangements with their eyes open. But, with more and more people establishing planned gifts each year, "most of the time" leaves much out of the equation.

Trouble brews when financial advisors are not forthright and, because they often have a financial interest in the transaction, they aren't always straightforward. For example, the advisor may earn money by managing or investing the assets in the trust or he or she may sell products, such as life insurance, to make the plan more attractive to the donor.

As sophistication sometimes leads to confusion, a married couple who wanted to make a planned gift—with the help of their advisors, as well as of the Ohio State University Foundation—went down a path they never should have entered.

IN 1956, RAYMOND and Margaret Martin bought a few acres of rural land in Columbus, Ohio, for $75,000. By 1985, the land was rezoned for commercial development, and the property's value had grown to approximately $1 million. The Martins tried to sell the land shortly after the rezoning, hoping to reap healthy cash proceeds to purchase a home in either Florida or Arizona,

They collected monthly option payments of $5,000 from a developer, but couldn't find a buyer for their property. The developer decided not to buy, and this left the Martins with an asset they couldn't sell, but on which real estate taxes still had to be paid.

In August 1989, when Raymond was sixty-five and Margaret fifty-nine, the Martins met William Clark, an insurance agent and financial planner who'd heard that they wanted to sell their land.

Clark met with the Martins several times. He told the Martins that they would do well to establish a planned gift—the charitable remainder trust—and then use some of the trust-generated income to buy life insurance that would benefit the Martins' five children after the Martins died.

When the property was appraised at $1,262,500 before the gift transaction, Clark and another advisor, Willis Wolfe, Jr., an attorney, estimated the trust income would be approximately $90,000 in the first full calendar year, with projected annual increases of 3 percent each year after that. The trust document called for an annual payout of 7 percent of the trust's value. That, along with the 3 percent after-payout growth prediction, meant that the advisors told the Martins the trust would earn 10 percent each year for the rest of their lives.

The Martins were delighted. They were told the trust would generate an income from the sale of the asset, the value of which would be unreduced by capital gains taxes. These taxes were calculated to amount to $363,000, if the land had been sold privately and not donated to charity.

The prospect of savings of that magnitude must have been quite appealing. Also, the trust payments were designed to be such that they would be enough to pay for a life insurance policy with a face value of $1 million, assuring that the Martins' children would have sufficient assets.

This is what financial planners call a "win-win-win" situation. The donors generate more income than they had before, and they receive a large income tax deduction, in this case approximately $300,000. That was one win. The second was that the charity, in this case the cancer center at Ohio State University, would one day receive a significant, although not precisely measurable, gift.

The third win, of course, was for the insurance agent. Premiums on the sale of a $1 million life insurance policy are significant, as are the commissions on the premiums.

The Ohio State University Foundation which serves as a conduit for gifts, and supports the university, its programs, and related entities—including the cancer center—would act as trustee to administer the trust. It would make sure the property would be sold correctly and that the money from the sale would be prudently managed.

With assurance from their advisors that the trust would generate income beginning immediately, the Martins signed the charitable trust document. Soon after, they bought $1 million worth of life insurance and put a deposit on a new home in Florida.

The Martins didn't know it, but the shadow of trouble hung over their gift even before the ink on the trust document was dry. A moment's luster would quickly tarnish. T. S. Elliot captured the concept well: "But our beginnings never know our ends."

★ ★ ★

IT MIGHT BE said that those who believe the false promises contained in computer-generated printouts deserve what they get. Most people are not schooled in the language of finance and investments, and when they see a graph or numbers that spew from a computer, they tend to believe what they see. This is especially true when the information is confirmed by trusted professional advisors.

Raymond Martin was an alumnus of Ohio State University, and the development office had no reason to doubt that he wanted to help the school with a substantial gift. On the other hand, university fundraisers weren't fully certain about his motives. Had anyone investigated, he or she would have quickly discovered that Mr. Martin's charitable intent was far less than his desire for financial gain. He had been led to believe that he'd personally benefit a great deal.

The Martins were not wealthy. Other than the undeveloped land and their personal home, they had few assets. Mr. Martin earned only $24,000 in 1990. To make a gift of a large portion of their estate, the Martins needed to make sure all of it would work correctly.

Nothing is wrong with seeking to profit from an investment, of course. What was wrong here was the convoluted manner by which charity was used to accomplish a goal wholly unrelated to philanthropy.

As it turned out, they should have made no gift at all.

The problem was not with the gift's essential structure; even though it was complicated, it was legitimate and legal. But legitimate and legal does not always mean appropriate. Expectations were wrongfully established by those who should have known better.

What drove this transaction—and the Martins were not in the driver's seat—was the desire for an insurance commission. William Clark, the insurance agent, did not make his living by persuading people to make charitable gifts. He made his living by selling insurance.

An essential component of the Martins' charitable plan—as it turned out, the most important part of the process—was for the trust to generate enough income to pay the insurance premiums. But first, the trust had to sell the land.

Remember, the assumption was that the land could be sold for $1.2 million, and that it would generate income of approximately $90,000 once things got going. Now, financial advisors and lawyers should know that land often sells for less than the appraised value. They should also know that there are fees associated with the sales process, the most obvious of which is a real estate commission. They also should realize that land doesn't tend to sell on the day it goes on the market. That the property had sat around unsold for many years while it was on the market might have been a clue.

But no, the computer wasn't programmed to take those realities into account.

A special version of the charitable trust had to be used, one that could accept land as an asset without ruining the trust. The kind of trust that was established pays only the net income generated by the trust, not a percentage of the trust as was shown on the computer printout. This is something almost no one in the general public is aware of, but it ought to be known by anyone parading about as a financial planner and talking about the benefits of charitable trusts. And it goes without saying—since it is so vital to the creation of expectations—that this nuance needs to be explained to prospective donors.

Alas, the charitable trust did not sell the land until more than two years after the trust was established, and more than two years after money was needed to pay the life insurance premiums, to say nothing of two more years of real estate taxes. This did not please the hopeful Mr. Martin. He didn't have enough income from other sources to pay the insurance premiums, so, to deal with this problem he had to borrow money from William Clark, the insurance agent. Martin also reduced the policy's coverage from $1 million to $250,000.

And when Martin did receive his first payment from the trust, it was far less than what he had been expecting. For the next seven years, through September 1999, the income never equaled the projected 7 percent payout, and of course its total return was nowhere near 10 percent.

At some point it occurred to the Martins that they had not been told the truth about their transaction, and they decided to try to undo what had been done. Although an upward economy made things seem brighter by 1993, in Martin's mind the damage was done. Enough time had passed with mounting debts and little financial relief from the trust. In July 1994, he sued.

★ ★ ★

NAMED IN THE suit as defendants were the Ohio State University Foundation; the treasurer of the foundation; William Clark, the insurance agent; Dennis Clark and Associates; and Great West Life Assurance Company.

In October 1999, the trial court agreed with the defendants' claim that they did no wrong and threw out the case. The Martins then appealed their case to the Ohio Appellate Court. The basis for the appeal was complex, but the key argument was that the trial court disregarded the Martins' claim that the advisors were guilty of fraud. The primary charge in the lawsuit, in fact, was that Martin was led to expect income to begin immediately from the trust. When it didn't, Martin couldn't pay for the life insurance or the newly purchased property in Florida.

The appeals court ruled that the trial court acted improperly. By parsing the phrase "fraud and negligent misrepresentation," the appeals court concluded that the advisors did in fact lead Martin to believe that income from the trust would begin immediately—which, of course, it hadn't.

The judge used as evidence the materials that the advisors had shown to Martin. A document called "Cash Flow Analysis" clearly indicated that the Martins would receive $21,000 in 1990 and almost $85,000 in 1991, with increasing amounts thereafter. Another document, "Estate Planning Ideas for Raymond and Margaret Martin," showed similar numbers. In that document, however, the trust was projected to pay an income of 8 percent, as opposed to 7 percent, per year. In a section called "The Martin Family Bank" it also showed the annual insurance premiums on the $1 million policy would be approximately $40,000 and would be payable for five years.

The appellate judge observed, "Not only did Clark and Wolfe make these direct representations, but they also made omissions that would have otherwise informed the Martins that they would not receive any payments until portions of the trust were sold."

No one except the direct participants knows how the actual conversations between the Martins and their advisors went. Not surprisingly, nobody wanted to talk about them. For this reason, the information on which this chapter is based has been taken from court documents, copies of exhibits used in the trial, and off-the-record conversations with an attorney involved in the case.

If we step back a moment to look at the situation's essence, we see a man and his wife, with a modest income and a significant but illiquid asset, who wanted to retire to Florida. The couple sought to sell the asset and buy new property where they could live for the remainder of their lives.

How could it be that people with such a simple and straightforward goal, and no intention of making a charitable gift, committed themselves to a gift of more than $1 million? Think of it: who would want to give away what they need to live?

It can happen when all the wrong elements get together, when advisors, whether they be paid professionals hired by the donor or representatives of the charity, do not see the whole picture from the donor's point of view. It can happen when other factors come into play, such as pressure from the head of the fundraising office or, in this case, when the income to be generated on the sale of insurance takes priority.

From the court transcript: "Appellant (Martin) elicited testimony from Clark that he would receive a seventy percent commission on his first year insurance premium, which originally was to amount to approximately a $30,000 commission to Clark in the first year of the policy. Clark was also to receive a three to five percent commission on all premiums paid . . . in the subsequent years."

Martin testified that no one had reviewed the terms of the trust with him. He also said he did not need other counsel because, in a sentiment bursting with pathos, he "knew Mr. Clark had put together the personnel required to close, and I trusted their integrity and knowledge. I had no reason to question anyone."

WHERE DID OHIO State fit into this mix? And why was the university's foundation part of the problem? In addition to the advisors and the insurance company, the foundation and its treasurer were named in the lawsuit. This is because the foundation essentially played the role of an accomplice in the transaction. Not only would the charity ultimately be the recipient of the trust gift when the Martins died, but also the foundation would act as trustee of the trust while they were alive.

In this case that was not a good thing, and Ohio State should have known better. Michael Fellows, at the time the director of trusts and estates at Ohio State, as evidenced by a memo he wrote to his colleagues, was well aware that this gift arrangement might not be in the best interests of the donor.

There was conflicting testimony as to whether Fellows ever told Martin that, after putting the property into the trust, there would be no income payments until the property was sold.

The foundation and its treasurer settled out of court with the Martins in December 1998 for $675,000. This amount represented the present value of the income that was shown to be due, based on the payout of the trust and the ages of Mr. and Mrs. Martin. This alone did not make the Martins whole, but the action compensated them as if they had received their projected lifetime income. At that point the trust just ended.

Why the foundation and not the university? Most public universities have private foundations to accept gifts. Each year the foundation makes its own gift to the university in support of the university's goals and budget. Since a public university's assets are those of the state, a foundation protects gifts from the whims of revenue-hungry politicians.

In fact, one source of confusion in the public university-supporting foundation structure is that it is often difficult to track which people, particularly those who raise money, work for which entity.

Ohio State and its foundation are charities, and the public, rightly or wrongly, has come to expect a higher standard of conduct from charities than from financial planners, lawyers, or anyone else with a profit motive. After all, as repugnant as the deal was, the insurance agent was only doing his job. He was selling insurance. But Fellows let the transaction take place. One might conclude, noting that the foundation acted as trustee, that he encouraged it.

Fellows wrote an internal memo to the treasurer of the foundation acknowledging that Martin, who was sixty-six years old at the time, had never set up a trust before and was untutored in these matters. According to the appellate court judge, Fellows also stated in that memorandum, "Mr. Martin needs our highest ethical consideration as he is not well educated in money matters and has chosen some rather middle level advisors." Further, Fellows wrote "His planners are rather mercenary." He also noted, "The illustration of a gift will serve to stimulate other gift inquiries. This is good in that it may open up other gifts to the university. It is dangerous in that we must maintain high standards."

A planned gift, despite the financial and tax benefits it generates, is not for those who have less interest in making a gift than in planning for their own financial security.

THE MARTINS NEVER did get to live out their lives together in peace. On November 16, 1999, two months after the arduous and unsatisfying trial began, Margaret Martin died of a heart attack.

THE NATURE CONSERVANCY

*"People who donate property and dollars to help protect the environment deserve
to know The Nature Conservancy won't betray them."*
SENATOR CHARLES GRASSLEY
CHAIRMAN, SENATE FINANCE COMMITTEE, JULY 17, 2003

FOR SEVERAL YEARS, The Nature Conservancy engaged in a program
that brought our tax code and social policy into doubt. When it was discovered by the general public, it intensified an already ongoing Congressional investigation into how charities work.

Based in Arlington, Virginia, a suburb of Washington, D.C., The Nature
Conservancy, or TNC, as it is often called, is the largest environmental
charity in the United States. With assets in excess of $3 billion, it is also
the world's richest environmental group.

Its mission is to "to preserve the plants, animals and natural
communities that represent the diversity of life on earth by protecting
the lands and waters they need to survive." TNC's slogan is "Saving the
last great places on earth," and it has developed a strategic, scientifically
based program called Conservation by Design, which identifies thousands of places worldwide that it feels need to be preserved.

The Nature Conservancy buys or receives land and then often holds
it in perpetuity, or takes other measures to make sure it will remain in its
natural state. According to its promotional literature, since its birth in 1951

TNC has protected almost 120 million acres of land and 5,000 miles of river throughout the world. More than 100 million of those acres lie outside the United States.

The approach is to protect private lands, encourage governments to conserve land, and obtain funding for wider conservation. TNC lists a wide variety of entities as partners: government agencies, other nonprofits, local owners, and corporations, as well as foreign-based groups.

The image of The Nature Conservancy is far from radical. Not for TNC the tree huggers who subsist only on granola bars and water and believe that no compromise should ever be made with corporate interests. The group takes the view that environmentalists and the corporate community can live side by side, and that good environmentalism can be good business.

To the public and among other charities, especially other environmental groups, TNC is revered as an organization that is smart, savvy, and practical, a group that does a lot to protect the earth's natural resources.

It came as a surprise, then, when, after a two-year investigation, the *Washington Post* published a series of highly critical articles about TNC in the spring of 2003.

AMONG SEVERAL REVELATIONS, the *Post* reported that The Nature Conservancy made some unusual arrangements with donors, many of them board members at the various local chapters throughout the country. The newspaper suggested that these people, who had, in fact, made gifts, acted improperly by taking a fraudulent income tax deduction for those gifts.

Here was the deal: TNC was interested in preserving natural land and keeping it from the hands of real estate developers. Indeed, it often purchases property and then creates a "conservation easement"—a legally binding restriction preventing the owner of the land from developing it. Many charities and towns use easements to ensure the future of natural and historic places.

Not all easements are the same. Some don't permit any development at all, while others, like the ones TNC sometimes places, might allow for limited changes. Often, that means a new owner can build a house, a home office, or a guest cottage, or install a swimming pool or a tennis court—things like that. Even with an easement restriction, property can be quite attractive to an individual who wants peace and quiet and, sometimes, leisure.

Even though there are different types of easements, the general idea behind them does not waver: the financial value—and the classic market-oriented appraisal deals with financial value—of the property is reduced.

As an example, TNC might buy a parcel of land for $1 million. It then places an easement on the property and tries to sell it. The easement's negative effect might be valued at $300,000, which means that the organization could expect to sell the land for only $700,000.

It's important to note that the property worth $1 million a while back is the same property that is now worth $700,000. Nothing physical has happened to the land or any of the structures on it. The financial value of anything that's not cash is affected by its potential, and property with an easement on it has a limited future from the point of view of a developer.

The new buyer, who must abide by the easement's restrictions, pays $700,000, not the $1 million TNC paid, because, according to an appraisal, that is what it is worth.

Not all buyers are bothered by easements, and not simply because the property costs less. Some people proactively seek property they intend to restore and maintain in its original natural splendor. That's the other dimension of the value idea. To those who don't like strip malls and McDonald's littering the landscape, and would never want to sell to a developer, the easement makes the property more valuable.

While The Nature Conservancy has accomplished its goal of preserving the land, it has incurred a cost—in this example, $300,000. And even though TNC imposed the value-reducing easement in the first place, wouldn't it be nice if it could get some of that money back?

Enter the donor. How about finding a purchaser, someone who is both a lover of natural places and sympathetic to TNC's cause, who will pay the $700,000 asking price for the property and then decide to contribute another $300,000 to the charity? This way, TNC, in addition to advancing its mission by making sure the property is protected from future development, is made whole in the transaction.

This technique is neither unusual nor illegal. Thus the charity received a letter in January 2003 from Jerry McCoy, one of the nation's top charity tax attorneys, approving the transaction. McCoy's letter stated, "I believe I can say with certainty that the buyer is clearly entitled to the deductions described."

The deductions he referred to were those available to donors who purchased property with a conservation easement and then took a charitable income tax deduction by making a gift of the difference to TNC.

The *Washington Post*, however, noted that many of the land buyers were people close to TNC, including some who were trustees of the organization. TNC acknowledged that "many of our conservation buyers have been trustees," but saw nothing wrong with that. The trustee-buyers, affiliated, by the way, with the state chapters and not directly with the national group, were natural donors—the very people who would appreciate both the conservation and the contribution aspects of the arrangement.

The Nature Conservancy also said that this type of arrangement amounted to a small fraction, less than 2 percent, of its overall land preservation transactions. That amounted to only 186 out of 12,000 deals since 1990.

The problem was the perception that this was an inside deal, available only to those close to the charity. Even so, TNC said, "The goal in every case is to find a suitable buyer, whether that person is a Conservancy trustee or not."

Then something else arose. When the *Post* reported a few comments from buyers who said that their gifts were part of the deal, TNC stressed that the charitable gifts were "not legally tied" to the transactions. That is, the charity, by defending itself on the basis of a legal definition, was leaving room for interpretation; there just might have been a wink and a nod, with the expectation that the lower purchase price would be supplemented by a gift to ensure that TNC got all its money back.

Running a $3 billion organization is not simple. The Nature Conservancy is big and has big plans, and big plans require big money. The charity says, and it's true enough, that it cannot raise or otherwise acquire enough money to do its job fully. So it was trying to figure out how to legitimately expand its reach by offering some donors the option of making up the difference in the transaction with a tax-deductible gift.

The charity does well by placing the easements, and it was protecting its financial health by matching the sale of certain pieces of land to those donors who were already sympathetic to its cause.

When an easement is put on land, property value is reduced. The buyer pays market value. Nothing amiss about that. The charity also receives a gift it might not otherwise get, and the donor takes a deduction for it. Nothing amiss about that, either. But because newspaper reporters without a solid understanding of charitable giving sniff around, they can come up with something that *looks* amiss.

This is true especially if the scribes omit certain information. Take the headline of one of the *Post*'s stories: "Nonprofit Sells Scenic Acreage to Allies at a Loss." You can't exactly avoid a loss in value with an easement, and you can't exactly protect land without an easement. Or take the story's subhead: "Buyers Gain Tax Breaks with Few Curbs on Land Use." Actually, the easements called for more than a "few" curbs.

The curbs in question were the very curbs that would make the land of less value to developers. The headline might as well have read "Nonprofit Does Job Well," or "Donors Receive Legal and Appropriate Deductions for Gifts to Charity."

But then, that wouldn't sell papers, would it?

THAT THE BUYER was an individual with no plans to develop the land, however, did not erase the problem of the perception of favoritism. It looked like The Nature Conservancy, a charity with tax-exempt status, was encouraging those closest to the organization, as it turns out, to take advantage of a great big tax loophole.

That summer, the Senate Finance Committee requested a lot of information from TNC, a whole lot more than a charity is usually required to give the IRS about its activities.

Within the category of land transactions, the committee requested a description and the location of the properties, the dates of land purchases and sales, the terms of the easements, the identities of those who sold property to the Conservancy and those who bought it, information about any relationship the organization may have had with the sellers or the buyers, and information about any donations of $1,000 or more by a land purchaser or seller.

The committee also asked for all appraisals of the properties, including appraisals made before TNC's purchases and after easements or other restrictions were imposed.

It was quite a laundry list—some might say a fishing expedition, considering the thousands of pages the request generated.

THE WASHINGTON POST uncovered a memo from a state trustee.

> Generally, the buyer puts too much value on it [for tax purposes]. Land donators almost always try to value their land at more than the [true] value. This is a business. We sort of wince and look away at some of the values buyers put on these transactions. We're not the IRS.

This didn't look good at all, and the Senate Finance Committee asked for "TNC's viewpoint on this statement."

It also wondered about the sentence, "This is a business," since The Nature Conservancy is not a business but a charity. Of course, any charity is also a business; it just doesn't have any shareholders.

While the sentence itself might not have made much of an impact, the memo's context placed TNC in a highly unfavorable light. The memo practically shouts out that donors are abusing the idea of an easement to take more of a charitable deduction than they would ordinarily be permitted. The higher the value of the easement, the lower the selling price after the easement is imposed, and if the donor is making a charitable contribution for the difference, the deduction is higher.

Thus, if the easement is determined to reduce the land's value by $400,000, as opposed to the $300,000 in the example above, the purchase price is only $600,000. Someone buying the land and making TNC whole with a total of $1 million thus receives a charitable deduction of $400,000. Calculating a larger reduction in the property's value, a move that might be seen as arbitrary, makes the public subsidize more of the cost. The memo suggested that fooling around with the easement value was common. Worse, that The Nature Conservancy knew this but looked the other way.

The picture darkened with the discovery of another internal memo: "If you look at our revenues from last year, they're up from the year before, mostly due to the valuation of easements, which can be viewed as subjective and a tool we used to inflate our income."

The substance of each of the memos was incorrect, and the fears expressed in each were unfounded. The Nature Conservancy puts easements on property by describing the restrictions, but it is not up to the charity to place a value on the easement. That's done independently. The memo addressing that point had the effect of making it sound as if the higher revenues were false and as though TNC artificially controlled the amount of false revenues it could report. That was not the case.

The communication was costly and careless. It put the organization in unjustified danger in the event that anyone wanted to examine TNC's records, as the *Washington Post* did.

ONE OF THE basic rules of charitable giving is that donors—not charities—determine what deductions they take. It is an extension of the rule that a taxpayer is responsible for calculating his or her own taxes. While a paid accountant can play that role, a charity cannot.

Charities find themselves in an awkward position, however, when a donor makes a large gift. Donors often ask charities to explain the tax consequences of their gift. Most charities will insist that the donor consult a tax advisor, but the best charities are knowledgeable and are eager to help the donor understand the tax benefits of a charitable gift. So advising the donor, even if only in an informal way, is not uncommon.

I've used the word "appraisal" a few times in the context of the TNC issue. One of the Senate Finance Committee's central concerns in the land deals was the accuracy of appraisals. Except for publicly traded stock, all charitable gifts of property—called "non-cash gifts" by the IRS—require a valid appraisal, as well as Tax Form 8283, where the results of the appraisal are summarized if the donor claims a deduction of $5,000 or more.

Real estate is a non-cash gift—literally, in the vernacular of the average person, a gift of property.

For an appraisal to be valid, it must adhere to several restrictions imposed in the tax regulations. Basically, the appraisal must be conducted by a professional who has no conflict-of-interest relationship with either the donor or the charity. Although charities may conduct or pay for their own appraisal, the donor, not the charity, is the party responsible for getting the appraisal. The idea is to provide authenticity to the process so the donor can't just make up a value.

The appraisal requirement came about in the mid-1980s, after Congress discovered that donors of artwork routinely, and by large amounts, inflated the value of their gifts. Back then, the IRS panel that examines donated artwork was aware that, on average, donors overvalued their gifts—and their deductions—by 1,000 percent. On average. These days, that happens far less often, because of the requirement for a qualified appraisal. The opinion letter from Jerry McCoy, the tax attorney, took that fact into account.

Despite the rules, the process still has some subjective components. Yet there's not a whole lot of room for malfeasance. Certainly, despite the impression the *Washington Post* left with its readers, and despite the questions from members of Congress and their staffs—who, let's face it, aren't really that informed about this process and aren't strangers to playing politics with confusing issues—donors can't willy-nilly determine their own land value, as was stated in the trustee's memo. In fact, the assertion that they "almost always try" was unfounded.

But tell that to the newspaper or to Congress.

When elected officials complain about the "abuse" in the charitable sector and point to the appraisal process as one of the big problems, they are probably not addressing the issue honestly or in an informed way. Charitable gifts of property are too important to charities, and to society, to attack because there's a variation in appraisal values. But there are people who are simply unsympathetic to the role charities play in the United States, who view a tax deduction as nothing more than a drain on revenues and would be quite happy, except for gifts of publicly traded stock, to eliminate the deduction for charitable gifts of property altogether.

Or at least lessen their market value at the time of the gift. Those people wouldn't mind "conceding" that donors should be permitted to deduct what they paid for the asset to begin with. But many types of property—land, privately held stock, jewelry, artwork, book and stamp collections—tend to rise in value over the years, and giving away that value should be acknowledged for what it is. It isn't an abuse.

There are abuses, of course, and they should be dealt with as they arise with more severe penalties for fraudulent appraisers than are now on the books, but the *idea* is not an abuse.

To do what several Congressional members and staffers have discussed during recent years would be to throw the baby out with the bath water.

As it is not up to the charity to determine appraisal values for their donors' gifts, so it is also not up to the charity to police its donors when they fill out their tax forms. The trustee should not have made that claim "we sort of wince and look away," and did so out of ignorance.

Again though, the *Post* reporters, not knowledgeable about the nuances of charitable giving, simply reported the words of the trustee.

IN ALL, THE Senate Finance Committee requested detailed information about eighteen categories of activity at The Nature Conservancy.

In addition to the easement-donation issue, of interest to the Committee were the loans to top-ranking officials, in particular a loan of more than $1.5 million to its executive director, Steven McCormick. McCormick had recently moved from California to take up his new position, and the charity loaned him money to buy a new home. The charity was, in fact, the mortgage holder.

The IRS pays attention to this kind of thing. It is interested in internal deals that might run against the public interest. At first, TNC reported that the terms of the loan called for an adjustable interest rate that started out at only 4.59 percent, lower than the market would provide to anyone else. After some public relations damage, it was learned that the loan was actually 7 percent.

Even though it turned out not to be the case, the lower-than-market–rate report made people nervous. When the difference is subsidized by a charity, it is subsidized by the public. When the beneficiary is a person in a position of authority at a charity—in this case, the executive director—and benefits too much, the problem becomes evident. It is called "private inurement." The rules are strict on this point, though the boundaries of the point itself are often subjective or unclear.

The IRS asks charities to report any loans it makes to those closest to the charity, such as key employees or members of the board.

McCormick's income was $420,000 from The Nature Conservancy

the year before the newspaper articles were published. The Senate Finance Committee wanted to examine that, too, and requested all minutes of the compensation committee that related to salaries and loans. Also, it asked, "Please provide a detailed discussion, including value, of any deferred compensation programs that TNC or its related organization operates for any of its employees."

The committee also asked for TNC's IRS filings for the preceding ten years.

Perception is always an important concern. There is an old adage about whether a decision should be made, or at least guided by, the concern about how it will look in tomorrow morning's newspaper. This is particularly true when the decision involves gray areas. A gray area would not involve a person receiving a deduction for a gift, but whether that gift opportunity, in the context of who might be most interested in it, is available and made known to only a few people, a few friends.

The Nature Conservancy forgot the adage, but it did something remarkable. Less than a month after the *Post* series was published, and before the Senate Finance Committee got into the act, the board of The Nature Conservancy met to discuss the newspaper's allegations.

The board brought in outside help—people intimately knowledgeable about the way charities ought to be run—and, after an independent report was issued, voted to make changes in the way the charity operated.

The board made a new rule that barred board members, trustees, employees, and their immediate family members from taking part in the conservation buyer program.

The board terminated its practice of providing loans to its employees.

The board announced that it would use independent advisors to assist in its "aspiration of making the Conservancy a recognized leader in governance and oversight."

Although it was wounded by the *Post* articles, The Nature Conservancy took them seriously. The board said, "We are committed to changing any of our practices that do not live up to our mission and values." There would be no more winking and nodding.

The Nature Conservancy did not run and hide. Its board acted with speed, efficiency, and sensitivity to public opinion.

THE LEGACY OF SOLFERINO

"Somehow or other a volunteer service had to be organized; but this was very difficult amid such disorder.

JEAN HENRI DUNANT, *A Memory of Solferino*

ALTHOUGH DONORS ANNUALLY contribute to hundreds of thousands of charities for a variety of reasons, perhaps nothing evokes our sense of largesse more than a disaster. To Americans, disasters in the United States were unlike those in the rest of the world. The fighting in Ireland and the Middle East, the famines in Bangladesh and Somalia, and the decades-long run of terrorism in Europe were all distinctly foreign, in concept as well as locale.

The devastating Christmas 2004 tsunami in East Asia, which killed more than 200,000 people, elicited great sympathy and support from Americans.

Then, less than a year later, America had its own tsunami in the form of a hurricane called Katrina. Tens of thousands of people died in her wrath. Measured by the number of lives lost, it was the worst natural disaster to befall the United States in a century.

While several charities are dedicated to eradicating problems in other parts of the world, the disasters that receive most of our support tend to be local: hurricanes, floods, and large fires.

The February 1993 bombing at the World Trade Center in New York, and then the April 1995 attack on the Murrah Federal Building in Oklahoma City, were different. They awakened Americans to what could happen here at home. But the first, for which one Ramzi Ahmed Yousef was convicted, was contained. The second was perpetrated by Americans Timothy McVeigh and Terry Nichols, whom the world came to think of as demented loners. Both tragedies were packaged and placed safely in the past, their causes eliminated.

That sense of safe distance, the idea of being safe, changed on September 11, 2001, when Americans experienced the worst national tragedy in most of their lifetimes. No other day saw so many die. No other day introduced such fear and uncertainty.

As television conveyed the news, millions of horrified and disbelieving people witnessed—helplessly watched—the terrible drama of three thousand men and women dying.

In the past, Americans believed the oceans protected us. Now we knew it wasn't so and we suddenly felt vulnerable.

No other day was filled with so much anguish. Almost 10,000 died at Gettysburg over three days, but they were soldiers, and no one, except those on the scene, was watching.

It is also true that no previous disaster sparked such a spirit of generosity. This was expressed with millions of donations to charitable organizations. Organized charity was at the ready, its resources quickly available for people needing help. The news from Connecticut alone:

- In an act at once simple and profound, shortly after September 11 one person walked into a Red Cross office in Greenwich and held out a check for $10,000. "I don't know what else to do," he said;
- Within forty-eight hours high school students in South Windsor raised $5,000 and a truckload of food and supplies;
- A Salvation Army drive for relief workers had a moving company in New Britain at one point filling a truck every twenty minutes with food and supplies to take to Manhattan;
- At a McDonald's in Darien, occupants in a long line of cars waited to drop off money. One volunteer said, "They may knock down our buildings, but they will never bend nor break the steel of the American spirit."

And that was but a sampling of what was taking place all over the country within just hours and days of the September 11 tragedy.

Within weeks of the attacks, more than 200 charities collected hundreds of millions of dollars, and hundreds of millions more came in during the following months. It was a record-breaking harvest of giving.

After six months, charities collected more than $2 billion. Nothing, except perhaps the post-World War II Marshall Plan, compared to the magnitude of the generosity Americans provided in the wake of September 11.

While September 11 will undoubtedly be remembered most for its impact on our foreign policy and national security implications, it is also true that the urge to help others, even before we looked around and learned that we were safe, was strong and focused.

Amid the rumors and fears of additional assaults, people gave. They telephoned and walked and drove to nearby charities to see what they could do.

One charity, the American Red Cross, stood out. It is one of the nation's oldest and most venerable charitable organizations. Within hours on September 11, both money and blood began pouring into the Red Cross. In less than a week, more than enough blood had been collected to care for those who needed it. Lines were so long in Washington, D.C., New York, and other major cities that many potential blood donors were turned away.

THE ORIGINS OF the Red Cross can be traced to Solferino, Italy, in 1859, and the death and bloodshed in the last battle of the second war for Italian independence. Although most people today are not familiar with the battle of Solferino, it was widely reported and widely known at the time.

Solferino is a town in northern Italy, a short distance southeast of Milan. The Austrians had occupied parts of that area for more than five generations, and the Italians were fed up with the brutality: rape, executions, even, so the story goes, the nailing of a six-year-old child to the door of a church. They finally were driven to rebel and exact revenge.

The armies of three countries—France, seeking a revenge that dated to Austria's role in the downfall of Napoleon Bonaparte, joined Italy to fight Austria—numbered approximately 270,000 men.

In a savage battle lasting fifteen hours—it began at 4:00 a.m. and ended at 7:00 p.m. on June 24, 1859—forty thousand men died or were wounded. The wounded and dying were shot and bayoneted by both sides.

The Geneva Conventions were still somewhere in the future. There were no rules of engagement, no mandated humanitarian principles to follow.

On that June 24, a man named Jean Henri Dunant, a Swiss business-man, happened to be in the nearby town of Castiglione, where many of the wounded and dead from Solferino were carried. Wounded soldiers lay abandoned, and medical supplies and services were grotesquely lacking.

Dunant, who years earlier had been instrumental in founding the YMCA in Europe, was so haunted by his memories of the butchery at Solferino that he wrote a pamphlet, *A Memory of Solferino.*

That essay was the beginning of the International Red Cross. Dunant wrote, "The feeling one has of one's own utter inadequacy in such extraordinary and solemn circumstances is unspeakable."

Another passage describes his despair.

> There was a shortage of medical orderlies, and at this critical time no help was to be had. Somehow or other a volunteer service had to be organized; but this was very difficult amid such disorder.

In 1864, shortly after *A Memory of Solferino* was published, the Red Cross Society was formed, and the Geneva Convention was signed by fourteen nations in Geneva, Switzerland.

The convention defined the rules for governing the care of the wounded and the treatment of prisoners. Although the United States sent delegates to the convention, it did not ratify the agreement until the early 1880s.

The Red Cross adopted as a symbol of neutrality a Greek cross com-posed of five equal squares, and it became the organization's interna-tionally recognized trademark of neutrality. Its deep, pre-Christian historic significance relates to the celebration of the human being. The Muslims don't like a red cross on a white background, however, because it reminds them of the Christian crusaders. This is why Muslim countries have a Red Crescent emblem. In 2006, Israel and Palestine were admitted to the International Red Cross and Red Crescent Movement. The Palestinian emblem is the Red Crescent; Israel designed a third emblem, called the Red Crystal.

Dunant, meanwhile, having sold his business interests to pay debts and unable to profit personally from his vision, declared bankruptcy in 1867. In 1901, although Dunant was living in poverty and was largely forgotten, the Nobel committee awarded him its first Peace Prize, shared with Frédéric Passy, another Swiss citizen.

Shortly afterward, the International Committee of the Red Cross sent the following message:

> There is no man who more deserves this honour . . . Without you, the Red Cross, the supreme humanitarian achievement of the nineteenth century, would probably never have been undertaken.

As poor as he was, Dunant did not spend the $10,000 prize money on himself. Instead, he left the money in his will for charitable causes.

ON DECEMBER 12, 1862, as Dunant was finishing his essay, a woman on a Civil War battlefield was writing her own story, its sentiment strikingly similar to that contained in *A Memory of Solferino*. Only she was contemplating what was to come. In a letter, she described the atmosphere, full of awful expectancy, on the night before the battle at Fredericksburg: "I thought I could almost hear the slow flap of the grim messenger's wings, as one by one he sought and selected his victims for the morning."

Her fears were well-founded. Death did come that next day to Fredericksburg, Virginia: 7,000 Union soldiers and 1,200 Confederate soldiers were killed.

That woman was Clara Barton, who started the American Red Cross in 1881. A remarkable and caring person, she helped wounded soldiers during the Civil War by going directly to the battlefield with medical supplies.

In 1869, after strenuous work with the suffragist movement, Barton suffered a breakdown and sailed to Europe to convalesce. It was then that she learned of the Geneva Treaty to protect sick and wounded soldiers. This treaty, although signed by many nations five years earlier, remained unratified by the United States.

At about the same time, she also learned about the International Red Cross, whose mission then was to protect the injured on battlefields. In a curious effort at recuperating from a breakdown, she made it a point to witness the horrors of war firsthand by traveling to the front in the Franco-Prussian War in 1870.

When she returned she pressed the case to get the United States to ratify the Geneva Convention and also tried to form a Red Cross organization in the United States. On May 21, 1881, a constitution was adopted for what was then called the American Association of the Red Cross.

On June 9 of that year, the new association selected Clara Barton as its first president.

In December 1881, President Chester Arthur surprised the new American Red Cross by calling for ratification of the Geneva Convention in his first message to Congress. He signed the Convention, and the Senate approved it in March 1882.

During her presidency, Barton authored what came to be known as the "American Amendment" to the Red Cross charter, a key provision that provided for disaster relief during peacetime as well as war. She also broadened the organization's mission to help victims of natural disasters such as floods and earthquakes.

The American Amendment, by the way, put Clara Barton at odds with European Red Cross leaders, who believed in limiting their activities to military conflicts.

TODAY, EVERYONE IN America knows the Red Cross. While the Red Cross has its tax exemption from the Internal Revenue Service, just like other public charities, it is also different. Unlike most other charities, Congress granted it a charter to maintain a special relationship with the federal government.

The Red Cross has the legal status of "a federal instrumentality" and carries out the purposes of the Geneva Convention in the United States. Those purposes include furnishing aid to the sick and wounded in armies during war, acting as a medium for communications between those who serve and relatives back home, and carrying on peacetime disaster relief.

In addition to spelling out its objectives, the American charter gave the Red Cross full legal status and protected its right to use the Red Cross emblem. It requires the charity to report annually to Congress on its activities and financial status.

By the turn of the century, many people close to the organization were concerned about the way the Red Cross conducted its business, and some of them did not approve of the way Clara Barton ran the place. They criticized her personal management style and, in particular, her financial record–keeping. They took their complaints to President Theodore Roosevelt, and on May 14, 1904, after twenty-three years as the first president of the Red Cross, Clara Barton was forced to resign.

Congress issued a new charter in 1905. Now more than one hundred years old, that charter is the one under which the Red Cross continues to operate today. It has been amended over the years, but the most important amendment was made in 1947, when a fifty-member Board of Overseers was created. Eight members are appointed by the president, and one of those serves as the chief executive officer. As the presidential appointees are often officials of the federal government, the Red Cross is as much a political organization as it is a charity.

Despite its special status, however, the Red Cross is not an agency of the government and, except under unusual circumstances, it does not receive government funding.

IN 2001, THE Red Cross raised $728 million to support a budget of $2.7 billion. By the end of January 2002, in a period slightly less than five months after September 11, 2001, the Red Cross raised $850 million for its Disaster Relief Fund. Eventually, the Relief Fund raised over $1 billion. By the beginning of November 2005—after only two months—the Red Cross raised $1.3 billion for Katrina victims.

That's the good news. But even that depends on whether you care about where the money went.

As it turns out, the legacy of Solferino would not be enough to protect even this celebrated charity from massive criticism. September 11, 2001, changed the world in many respects, and one is the way we now look at how charities raise their money and what they do with the funds they receive. In the aftermath of September 11 the Red Cross received severe criticism—much of it justified—for misdirecting the money it raised.

Was it ignorance or arrogance or something else that led to the accusations that money, so generously donated to help at a most vulnerable time, was being put to purposes other than those for which it was intended?

It is true that the acute and effective public outrage forced upon the Red Cross generated a sobering self-examination that ultimately led to a change in the way it does business. But the questions remain, especially after the Hurricane Katrina disaster. Did the Red Cross change enough? And what, after all, should donors expect of a charity after it has taken their money?

THE RED CROSS AND
PUBLIC OPINION

"I will never, ever wear the Red Cross vest again"
BETTY BRUNNER
A RED CROSS VOLUNTEER FOR THIRTY-SEVEN YEARS,
UNTIL SHE QUIT IN DISGUST AFTER HURRICANE KATRINA

NEITHER JEAN HENRI Dunant nor Clara Barton would have been pleased. While the American National Red Cross has performed some very good work since it was founded in 1881, its responses to two huge disasters in the United States four years apart—9/11 and Hurricane Katrina—combined to create an organizational disaster.

For different reasons, in its response to each cataclysm, the Red Cross fared poorly. It's almost as if it wanted to taunt the public, to dare donors into their generosity.

We begin with the aftershocks of September 2001, and then go to the wake of September 2005.

WITH A WIDESPREAD profound desire to help after 9/11, donors needed little time before their efforts took tangible shape with offers of food and shelter, as well as a river of money.

In the weeks that followed the attacks, more than three hundred new charities sprouted up to aid the victims. These joined the several hundred already-established charities that were collecting funds to help.

The charity at the center of it all was the American Red Cross. Even President Bush appealed to Americans to send their dollars to the Red Cross. It was the only charity advertised by the president, and he did so several times in his speeches and at his press conferences.

The Chronicle of Philanthropy reported in late 2003 that its survey of the year before showed that the Red Cross raised the most money of any charity in the United States, replacing the Salvation Army for the first time in the survey's twelve-year history. In the days following 9/11, the Red Cross established the Liberty Disaster Fund to receive the outpouring of money. In less than four months it raised more than $667 million.

Approximately $2.7 billion would eventually be donated to charities that said they were helping terrorist victims. Of that amount, the Red Cross raised $988 million.

How the money would be used stirred up quite a controversy, and it continues to have implications for donors and charities everywhere to this day.

Although the donated money did a lot of good, had people not paid attention it also would have gone places that donors never intended. As far as the public was concerned—after all, the Red Cross advertised it this way—the Liberty Disaster Fund was specifically formed to help *only* those affected by the 9/11 disaster. But then, much to the public's surprise, the Red Cross said it didn't see it that way at all. Indeed, more than $250 million dollars had been allocated to other purposes.

Exposed, the Red Cross referred to the fine print, which said that the funds would be used "for this tragedy and the emerging needs from this event."

It would be an understatement to say that many contributors felt betrayed.

Congress held hearings. After stern and often angry questioning from members of the Committee on Energy and Commerce of the House of Representatives, the president of the Red Cross, Dr. Bernadine Healy—whose departure from office had already been announced—said that the phrase "emerging needs" clearly meant that victims of other tragedies were intended to be helped with the money in the Liberty Disaster Fund.

Few in the room agreed. Representative Bart Stupak, a Democrat from Michigan, said, "I think you took advantage of a very tragic situation." Stupak also said that the Red Cross "opportunistically seized on a horrendous act of terrorism to further its own long-term institutional needs, such as improving its telephone and technology systems and building its reserve of blood."

Representative Bill Tauzin, the committee's chair, accused the Red Cross of "siphoning millions of dollars away from thousands of victims' families, misleading millions of donors and using bad judgment that could imperil the fundraising efforts of all charities."

Another committee member said that the Red Cross had willfully trampled on the intent of those who gave money out of a heartfelt desire to help victims and their families.

Another accused Dr. Healy of engaging in "just plain spin."

Dr. Healy explained that there had been internal discussions on how the Liberty Disaster Fund contributions would be used, and that the decision to withhold money for future events came only after much debate.

After the hearing, she was quoted in *The New York Times* as saying of the House committee members, "I don't know why they didn't get it. I think they went in with their own spin."

The truth was, however, that the Red Cross didn't get it. At times when the public response was so emotional, it cold-bloodedly and inappropriately deceived the public. The message in the big print—the words everyone reads, the words the Red Cross knew would get the money—was never unclear: give to the Liberty Fund to help the victims of 9/11.

THE RED CROSS already had other image problems that foreshadowed what it experienced after the attacks. In an article entitled "Red Cross Has Pattern of Diverting Donations," written a week after September 11, the *Washington Post* chronicled several disasters during the prior decade for which local officials had to pressure the charity to make sure victims received the money donors intended.

San Francisco

The Red Cross faced severe criticism after the San Francisco earthquake in 1989. A Red Cross representative visited Mayor Art Agnos shortly afterwards, but the representative "wasn't talking about disaster relief," Agnos said. "He asked me to cut a commercial to raise money." The Mayor declined the request but that didn't deter the Red Cross, which advertised for donations and raised nearly $55 million for earthquake victims.

Mayor Agnos thought this might be an opportunity to rebuild, so he asked the charity for $7 million for homeless shelters. He was turned down.

Agnos reported: "I asked, 'Where the hell are you putting all of this money?' When I asked, they answered in generalities. Finally, it dawned on me that they were stonewalling me."

While the earthquake still captured the attention of the media and the public, Agnos accused the Red Cross of using bait-and-switch tactics—soliciting earthquake donations and then piling the money away in its general disaster relief fund.

The Red Cross responded by saying that it would increase spending in Northern California and that it would indeed provide Agnos with $5.4 million for homeless shelters. Of the $55 million raised, about $12 million went to the relief effort.

As was the Red Cross's policy, its fine print noted that some funds would be used for other disasters.

Oklahoma City

After the 1995 Oklahoma City bombing, the Red Cross spent only $3 million of the $13 million it collected for the victims and their families. The charity knew within two days that it had collected much more money than it would need. Ignoring what the donors had contributed for, a Red Cross spokeswoman said that they had allocated about $2.6 million for Oklahoma City victims and the rest would help address less-publicized disasters.

The Midwest

After the Red River flooded in Minnesota and North Dakota in 1997, the Red Cross released all the donated money, but only after being confronted by public protest hearings.

The Red Cross collected $16 million, but, according to then-Minnesota Attorney General Hubert Humphrey III, more than a year later $4 million remained unspent.

"You don't have someone who is outright trying to defraud people in this process," Humphrey said. "But when you make appeals at a time of great emotion and stress, you have a significant responsibility to see to it that you use the funds for the purpose you state."

San Diego

The way collections were handled after a wildfire in 2000 in nearby Alpine, California, generated deep criticism of the Red Cross. The San Diego chapter solicited donations and within two weeks it told its board and San Diego news media that $400,000 had been collected. However, the families who had lost homes did not receive most of the money donated for their benefit.

A confidential audit revealed that as of September 2001, the San Diego chapter had spent $123,000 on fire relief and that less than $10,000 of that had gone directly to victims. Yet donors had given nearly $188,000 for the victims.

Despite its limited assistance to victims, the chapter quickly wrote to one major donor, San Diego Padres owner John Moores, to ask if it could move the $100,000 he collected for the Alpine fire into a fund for other emergencies. The chapter explained that it had already addressed the Alpine victims' immediate needs.

Moores's office told them: "Use it for what we gave it for—the Alpine fire." Moores's executive assistant, Beverly Stengel said, "I was really angry."

Responding to local demands for an accounting of the fire money, the San Diego chapter released an edited version of a headquarters audit, a version that omitted several critical passages, only to have the full version later provided anonymously to the *San Diego Union-Tribune*.

The Sycuan Band of the Kumeyaay Nation, a Native American tribe that donated $50,000 for the disaster, said that the Red Cross "has at best mismanaged the funds collected and at worst exploited a tragic situation."

A WEEK BEFORE Bernadine Healy responded to questions on Capitol Hill, Bill O'Reilly roundly criticized the Red Cross on his television show, *The O'Reilly Factor*. "The Red Cross believes it has the right to do other things with your donations," he said.

The Red Cross said that it needed a lot of money to do its work.

That's true enough, of course, and it's also true, and more to the point of the criticism, that the Red Cross does not—and most of the time cannot—raise funds retroactively. That is, it needs money in the bank for the next disaster.

The problem, though, was that the money was solicited on the premise that it would be used on behalf of the victims. Using 9/11 as the marketing platform would generate the most public sympathy and the most money.

Crass as that sounds, that kind of marketing is not all bad. The Red Cross's mission is to provide "relief to victims of disasters and help people prevent, prepare for, and respond to emergencies." Take note of the need to be prepared.

The Red Cross, like businesses selling a product, and like other charities raising money, needs to sell the sizzle before it sells the steak. Helping the 9/11 victims was so much more effective an appeal than one asking to help people in some future, unknown disaster.

O'Reilly's guest that night was Renata Rafferty, a consultant and author of a book about what people should know about charities before making donations. They got to talking about what charities do with donated money.

"When you send a check to a rescue mission to pay for a Thanksgiving dinner," she asked, "do you honestly believe that money is being used for turkey and stuffing?"

The intended answer was no. You can't expect a dollar to work its way through the labyrinth of a charity's finances to have all of it go to the specific, stated purpose of the appeal.

Yet O'Reilly responded, "Yes. I do."

A simple question often reveals a big problem, and at that moment a small ax felled a large oak tree. Renata Rafferty's response to a question about Thanksgiving turkey for the homeless exposed how donors who contribute funds for a specific cause are often misled.

While charities legitimately and necessarily disperse donations throughout their operations to better perform their good work for society, they also give the impression that every cent is going directly to the cause. Thus a question intended to elicit one response actually elicited another.

"When I give money to help the families," O'Reilly declared, "I believe that money is going there. Otherwise it's 'fraud in the inducement.' But," he went on, "the Red Cross says, 'I'm going to give a little money over here and a little over there.'"

He admitted to being outraged—not an unusual demeanor for Bill

O'Reilly—and reported that the Red Cross said it had earmarked $50 million for a blood readiness program and $26 million for community outreach, an effort, he asserted, that was not connected to any tragedy. He also noted that $29 million was being spent on phones, database management, contribution processing and other overhead.

That was not much, actually, considering the Red Cross's budget was well over $2 billion at the time. It takes a lot to keep the place going. But you never hear the Red Cross, or any other charity, willingly disclose its administrative costs.

The Red Cross was not the only target of criticism. *The New York Times* reported that the Salvation Army wasn't fulfilling its promise to pay victims' bills. Its difficulty was attributed not to insufficient funds but to administrative delays and failures.

When a charity makes a promise to help, that promise fuels people's hopes and expectations, particularly when the difference between the promise and its fulfillment is the difference between sleeping on the street or in a warm bed.

During his show, O'Reilly announced that until he got an acceptable report about how much would be going to the families, he would "not give the Red Cross another penny." He encouraged his viewers to do likewise.

"That organization," he said, "has done a lot of good in the past, but they are blowing it this time around and blowing it badly."

Donors to the Liberty Disaster Fund made their gifts in the belief that their dollars would aid the survivors. They were fooled; the charity misled those who gave.

In the wake of America's most vulnerable moment, the highly esteemed American Red Cross created the biggest public relations fiasco of any charity ever. It deceived the public on how it would use the hundreds of millions of dollars given for a specific purpose. A lie is a lie no matter who says it, or what fancy language cloaks it.

AFTER THE CONGRESSIONAL hearings and relentless media criticism, the Red Cross backed down. At a news conference in November—and after Dr. Bernadine Healy was gone—Harold Decker, the new chief executive officer, said, "We deeply regret that our activities over the past eight weeks have not been as sharply focused as America wants, nor as focused as the victims of this tragedy deserve. The people affected by this terrible tragedy have been our first priority, and beginning today, they will be the only priority of the Liberty Fund."

The Red Cross ran a full-page ad in *The New York Times* with the heading "The American Red Cross Hears America." In it, the charity apologized for its lack of focus, a focus that "the people affected by this tragedy deserve and as our generous donors intended."

Less than a year after September 11, the Red Cross changed its policies relating to honoring donor intent. Donors now are asked how they want their money spent, and the Red Cross honors it.

The language on its disaster-relief solicitations says: "You can help the victims of [this disaster] and thousands of other disasters across the country each year by making a financial gift to the American Red Cross Disaster Relief Fund, which enables the Red Cross to provide shelter, food, counseling and other assistance to those in need."

That's a start. Note the "thousands of other disasters" part, which is intended to say that donors are helping in this disaster but that a portion of their money can and most probably will be used for others.

While this was a good and necessary step, much damage had been done. The public came to distrust America's charity, and, as we all know, broken trust, absent a miracle, is often irreparable.

It was a disaster, not a miracle.

Hurricane Katrina came through New Orleans and the rest of the Gulf Coast leaving no doubt that Mother Nature can still do what she wants. The president looked at the damage from high above, safe within his high-technology airplane, perhaps wondering why no technology can stand up to something so primitive as wind and water. Yet there she was, brewing up a storm that would take the region and the country into a different consciousness altogether. The whole Gulf Coast region, and most notably the fabled city of New Orleans, would be dramatically changed, probably forever.

Once again the Red Cross was on the scene. This time, though, the question wouldn't be how the money was spent, although some wondered why the charity needed so much to do its job of providing short-term care, while other charities, whose job was to provide far more costly long-term assistance, were able to raise so little. This time the question was: Why did the Red Cross do such a lousy job?

It got so bad that Alabama's governor, Bob Riley, asked to take over the responsibilities of the Red Cross in his state.

It got so bad that the state of Louisiana investigated Red Cross volunteers for stealing money that was meant for the hurricane victims.

It got so bad that nearly fifty people were indicted for authorizing payments to fictitious storm victims.

It got so bad that the Red Cross president, Marsha Evans, resigned. Her resignation was seen as just the leading symptom of a dysfunctional organization.

It got so bad that the chairman of the Senate Finance Committee, Charles Grassley, would threaten to revoke the Red Cross's status as the only charity chartered by Congress to help Americans in disasters.

It got so bad that Senator Grassley also threatened to overhaul the Red Cross board.

The most important charity in the United States has to have important people on its board, so the president gets to appoint eight of the fifty board members. Six of those eight important people, however, had never attended any—not one—of the twenty-three board meetings held between October 2000 and May 2005. One of the other two showed up just once.

The vast majority of the rest of the board had been chosen by region. Chapter representation is democratic, which has its merits but also means that the organization is subjected to other levels and types of political pressure.

Even without the absences of the White House appointees, things were dire; the bad news during the months after Katrina hit was deadly enough. But it would have been nice to have board members who actually care about the charity they serve and govern.

By the way, the only person to make the meetings during those five years was the one the president personally appointed to serve as head of the board.

CONGRESS, SWEPT UP in the emotion of the moment, did something unique for people who wanted to donate to charities helping Katrina victims.

There's a provision in the tax code restricting a donor's deduction in any one year to fifty percent of his or her income. For example, a person who earns $50,000 cannot deduct more than $25,000 of charitable gifts. In the fall of 2005, Congress passed a law that provided a one-time exception to this rule. The limit for deducting charitable gifts would be 100 percent of the donor's income.

Congress being Congress, however, the law didn't hit the nail on the head. The idea was to encourage increased giving for Katrina victims, but the law ended up applying to donations to any charity.

A lot of people, particularly rich people, took advantage of the rule. To be sure, some of the extra money donated to charities as a result of the relaxed deduction limit went to help people on the Gulf Coast, but a lot didn't.

But that wasn't so bad. If you want to help a charitable cause, but in the process you help a lot more, what's the harm? There's harm in the extra money it costs, but it would seem by what happened that the cost was outweighed by the general benefit to society, Katrina victims being an important part of the equation.

As it turns out, one of those people who took advantage of the new, temporary law was Vice President Richard B. Cheney. It so happens that in 2005 the Cheneys made charitable gifts of almost $7 million. Cheney's income that year was almost $9 million, which was huge, even for him, because he cashed in on the Halliburton stock options that he had been given before he became vice president.

The decision to make charitable gifts of the options, once they became real money, was made in 2001, so there was never any question that he would not personally benefit from the extra cash. The gifts were structured so that he would not pay any more or any less in taxes than he would have if the gifts had not been made.

The Cheneys gave money to the George Washington Medical Faculty Associates, the University of Wyoming, and to Capital Partners for Education, which helps low-income high school students in Washington, D.C. There was nothing for the Red Cross or any charities helping Katrina victims, but his gifts were driven by what normally drives donors: a personal interest in the charity. George Washington Hospital is where his heart had been attended to. He earned his bachelor's and master's degrees from the University of Wyoming. And he and his wife have an interest in the education of poor, inner city high school students.

Seven million dollars is a lot more than 50 percent of $9 million, but even though he was able to do this all in one year, because of the temporary change in the law, there was nothing illegitimate about the tax consequences of the Cheneys' charitable gifts. The legislation, designed for one purpose, simply helped many other causes.

President Bush gave over $75,000 to charities in 2005—including the Red Cross.

EVEN MORE THAN after 9/11, the money poured in after hurricanes Katrina and Rita. The Red Cross received over $2 billion of the more than $3 billion that was raised.

By the way, foreign countries sent $126 million to help in the hurricane relief effort. Seven months later, however, only $10.5 million of that had been spent because of confusion in the federal government at the departments of Homeland Security, Defense, State, and Education. By far the single biggest foreign contributor, making gifts of over $100 million, was the United Arab Emirates.

From somewhere in its vast budget, the Red Cross found $500,000 during the three years after 9/11 to enhance its image. While spending money on public relations is not uncommon, even at charities, one has to wonder how Hollywood actors could tell a more convincing story than the Red Cross itself through its good work.

In any event, the money was probably all wasted. Regardless of how good the work was, or how much reform the organization undertook after the scathing criticism it received when it mishandled donations intended for 9/11 victims, by the time Katrina hit, the Red Cross was in deeper trouble.

It took a Brit to tell the story. International Red Cross teams from Spain, Britain, Finland, and the Netherlands were asked to travel to the Gulf Coast to help out. Michael Goodhand, the head of international logistics at the British Red Cross, nailed the problem just two weeks after the hurricane.

On September 15, Goodhand reported on what the teams had observed. A death sentence for the American Red Cross might have been more merciful.

The only good news in the report was its introductory praise of the Red Cross volunteers, approximately 235,000 of them: they were the "best any of us have experienced in over 65 years of international disaster relief." (The crimes of a tiny fraction hadn't yet been committed.)

After that, it was a most damaging report.

The report said the Red Cross placed "volunteers in some critical managerial and programme positions for which they do not have the requisite skills," creating "an inability . . . to meet the needs of those we serve."

The ability to assess those needs is "woefully lacking," it said. Examples of the problem included people asking for prepared meals, known in Red Cross vernacular as "Meals Ready to Eat (MRE)" but "volunteers had only bananas to give them, and volunteer drivers asking for water and juice to distribute and having only"—this is not a joke—"bleach to give them." In dry understatement, the report said, "This cannot be acceptable. Distributing bananas because there were no Meals Ready to Eat and delivering bleach when people were asking for and prioritizing water and juice are indicative of the breakdown of the system."

A survey, which the report concedes was not scientific but was nonetheless representative, listed the items most requested by the storm victims, as well as their availability in the area warehouse:

Item:	Warehouse stock:
Juice	Zero
Feminine hygiene items	Zero
General hygiene items	Zero
Household cleaning items	Zero
Gatorade (to address dehydration)	Zero
Insect repellent	Zero

"The demand for these needs," said the report, "is entirely predictable. The most basic assessment and relief plan of action would have these items identified as a priority requirement." In fact, the report said, it was even worse. Not only did the Red Cross not have in stock the most requested and basic items, but also, "There was no inventory list available to identify what was in stock."

So the homeless went without. The report suggested that the Red Cross, as a last resort, could have simply gone to the grocery store to buy the stuff. With unaffected towns only eighty miles away, it was a "lost opportunity to a speedy response."

The superb volunteer base was "let down," it said, "because of the inability of some management to recognize and address its own shortcomings." The report pointed out that it is not only typical but also required to have a formal plan of action, but that "no such plan was ever seen."

Then there was the issue of incompetent personnel. The report described them as not "suitably experienced," which "ensures these shortcomings are rarely noticed and remedial action almost non-existent."

The international team saw that the relief planning system wasn't working and was aghast at the inexperience, and noted, perhaps with modest relief of its own, "The volunteer Relief Coordinator for the operation was replaced after one week because Katrina was the first relief operation he had ever coordinated."

The members of the international team acknowledged that the management of crises is very difficult. They should know: they're professionals at this sort of thing, as people at the Red Cross are supposed to be. Even so, the report noted that the American Red Cross didn't even measure up to other charities that don't spend their time that way.

"The Red Cross publicly describes itself as a disaster response organization. It has disaster preparedness plans, it has relief and logistics functions, and yet its volunteer appointees in those functions could not perform where, for example, the Southern Baptists could."

The well-intentioned but incompetent Keystone Kops come to mind with this example: a volunteer charged with a fleet of more than one hundred cars lost control of all of them. "Keys and rental documents could not be matched and the vehicles were thought to be 'somewhere in the car park' but with no guarantee they had not already been dispatched."

Then, on logistics: "There is good reason why the functions of logistics . . . are recognized as professions. Failure to deliver, in time, the right goods to the right place can endanger lives every bit as much as an incompetent doctor."

The problem was made worse, stated the report, because the Red Cross didn't take advantage of "the significant skills and experience of the various international teams that responded to the request for support. These resources were largely ignored, marginalized and squandered," which, it was pointed out, was particularly egregious, because there were hungry, homeless people in other parts of the world who needed that help.

At one point, the Red Cross decided to increase the Meals Ready to Eat per person from one to three, because trucks with many meals were on their way. It was then that race, the topic of so many headlines in Katrina's aftermath, was also exposed as an issue at the Red Cross. "Only when the relief managers were asked to consider the implications of the last family receiving one MRE per person being black, and the first family to receive 3 per person being white, was some comprehension of the issue realized."

Voluntary service is the cornerstone of the Red Cross, the report said, but, "As long as American Red Cross believe they can manage major domestic disaster response programmes with well-intentioned but volunteer amateurs, their programme will remain amateurish and their service to those affected sub-optimal."

The report's conclusion was short: "Hurricane Katrina has exposed some limitations of the American Red Cross. The systems have not been changed, the inappropriately skilled personnel are still in place, and women who survived Katrina are still awaiting sanitary towels."

By April of the year following Katrina, the Red Cross promised some changes. It would spend $80 million to improve operations. It had created a system to serve 2,000,000 families and handle 100,000 cases a day so that people in the future wouldn't have to wait so long. It also said it would improve its logistical management and planning, work on its relations with minorities, and eliminate its reluctance to work with other groups.

One has to wonder, though. The promise to change came just days after the report by the International Logistics team was made public. It became public, by the way, because—and perhaps only because—

someone at the Red Cross anonymously gave the team's report to *The New York Times* a week earlier. One has to wonder if any changes would have been announced without the publication of that report. You might think that, given all the bad news of the prior seven months, to say nothing of its tarnished reputation after 9/11—the Red Cross would of course have changed its ways.

I asked to interview key people at the Red Cross in Washington, D.C. I told them I wanted to go beneath their press releases, that I would go where newspaper reporters would not normally go, that my questions would be informed by decades of working with all sorts of charities across the country, and that the result, while honest and critical, might even be compassionate. I was told, "No. No thank you. We'd rather just put all this in our past. We want to get on with things." (I did talk with people connected to the Red Cross; they weren't at the top of the organization, but they knew what was going on and could see the problems.)

Think of people or organizations you know or have known that are in that kind of denial. They typically deal with their issues by simply sweeping current and ongoing problems into the past.

Politicians do that all the time. In sound bytes filled with false bravado and insincere optimism, they spin their troubled reality into something else altogether.

Despite the most seasoned effort, however, the truth tends to emerge. Tim Kellar, the administrator of Hancock County, Mississippi, was quoted as saying in the weeks after Katrina, "The Red Cross has been my biggest disappointment. I held it in such high esteem until we were in the time of need. It was nonexistent."

HOW MUCH HAD changed in the many years since the problems in San Francisco, Oklahoma City, the Red River in the Midwest, and San Diego? Not much.

After 9/11, Bill O'Reilly said he wouldn't give the Red Cross another penny until it came out with an acceptable report on how it was using the money it received. As a result of the Katrina debacle, we might be wise to go one step further. Why not embargo the Red Cross completely. Nothing from anyone, even though the president mentions it often, until it comes out with a full report, written by independent experts, on all its operations. Until there's an overhaul of its board and senior management, as well as a meaningful apology to the people of the United States.

In the meantime, Congress can give it some money, and other charities can take up the slack. Maybe it's time for this charity to look in the mirror and ask itself, "Why are we so special? What we try to do is special, but why do we think we're the only ones who can do it?"

Who knows? Maybe we'd find out we can get along without the Red Cross. Maybe somebody else can do a better job. After all, distinguishing between juice and bleach for a thirsty person can't be all that difficult.

15

UGLY TIFFANY

*"They're not going away. If you create some healthier products, they'll
go after all the unhealthy ones you still make."*

RICK BERMAN, FOUNDER OF THE CENTER FOR CONSUMER FREEDOM, QUOTED IN THE NEW
YORK TIMES ON JUNE 12, 2005, RESPONDING TO EFFORTS BY THE CENTER FOR SCIENCE IN
THE PUBLIC INTEREST TO ADDRESS FOOD SAFETY ISSUES IN THE UNITED STATES.

*"We respectfully request that the IRS revoke the tax-exempt
status of the Center for Consumer Freedom."*

FROM A LETTER TO THE IRS, CITIZENS FOR RESPONSIBILITY AND ETHICS IN WASHINGTON

OBESITY IS A growing problem in the United States. So says the Centers
for Disease Control and Prevention, the federal agency charged with protecting the nation's health. The CDC is supported by considerable scientific research and authority when it takes that position.

Between 1980 and 2000, obesity rates doubled among adults. This
means that 60 million of us—thirty percent of the adult population—
are obese. Similarly, according to the CDC, since 1980 the overweight
rate (fat but not obese) has doubled among children and tripled
among adolescents. Many are the health issues: Diabetes and heart disease, for example, rise rapidly with the increase in obesity.

The CDC estimates that only twenty-five percent of adults and less
than twenty-five percent of adolescents eat a healthy diet, and that less
than fifty percent of adults and less than two-thirds of young people get
enough exercise.

In 2004, the CDC reported that 400,000 deaths in the United States each year can be attributed to obesity. The following year, however, the CDC revised its estimate downward and said that the number is actually closer to 112,000.

The two reasons the CDC gave for its dramatic, downward adjustment were that it had newer data, and it used different methods to analyze the data. The problem is complexity. The scientists who know the most about this issue admit that counting the actual number of deaths from obesity-related causes is impossible. Almost every aspect of public health policy—including mountains of research and statistical analysis—is complex and subject to differing opinions.

But this doesn't mean that obesity is less of a problem than it was before the first estimate was announced. Even though the actual number of how many people die from obesity each year is "only" 112,000, that number is substantial, especially when you consider the research showing that many, if not most, of these deaths could be prevented by better eating habits and more exercise.

From this, you might conclude that a good step in staying healthy is to eat healthful foods. Combined, a good diet and regular exercise provide a healthy lifestyle.

We all know this, right?

NOT THE CENTER for Consumer Freedom. Based in Washington, D.C., the Center attacks the CDC and others it calls the "food police" for "spreading unwarranted hysteria about the so called 'obesity epidemic.'" It prides itself on correcting what it calls "obesity myths."

The Center for Consumer Freedom was started in 1995 when Richard Berman, a lobbyist and attorney, formed an organization he called Guest Choice, CCF's predecessor. It began with a $600,000 gift from the Philip Morris tobacco company. The purpose of Guest Choice was to create a charity to fight the nationwide campaign to ban smoking in restaurants.

In 2001 Berman changed the name to The Center for Consumer Freedom to broaden its scope. It would lobby about food and beverage issues in addition to campaigning to "protect" smokers from excessive regulations on cigarettes.

Berman is a 1964 graduate of Transylvania University in Lexington, Kentucky. According to the school's Honor Roll of Giving, he is a significant supporter. He received a law degree from the College of William and Mary in Williamsburg, Virginia.

In 1967, he started his law career as an attorney representing Bethlehem Steel. In 1975, he became the senior vice president of Steak and Ale, a restaurant chain. In 1986, he launched his own consulting firm, Berman and Company.

The for-profit Berman and Company exists today and Berman remains its president, even as he acts as executive director of the nonprofit Center for Consumer Freedom. The central idea at CCF is that the government should promote personal responsibility and consumers should be protected so they can make their own choices.

Fighting what it calls the "food cops," whom it characterizes as the "militant activists, meddling bureaucrats, and violent radicals" who think they know what is best for people, CCF's position is that the whole fat fear—in fact the whole matter of telling people how to eat and live—has gotten so out of hand that someone must come to the public's rescue.

CCF claims the support of over 1,000 "concerned individuals." It retains anonymity for both its individual and corporate donors to protect them from "violence" on the part of "activist groups."

Although any group that educates people about good health is fair game, CCF's main antagonist is the Center for Science in the Public Interest.

CSPI was started in 1971 by three men with an interest in nutritional science. Today, one of those men, Michael Jacobson, who earned a Ph.D. in microbiology from the Massachusetts Institute of Technology, is CSPI's executive director. Articulate and passionate about nutrition and food safety, he has written more than a dozen books on nutrition.

Among other things, CSPI is responsible for the sodium labeling requirement by the Food and Drug Administration in 1982 and the National Labeling and Education Act of 1994, which requires food companies to include that nutrition information panel on the label of almost all food packages you buy at the supermarket.

CSPI began small and today derives a significant portion of its funding from its award-winning newsletter *Nutrition Action Healthletter*. Gifts from foundations, which are listed on its Web site, and more than 100,000 individual donors comprise the remainder of CSPI's annual revenues. It accepts no corporate contributions over $250 and no government grants of any amount.

The central idea at CSPI is that people have a right to know what goes into the food they eat.

AS EVERYONE WHO examines a charity should, let's look at the mission statements of each group. First, CCF:

> The Center for Consumer Freedom is a nonprofit coalition of restaurants, food companies, and consumers working together to promote personal responsibility and protect consumer choices.
>
> The growing cabal of "food cops," health care enforcers, militant activists, meddling bureaucrats, and violent radicals who think they know "what's best for you" are pushing against our basic freedoms. We're here to push back.

Now, CSPI:

> The Center for Science in the Public Interest is a consumer advocacy organization whose twin missions are to conduct innovative research and advocacy programs in health and nutrition, and to provide consumers with current, useful information about their health and well-being.

Whereas CSPI wants to provide *useful information*, CCF wants to *push back* against what it calls the *food cops*, and to protect consumers from *militant activists, meddling bureaucrats, and violent radicals.*

Each organization also sets out its goals.

CSPI's:

- To provide useful, objective information to the public and policymakers and to conduct research on food, alcohol, health, the environment, and other issues related to science and technology;
- To represent the citizen's interests before regulatory, judicial and legislative bodies on food, alcohol, health, the environment, and other issues; and

- To ensure that science and technology are used for the public good and to encourage scientists to engage in public-interest activities.

Since 1971, the Center for Science in the Public Interest has been a strong advocate for nutrition and health, food safety, alcohol policy, and sound science. Its award-winning newsletter, *Nutrition Action Healthletter*, is the largest-circulation health newsletter in North America, providing reliable information on nutrition and health.

Because of CSPI's leadership in the areas of nutrition, food safety, and other issues:

- A new federal law was enacted that sets standards for health claims on food labels and provides full and clear nutrition information on nearly all packaged foods.
- Millions of Americans changed their food choices at popular restaurants thanks to CSPI's widely publicized studies on the nutritional value of restaurant meals. Thousands of restaurants have added healthier options to their menus.
- Major fast-food chains have stopped frying with beef fat and many have introduced more healthful foods.
- Scores of deceptive ads by companies such as McDonald's, Kraft, and Campbell Soup have been stopped.

With support from 900,000 members, CSPI is vigorously pursuing its mission in the new century.

CCF's:

So what exactly is "consumer freedom"?
Consumer freedom is the right of adults and parents to choose what they eat, drink, and how they enjoy themselves. Defending enjoyment is what we're all about!

Do you have a bias?
Yes! We believe that only you know what's best for you. When activists try to force you to live according to their vision of society, we don't take it lying down.

Does that mean you're against vegetarians?

Of course not! Everyone should have the right to make their own choices about what to eat and drink—whether it's a garden salad and bottled water, or a prime rib steak and a cocktail. We respect your personal choice. All we ask in return is the same.

But you are opposed to "good" groups. Doesn't that make you the "bad guys"?

We speak up whenever activists propose curtailing consumer freedom. What makes us different from many organizations is that we aren't afraid to take on groups that have built "good" images through slick public relations campaigns. Remember: even an ugly baby can be named "Tiffany." Just because they claim to be "ethical" or "responsible" or "in the public interest" doesn't mean they are. And when they talk about throwing bricks through windows, taxing your favorite foods, or throwing the book at popular restaurants with tobacco-style lawsuits, we make sure you know about it.

Who funds you guys? How about some "full disclosure"?

The Center for Consumer Freedom is supported by restaurants, food companies and more than 1,000 concerned individuals. From farm to fork, our friends and supporters include businesses, employees and consumers. The Center is a nonprofit 501(c)(3) corporation. We file regular statements with the Internal Revenue Service, which are open to public inspection. Many of the companies and individuals who support the Center financially have indicated that they want anonymity as contributors. They are reasonably apprehensive about privacy and safety in light of the violence some activist groups have adopted as a "game plan" to impose their views.

While CSPI is proud to have initiated the food labeling standards that help consumers know what's contained in the food they buy, CCF is proud to *defend enjoyment.*

Mike Jacobson, mild and soft-spoken, has spent more than thirty years overseeing the publication of its newsletter. Men and women of distinguished science organizations have come to know and respect the work of CSPI. As a result, CSPI's reputation has grown over the decades.

That well-earned respect has filtered into the media. CSPI is in the news somewhere almost every day of the year. *The New York Times* once said, "The Center for Science in the Public Interest has consistently shined a bright light on the nutritional ills of the standard American diet."

IN THE SUMMER of 2005, CSPI held a news conference where Mike Jacobson announced the results of its updated soft drink study, "Liquid Candy."

The study concluded that Americans "drink twice as much soda as we did thirty years ago and five times as much as fifty years ago." Teens, he said, get "eleven percent of their calories from soda pop." Also, he said, "the average teenage boy is drinking the equivalent of two 12-ounce cans of soda pop a day, and the average girl 1.5 cans."

He noted the nutritional deficiencies in sodas and said the soft drink industry should be required to place health messages on cans and bottles so that everyone would know the potential consequences of drinking too much soda.

The soft drink industry is doing everything it can to persuade the public that sodas are a healthy product. "Liquid Candy" quotes a paper written by the industry's association: "Drink plenty of fluids: consume at least eight glasses of fluids daily, even more when you exercise. A variety of beverages, including soft drinks, can contribute to proper hydration."

The study also quotes a comment made in 1998 by M. Douglas Ivester, then Coca-Cola's chairman and CEO: "Actually, our product is quite healthy. Fluid replenishment is a key to good health . . . Coca-Cola does a great service because it encourages people to take in more and more liquids."

Another presenter at the news conference, Lucy Nolan, the executive director of End Hunger Connecticut! and a mother, recounted how the governor of Connecticut had recently vetoed a bill to limit soft drinks and fast foods in public schools. The wishes of 70 percent of Connecticut adults and an onslaught of e-mails and phone calls to the governor's office were no match for the soft drink lobbyists who held sway that summer over the pen of Governor M. Jodi Rell.

The mood changed a year later. In the spring of 2006, Connecticut banned all soft drinks, including diet and sports drinks, from its public schools. That fall, the country's top three soft-drink companies—Coca-Cola, PepsiCo, and Cadbury Schweppes—which controlled 90 percent of school sales, agreed, in the face of mounting public pressure and threatened legal action by CSPI, to voluntarily remove their sodas from cafeterias and vending machines in schools around the country.

On the same day of CSPI's "Liquid Candy" news conference, in a full-page advertisement in the *Washington Post* that looked much like a mock food label, CCF accused CSPI of serving up "Junk Science (56%), Scare Tactics (41%), and Sensationalism (28%)." Balance, objectivity, and fairness received zero percent each.

A few weeks earlier, a spokesperson for Kraft Foods said in a *Times* article that his company has a "responsibility to address consumers' concerns over obesity, so we're responding by reformulating many of our products, providing more product information, creating smaller sizes and adjusting our marketing practices."

Berman would have none of it. He said in the same article that the response was nothing more than "appeasement." He then said, "You can't accommodate these people"—meaning CSPI. "They're not going away. If you create some healthier products, they'll just go after all the unhealthy ones you still make."

Got it? Berman is worried that people will be protected from unhealthy foods.

ACCORDING TO CCF, obesity is no big deal. Nor are over 100,000 obesity-related deaths every year.

In the booklet, *An Epidemic of Obesity Myths*, in which CCF claims to tackle "seven myths driving the current hysteria over excess flab," one of the myths is, "You Can't Be Overweight and Healthy." One of the quotes in the booklet is, " ... people can be fit even if they are fat."

That is true. It is also true that if a person runs blindfolded across a busy highway, he or she might not get hit and killed by a car. But the possibility of not dying isn't an argument to do that. Similarly, even though no one disputes that all sorts of body types and sizes have the potential for encasing healthy humans, the argument made by government health agencies and by most doctors isn't that there are no exceptions, but that the vast majority of overweight people are less healthy than they need to be, and that eating a healthy diet is certainly one way to be healthier.

Another stand-alone quote: "Rising cigarette prices account for as much as 20 percent of increasing BMI [Body Mass Index]."

That still leaves 80 percent.

The quote is clearly intended to show the tobacco industry in a favorable light.

You might think that if only cigarettes were less expensive, people wouldn't be so fat.

CCF ignored the part of the study where the authors acknowledge that obesity has sky-rocketed over the last generation, that a large part of the reason is the huge increase in fast-food restaurants, and that obesity is in fact a public health issue.

Since there aren't any legitimate scholarly works promoting fast food and smoking—at least not for health reasons—CCF is left to extracting out-of-context quotes, perhaps hoping that people will be swayed by the source's legitimacy.

EVEN THOUGH CCF does not reveal the sources of its corporate support, how it gets its money is no secret. But, although charities accept donations all the time from businesses, it's not normal for a charity to act as part of a business's media arm.

The government recognizes as nonprofits—but not as public charities—business leagues or trade associations. The National Restaurant Association is one such group and the American Beverage Association is another. They support the interests of the restaurant and beverage industries before Congress and regulatory bodies.

You might wonder—when the food, beverage and tobacco industries have their own money and influence, and their own trade associations—why there's a need for Center for Consumer Freedom at all.

A nonprofit group in Washington, D.C., Citizens for Responsibility and Ethics in Washington—CREW—wrote to the IRS in November 2004 to ask the commissioner to revoke CCF's charitable status.

CREW alleged that CCF is in violation of the tax laws governing charities because it has engaged in electioneering, pays too much money to its founder and to his consulting firm, and has continuously embarked on activities in which charities are not allowed to engage.

In a series of editorials in 2003, CREW notes, CCF openly opposed the candidacy of Dennis Kucinich, who was seeking the Democratic presidential nomination. Kucinich was characterized as "brutal," "vain," a "yappy little demagogue," "an obnoxious little twerp," and "the nutty Presidential candidate." Actually, in its editorials CCF didn't claim authorship of these characterizations. It quoted other editorials that said those things.

There are those who may agree that Dennis Kucinich is vain and an obnoxious little twerp, but charities tread uncertainly when they say those things, even when they only quote others that say those things.

Many charities express their points of view, but their safe harbor from getting too political is the issue, not the candidate. Publicly advocating a position relating to a charity's mission is permitted but taking pot-shots to oppose a candidate running for public office is not.

CITIZENS FOR RESPONSIBILITY and Ethics in Washington also noted that there was an "insidious relationship between Richard Berman, Berman & Company, the Guest Choice Network, and CCF."

Guest Choice Network, you'll recall, was the predecessor to the Center for Consumer Freedom. It was also run by Berman. It had no employees.

In its application to the IRS, it claimed to educate "the public about threats to freedom in the hospitality and service industries," just like CCF claims to do today.

But what's really interesting is that in the three-year period from 2000 through 2002, the total payments either to Berman as an individual or to his consulting firm totaled almost $2 million. This represented more than 70 percent of the charity's expenditures.

Berman runs yet another nonprofit, called the Employment Policies Institute, which, as of the date of the CREW letter, had no employees.

EPI's mission statement goes like this: "The Employment Policies Institute is a nonprofit research organization dedicated to studying public policy issues surrounding employment growth. In particular, EPI focuses on issues that affect entry-level employment."

Critics say EPI is an industry front and that its real objective is to keep the minimum wage as low as possible.

EPI paid Berman and his company almost $5 million between 1997 and 2002.

CREW wrote: "The payments to Berman and BCI [Berman's consulting company] by the Guest Choice Network, the Center for Consumer Freedom, and the Employment Policies Institute from 1997 to 2002 total $6,801,322, or 72% of the $9,505,384 combined annual expenditures of those supposedly tax-exempt organizations."

That's a lot of money and a significant percentage. No wonder CREW concluded that the nonprofit is little more than a front for the interests of the for-profit.

Is Berman & Company the only consulting source for the nonprofits that Berman runs? That is, could another firm have been hired so as not to create this sense of a huge conflict of interest, which seems like it plays itself out for tax purposes as private inurement?

In a letter to the IRS, CCF claimed Berman's consulting firm was needed to manage CCF "because of the great knowledge and resources available within Berman [the company]," and, "It would be cost-prohibitive for CCF to employ these individuals directly."

But then CCF calculated the amount to be paid to Berman's company by multiplying an employee's hourly rate by a factor of three.

While that method of determining a billing rate may be industry practice for a consulting firm, it isn't less expensive than hiring people full time for a full-time job. Hiring employees for less money could hardly be cost prohibitive.

At the direction of the guy in charge of both organizations, the charity was paying a premium price to the for-profit firm.

And, yes, as you might expect, the nonprofit and the for-profit organizations have the same address.

THE FINAL MAJOR assertion in the letter from Citizens for Responsibility and Ethics in Washington was that CCF does not engage even in charitable activities. In 1995 Philip Morris funded Guest Choice Network, the predecessor to CCF, "expressly for the purpose of trying to protect the interests of the tobacco, alcohol, and chain restaurant industries, all within the guise of 'consumer freedom.'"

Berman pitched his proposal to Philip Morris this way: "The concept is to unite the restaurant and hospitality industries in a campaign to defend their consumers and marketing programs against attacks from the anti-smoking, anti-drinking, anti-meat, etc. activists . . ."

Philip Morris wanted to keep things secret and said so in a hand-written note on a type-written memo. But that memo is not secret today because tobacco company documents were made public in 1998 as part of the $206 billion Master Settlement Agreement signed by the tobacco companies and the attorneys general of forty-six states and five United States territories.

Because of this forced disclosure—but probably only because of it—we know that between 1995 and 1998, Philip Morris contributed $2.5 million, as CREW's letter put it, to "this clandestine industry marketing program misleadingly named the Guest Choice Network and the Center for Consumer Freedom."

As INDEPENDENCE DAY in 2005 approached, CCF wrote on its Web site, "Far too few Americans remember that the Founding Fathers, authors of modern liberty, greatly enjoyed their food and drink. . . . Now it seems that food liberty—just one of the many important areas of personal choice fought for by the original American patriots—is constantly under attack."

Who knew?

On Independence Day that year, the economist Paul Krugman, said of CCF in his opinion column, "It sounds like a parody, but don't laugh. These people are blocking efforts to help America's children."

While Congress allows all ideas under the charitable umbrella, you have to wonder why the Center for Consumer Freedom shares the same tax-preferred space as the Center for Science in the Public Interest.

PART IV
CHARITY AND YOU

MONEY AND MISSION

*"You expect a man of millions to be a man worth hearing, but as a rule they
don't know anything outside their own businesses."*

THEODORE ROOSEVELT

ON APRIL 17, 1991, the president of Yale University and the dean of Yale
College announced that the school had received $20 million, the largest
gift in its 290-year history. The donor, Lee Bass, a member of the undergraduate class of 1979, had been an alumnus for only twelve years.

He gave the money to promote the study of Western Civilization. The
dean, Donald Kagan, called the Bass gesture in the *Yale Alumni Magazine*,
"a splendid contribution to the future excellence of Yale College and the
University."

IN THE SPRING of 2001, Catherine Reynolds, whose vast wealth comes
from a company that provides student loans, announced that the foundation she created in her name would donate $38 million to the
Smithsonian Institution's Museum of American History, to create a
permanent Hall of Fame of American Achievers.

That was to be only the start of an ambitious plan to give between
$500 million and $750 million to Washington cultural institutions
over the next decade. "The foundation was created out of a very

entrepreneurial business," Reynolds said in an interview with *The New York Times*, "and that is the spirit and culture we want to apply to the philanthropic world."

ON SEPTEMBER 18, 1997, Ted Turner, the founder of Cable News Network, announced that he would give an unprecedented $1 billion to establish the United Nations Foundation and the Better World Fund.

At the time, his was the largest single charitable pledge ever made. Turner, whose net worth had grown from $2.2 billion on January 1 to $3.2 billion nine months later, said that he would give $100 million a year for the next ten years to programs approved by the United Nations.

Former United States Senator Timothy Wirth was named to direct the foundation. Wirth identified three programs it would support: Women and Population, Children's Health, and the Environment.

ON FATHER'S DAY 1993, Walter Annenberg said that he would give $100 million to the Peddie School, a small college preparatory school in Hightstown, New Jersey. Thus, in a single day, the school's endowment rose by a factor of six, from $17 million to $117 million. The gift catapulted the school from relative financial mediocrity to one of the wealthiest private schools in the nation.

Aarti Kapoor, a senior at the school, said at a memorial service for Annenberg in 2002, "It's hard to even comprehend how this man helped so many people, so much."

LARGE GIFTS TO charity always make news. It's part of our culture to chronicle what the rich and famous do, and that includes their philanthropy. Rarely a week goes by when some mention isn't made of someone's largesse in at least one of our major newspapers.

Andrew Carnegie, who amassed his fortune in steel, believed, not unlike Ted Turner a century later, that the rich had a moral obligation to give away their fortunes. Carnegie felt that what a family doesn't need ought to be distributed to the community and, furthermore, that the money should be given during one's lifetime to make sure that it accomplishes the most good.

"Rich men should be thankful for one inestimable boon," he said in

1889. "They have it in their power during their lives to busy themselves in organizing benefactions from which the masses of their fellows will derive lasting advantage, and thus dignify their own lives."

BASICALLY, THOSE WHO make large charitable donations take one of three routes. First, and most common, they give their money directly to the charity. A donor makes a gift to a university, a museum, a faith-based organization—whatever, as long as it's a charity that's already established—and he or she helps support that charity's mission.

The second way large donors express their charitable impulse is by giving their money to what has come to be called a "donor advised fund." In addition to a growing number of charities that have established for donors to help other charities, some commercial organizations, such as banks, have created nonprofit arms to handle these gifts. The idea is that the donor can make a tax-deductible gift today and then, at some later time, direct—or advise—where the money will go.

In this way, the fund acts much like a parking space for the money. The donation arrives at the fund, which means it's a tax-deductible gift. But it is not sent to help a particular charity until the donor decides which charity should receive it.

Why would a charity establish a fund from which a donor can help other charities? The goodwill and administrative help will increase gifts from that donor to that charity. Or at least that's the idea.

Donor-advised funds are a relatively new concept, and the rules governing them are not yet well established, although Congress has recently looked into how abuses can be prevented. The biggest potential abuse is the possibility that too little money gets distributed to charities that will actually use the money to serve society.

The third way for large donors to express their philanthropy is to create their own foundations. Once the foundation is established, it, too, acts as a parking lot, and the board decides where the money will go. Smaller foundations, often called family foundations, are usually run by the donor and family members.

The IRS has complex rules defining foundations and their payout requirements. As a parking lot, a foundation doesn't actually do any good until it sends money to charities that use it, so the government is keen on making sure society benefits. The rules call for at least five percent of the foundation's assets to be distributed every year to real charities.

Because foundations require much technical expertise and are expensive to operate, this third path is not usually a good way for people with less than several million dollars to earmark for charity.

The typical donor, the man or woman who gives $5 or $10, $100, or even several thousand dollars annually to his or her favorite cause, doesn't use that money to establish a personal foundation.

No matter how a large charitable gift is, almost always large doses of two ingredients come in the same donor package: generosity and ego.

Both will probably always be present, but something has changed over the years. In the past, a donor would want to help a charity do what it—the charity—wanted to do. While that is still usually the case, more charities are talking with potential donors who want to use their gifts to pursue their own ideas, and when they can't do that, if they're wealthy—more than ever before they're likely to start a foundation.

The key is control. True, in the past many donors charity to further their own views of the world—Rockefeller, Carnegie, Harkness—but they were noteworthy because they were unusual.

But even though the number of family foundations has grown enormously over the past several years, many wealthy donors still try to make their mark within an existing charity. This can be good when the donor's aims are the same as the charity's, but it can lead to problems when they aren't. Also, large donors, many of whom have made their fortunes controlling businesses, want to see results. They want charities to prove the money is being spent well. They also tend to think, as Catherine Reynolds expressed it, that entrepreneurialism should be the guiding spirit in philanthropy.

Business Week magazine published a cover story in December 2002 that discussed what it called the new face of philanthropy. It described a world where donors "are more ambitious, get more involved, and demand results." Among donors, the magazine said, a "new philanthropy" has emerged, one that "displays an impatient disdain for the cautious and unimaginative check-writing that dominated charitable giving for decades."

Business Week offered a glimpse at the new world through its lens:

- It's more ambitious: Today's philanthropists are tackling giant issues, from remaking American education to curing cancer.

- It's more strategic: Donors are taking the same systematic approach they used to compete in business, laying out detailed plans that get at the heart of systemic problems, not just symptoms.

- It's more global: Just as business doesn't stop at national borders, neither does charitable giving. Donors from William H. Gates III to George Soros have sweeping international agendas.

- It demands results: The new philanthropists attach a lot of strings. Recipients are often required to meet milestone goals, to invite foundation members onto their boards, and to produce measurable results—or risk losing their funding.

By harking back to the individualistic style of giving practiced by Andrew Carnegie, *Business Week* giddily declared, these donors have ushered in a new era of philanthropy.

IN 1995, JUST four years after he made the largest gift ever to Yale University, Lee Bass asked for his money back. In one of the more humiliating moments in the long and storied history of Yale, president Richard Levin returned the gift.

Bass was distressed by his impression that Yale had become a liberal place and that the faculty just plain didn't want to put together a new curriculum for the study of Western Civilization.

He had been given to understand that Yale would create a comprehensive program, enhancing its already robust syllabus that addresses Western Civilization issues.

When this didn't happen, Bass demanded the return of his gift.

If that were the whole story, Bass would have been totally justified. A gift accepted deceptively should be returned.

The Bass family is politically conservative. Its wealth came from the oil fields of West Texas when Sid Richardson, Bass's great-uncle, made several major oil strikes. In the mid-1980s, after they received a multi-million-dollar inheritance, Bass and his brothers invested in Texaco and Disney. These two timely investments made them billionaires.

By the beginning of the 1990s, Lee Bass was inspired to ensure that more traditional teachings of history would endure alongside less traditional courses at Yale. A series of missed communications and both a new president and a new dean of the college, each of whom was heavily involved in acquiring the gift, along with the sense that the Yale faculty really didn't want to offer more of the traditional courses, led to Bass's unease with the way his gift was being stewarded.

Despite the delays, Yale was more than ready to put the gift to the purposes outlined by Bass. But some felt that Bass wanted to put Yale's feet to the fire. They sensed he would use this as an opportunity to make a statement for conservatism. He'd embarrass Yale, the thinking went, exposing the university as an ultra-liberal hotbed that had little concern for traditional values.

Believing that he was in an advantageous position, Bass made an eleventh-hour demand that he may have thought Yale would not refuse. But it did refuse. The deal-breaker came when Yale's president, Levin, traveled to Texas, and Bass told him that he, Bass, must have approval over who would be teaching the courses he was endowing.

In other words, the donor of a $20 million gift wanted to control the faculty Yale hired. This was unacceptable to Yale, as it should have been, and is the reason the gift was returned.

While conservative commentators saw this as a university president who, by stalling on the Western Civilization courses, capitulated to left-wing faculty ideologues, others saw it as the right thing to do. The *San Francisco Chronicle* declared that "Yale University officials are to be commended for returning a $20 million gift that, in the end, contained too many strings," and *The New York Times* opined that "it does not pay to pander to a donor's political quirks in the hope of finding a way around his intent."

IF YALE UNIVERSITY was too esteemed to pander to a donor's quirks, the Smithsonian Institution in Washington, D.C., would seemed be absolutely airtight on that point.

In 1826 the British scientist James Smithson named his nephew as beneficiary of his will. He said that, should the nephew die without heirs, his entire estate, except for a small annuity for a former servant, should go "to the United States of America, to found at Washington, under the name of the Smithsonian Institution, an establishment for the increase and diffusion of knowledge among men."

The nephew died without heirs.

Although his bones rest in the lobby of the Smithsonian Castle, while he was alive Smithson never set foot in the United States. Nor did he know anyone here. The Smithsonian says, "Some think his bequest was motivated in part by revenge against the rigidities of British society, which had denied Smithson, who was illegitimate, the right to use his father's name. Others have suggested it reflected his interest in the Enlightenment ideals of democracy and universal education."

Smithson died in 1829, and six years later, President Andrew Jackson announced the bequest to Congress. On July 1, 1836, Congress accepted the gift, which amounted to more than $500,000 (an amount exceeding a billion dollars in today's purchasing power) and pledged the faith of the United States to the new organization.

Yet no gift, it seems, even one with all the right motives behind it, is easy.

After eight years of heated debate, an Act of Congress established the Smithsonian Institution as a trust. It was to be administered by a Board of Regents and a secretary of the Smithsonian. The secretary at the Smithsonian is its chief operating officer.

Today, the Smithsonian is the world's largest museum and research complex. It includes nineteen museums and eleven research centers. Approximately 70 percent of its funding comes from the federal government. The other 30 percent comes from public donations.

In 2001, Lawrence Small, the secretary of the Smithsonian, described the organization's mission on the Smithsonian's Web site, as follows:

> The Smithsonian is committed to enlarging our shared understanding of the mosaic that is our national identity by providing authoritative experiences that connect us to our history and our heritage as Americans and to promoting innovation, research and discovery in science. These commitments have been central to the Smithsonian since its founding more than 155 years ago.

By the measure of most, Catherine Reynolds's gift would further the lofty mission as described by Small. She announced her $38 million gift in May 2001 amid hoopla and fanfare. Yet by early February of the following year, she had withdrawn her commitment.

The gift was to the Museum of American History. It was intended to create something called a "Hall of Fame of American Achievers," one hundred people who have achieved much during their lifetimes.

That was to be only the first step, however. She planned to donate several hundred million dollars more to other cultural groups in Washington. She would direct the gifts, but they would be made from the Catherine B. Reynolds Foundation, which at the time had assets valued at approximately $500 million. She said in *The New York Times* on May 10, 2001, "The foundation was created out of a very entrepreneurial business; that is the spirit and culture we want to apply to the philanthropic world."

That same article said that the gift would finance "an interactive exhibition that tells the life stories of eminent Americans, describes their personal characteristics that contributed to their achievements and highlights those achievements." Examples of those who might be honored included "the Rev. Dr. Martin Luther King, Jr.; Michael Jordan; Jonas Salk; Steven Spielberg; Oprah Winfrey; Martha Stewart, the home fashion guru; Dorothy Hamill, the ice skater; Frederick W. Smith, the founder of Federal Express; and Steven Case, chairman of AOL Time Warner."

The Smithsonian even went along with Reynolds's desire to define "achievement" in her own way—that is, with a firm, almost consistent nod to the commercial aspects of success, to say nothing of her desire to impose her own whims on the process. She insisted on a substantial say about who would be honored in her Hall of Fame.

This caused many people, inside the museum and out, to criticize the Smithsonian for accepting the gift. They felt that Reynolds was demanding too much control and, in doing so, was undermining the integrity of the museum.

"The question is, at what point will the public say, 'This is just a corporate museum'?" asked Barney Finn, a curator who spent nearly four decades at the museum. "If they get the impression we're just renting space, we might as well throw out the name Smithsonian. It won't mean anything anymore."

But the Smithsonian did accept Reynolds's control as part of the gift—the opposite of what Yale did when Lee Bass wanted to approve faculty hiring in exchange for his gift.

Then things got complicated.

As it happens, another donor, a California real estate developer named Kenneth Behring, had already given the Smithsonian $80 million, a quarter of which was to create a "thematic hall'" that would focus on "American legends and legacies." It would be "a tribute to deceased individuals who made great contributions to our country and who truly epitomize the 'American spirit.'"

The two exhibits, it turned out, would compete with each other—a conflict for some reason not known when the Reynolds gift was accepted. This did nothing to quell the criticism that had been brewing among the museum's employees.

All was well, however, according to senior officials who spoke up at the time. Everything could be worked out to everyone's satisfaction, and the Smithsonian assured the public that the $80 million and the $38 million gifts would live in harmony, attached strings and all.

Even so, both the Reynolds and Behring gifts continued to be criticized. Then Spencer Crew, director of the National Museum of American History, resigned. While he said nothing publicly against the gifts, insiders said he was offended about not being included in the negotiations.

Some museum professionals contended that Small was permitting "wealthy donors to dictate the nature and content of the museum's exhibitions."

A group of curators, historians, and researchers, headed by Chief Justice William Rehnquist, wrote a letter to the governing board of the Smithsonian to complain. The letter said that the two gifts breached "established standards of museum practice and professional ethics."

In addition, the Organization of American Historians asked the Smithsonian to reconsider the Reynolds agreement. They were concerned about the role of private donors in shaping museum exhibitions.

In January 2002, one hundred seventy scholars complained that Small had commercialized the museum.

Three weeks later the Reynolds Foundation announced that it was withdrawing its offer.

FOUR YEARS AFTER its largest gift, Yale lost it. Less than one year after receiving a significant commitment, the Smithsonian lost it. These experiences may have been good for the purity of each charity, but the ordeal gave rise to the issue of linking money and mission.

Money not only runs the engines of commerce, it also defines society and our culture. Those who possess or control large amounts of it tend to think that they have an ability, expressed either as commercial prowess or fortunate genes, that can be translated to the mosaic of philanthropy.

It is also true that without money there would be no philanthropy, at least not in the sense of donating financial resources to help others. Since charities pursue their missions with other people's money, they can fall into the trap of bending their missions, even just a little, to build up their often empty bank accounts. As we have seen, even charities with immense bank accounts are susceptible to what some might call greed.

Moneyed donors often express their philanthropy through the prism of their own ideologies. An almost invisible line exists between helping a charity do what it needs to do and shoving ideas down the throat of an already hungry charity.

That's why the gifts of Ted Turner and Walter Annenberg serve as refreshing antidotes.

TED TURNER'S $1 billion gift to benefit the United Nations, pledged in September 1997, was one of the largest single donations ever made to a charitable cause. The gift established a foundation that Turner promised would aid refugees and children, clear land mines, and fight disease.

Turner said the gift would be made over ten years at the rate of $100 million a year. Ted Turner was a risk-taker, and the billion-dollar pledge was something of a risk. He committed himself to turn over one-third of his total wealth to charity. He urged other wealthy men and women to do the same.

Turner had an agenda: He wanted the United States to pay the $1.5 billion dollars in back dues it owed the United Nations. But while he used the stage and his microphone to admonish the United States, dues payment was not a condition of the gift.

As with many wealthy donors, Turner didn't want his gift used for administrative expenses and said that the money would not be spent that way at the United Nations. For that, he said, "the United States has still got to pay up what it owes." By that, he meant that his money wasn't going to be used to pay America's debt.

Even so, a few years later, just weeks after the September 11 attacks in 2001, Turner presented a check for another $31 million through his foundation to augment almost $600 million Congress had authorized for payment to the United Nations.

In an interview in 1997 with Larry King on CNN, the network that Turner started in 1980, he said, "There are a lot of people who are awash in money they don't know what to do with. It doesn't do you any good if you don't know what to do with it. I have learned, the more good that I did, the more money comes in. You have to learn to give. You're not born as a giver. You're born selfish."

He also told King's audience that the donation represented what he would have earned in interest over the years from his $3 billion in holdings. In the middle of a remarkable stock market rise, he was able to say, "I'm no poorer than I was nine months ago, and the world is much better off."

Turner has a sense of humor. When he announced his gift, he also pointed out that he was about to be listed as one of the twenty-five wealthiest people in America on the Forbes 400, but that his large gift would reduce his net worth and kill that honor.

Five years later, in 2002, Ted Turner was not as wealthy as he had been, and no doubt expected to be. Yet he was still happy that he made the gift. Time Warner stock took a nosedive after its merger with AOL, and Turner, who owned the lion's share of that stock, saw his fortune dwindle. He told *The New York Times* on December 12, 2002, "When I had the money before the stock collapsed, I gave away a lot of it, and I'm glad I did because at least when I had it, I gave it away. You know, I did something with it. I've been crushed by the stock collapse. If I'd hung on to the money and not given it away, I still would have been wiped out, totally wiped out."

"Wiped out" is a relative term. But isn't it nice to see a person who made a large gift and subsequently lost a lot of money still happy about his generosity? It would be easy to criticize Turner for giving away, as he pointed out, money that he had gained in just the prior nine months, easy to say that such a gift is not really much sacrifice at all. But, years later, after the stock market had fallen dramatically and when no recovery was in sight, the donor hung on to the original motive and joy of the gift.

The only acknowledgment of difficulty came when he announced that he would need a total of fifteen years to make good on the pledge, as opposed to the ten years he originally planned on.

Although the payment of dues was not a condition of the gift, Turner's action shamed the United States. It could be argued that he stepped over the line when he cajoled Congress to pay its back dues, which at the time were over $1 billion. While that might be debated, it is also true that the dues were actually owed, so Turner wasn't doing anything extraordinary, except perhaps rankling some who think the United Nations is a waste altogether. And he certainly wasn't asking the United Nations to change course to anything more ideologically narrow.

In fact, his gift inspired millions of dollars of other gifts to help the United Nations at a time when the organization was fraught with debt. The gift was made for pure reasons: Ted Turner would like to see a better world, as measured by a cleaner environment, healthier children, and the expansion of women's rights throughout the globe. He left it up to the United Nations, however, to figure out how best to go about doing that.

ALTHOUGH TED TURNER'S gift was intended to help humanity on a large stage, Walter Annenberg's $100 million gift to the Peddie School in 1993—a smaller gift on a smaller stage—may make as great an impact.

The Peddie School was founded by the Baptists in 1864 as a girls' seminary. By 1922, it was accepting boys too. Peddie accepted Annenberg in an era when not many private schools were admitting Jews.

As he gained fame and fortune during his long life, he nursed nostalgic affection for Peddie. In fact, on occasion he said he remembered his years at Peddie as the happiest time of his life.

Annenberg became wealthy at an early age. By the time he was eighty-five years old, he had contributed more than $2 billion to educational causes. His wealth came from publishing, primarily *TV Guide* magazine, which he founded and owned.

Annenberg was a decent man and his philanthropy benefited many charities, ranging from the United Negro College Fund to the

Metropolitan Museum of Art. To the Met he bequeathed his art collection, the largest gift to the museum in its prior fifty years.

On June 19, 1993—Father's Day—Annenberg pledged a total of $365 million to the University of Pennsylvania, the University of Southern California, Harvard University, and the Peddie School. Nevertheless, some people thought he was a "timid" philanthropist.

Some also hold to the notion that he was really paying penance for his ruthlessness as a businessman. In the event, Annenberg is only one in a long, long line of philanthropists who acquired their wealth by ruthlessly taking advantage of others.

A large university is one thing, but what would a small college preparatory school do with the money? It would be used for scholarships and faculty salaries. Every school needs money to accept all the students they would like. It is a sad fact that the vast majority of schools and colleges cannot admit all who are qualified. Surprising as it may seem to those who think of themselves as members of the better class, not all wealthy kids are all that smart. A slew of poor kids, given the chance, can do very well academically.

At Peddie, the gift would be used for scholarships and faculty, and today the school is among those in the country most able to provide scholarship assistance. *The Star Ledger* in New Jersey reported on July 7, 2003, that the year before, Peddie provided about $4.1 million in scholarships distributed to 42 percent of the students. Before Annenberg's gift, Peddie had been providing about $1 million to 25 percent of its students.

How remarkable that one person making one gift on one day can quadruple scholarship aid so that almost twice as many students are able to benefit. In the parlance of the charitable world, the gift was transformational.

Annenberg was very close to his father, Moses Annenberg. On his desk, wherever he worked, the son placed a plaque that read: "Cause me good works on earth to reflect honor on my father's memory."

When Walter was a young man working with his father in the newspaper business, indictments were sought for both men on tax evasion charges. Moses made an arrangement with the federal prosecutor by which he would plead guilty and serve a prison sentence in exchange for granting immunity to his son.

Moses enrolled Walter at Peddie so that he would be prepared for the world of business. It was a gesture Walter Annenberg never forgot. *The Peddie News* reported that in 1943 he said:

> I have never felt upon graduating from Peddie, a student was just entering life; he had already seen a good deal of life right here. Rather, he was given the opportunity to show what stuff he was made of, and how well he had learned the lessons in leadership and citizenship so well taught.
>
> For myself, I always keep in mind with gratitude and reverence, my great debt for the privilege of having been one of the graduates of The Peddie School.

Most charities would kill for that kind of testimonial.

Since receiving the gift, the school has struggled. It hasn't struggled in the usual way, but in a way that a thoughtful person must struggle when he or she is suddenly confronted with a life-changing event. Once the euphoria wore off, much like Robert Redford's character in the movie *The Candidate,* the staff, the faculty and the trustees asked, "What now?"

The money was safely in the bank. What would the school with such humble origins do? For one thing, fundraisers for the school had to persuade other alumni and donors that it still needed annual gifts. This gift would provide an income for scholarships and faculty salaries, but it could not be used for other needs. As difficult as that story might be to tell and sell under the circumstances—"You have enough now, right?"—alumni giving has gone up over the years since the Annenberg gift, the result of honesty and good communication.

Even so, Peddie has changed. The director of development at the time, Brian Davidson, wrote, "This financial aid endowment has enabled students from all over the world to pursue a course of study that would have been unattainable to them otherwise. Because of Walter's desire to see Peddie be accessible to all, today the school is more diverse, innovative and global."

Annenberg's only restriction on his massive gift was that it benefit both students and teachers. Beyond that, he left it up to the school.

SOMETIMES THE HEIRS of a donor think that the charity isn't honoring the gift's original purposes. As the idea of charities staying true to a donor's intentions has become stronger over the years, so has it also led to more friction—friction that finds its way to the courtroom.

In New Orleans, Tulane University, closed for half a year after hurricane Katrina hit, closed its women's college, Newcomb College, as part of a reorganization at the university in the wake of sudden devastating financial pressures. The university, which is fortunate in being both well endowed and on high ground, found an opportunity in the catastrophe and made changes that it felt would be more fiscally efficient and also improve the experience for undergraduates.

Losses totaled $300 million at Tulane, and the board voted to close both Newcomb and Tulane colleges and combine them into Newcomb-Tulane College.

By the way, the *college* at a university generally means the place where the undergraduates learn. A university in this country generally means the place has well-established graduate schools and programs, in addition to the undergraduate school. Tulane University will continue as it always has; the difference is that the undergraduate schools—Tulane College (which is where the men were) and Newcomb College—are now one place.

Josephine Newcomb established Newcomb Memorial College in 1886. It was the first degree-granting college in the United States at an established university. Although women weren't drawn to Tulane because of the college, by the time they were graduated, almost all of the women felt a strong bond to it.

The college was established with a $100,000 gift—around $2 million today—and at her death fifteen years later Newcomb left $2 million to the college in her will.

Two of her heirs felt that Tulane was breaking its word by reorganizing.

The heirs' attorney said to *The Times-Picayune* that Tulane agreed to the restriction of enriching Newcomb College when it accepted the gift. "There's no question that there were restrictions that Tulane understood," he said.

The university's position was that it was continuing Newcomb's legacy and traditions by keeping the Newcomb names on the building, and, more significantly, setting up the Newcomb Institute "as an umbrella organization for activities to benefit undergraduate women, as well as the Newcomb Scholars program, designed to honor undergraduate women for their work outside the classroom in research and community work."

PRINCETON UNIVERSITY'S WOODROW Wilson School of Public and International Affairs, perhaps the most highly respected school of its kind in the world, was sued by the son of the man who gave the money to start the school. Claiming that Princeton "mugged" the family, and demanding "justice," William Robertson filed suit against the university, asking for all the money that had been put into the endowment, plus all of its earnings over the years so he could put it somewhere that would do right by it, as, apparently, Princeton had not. .

In 1961 Charles Robertson, an alumnus, and his wife donated $35 million to Princeton to start the school of public affairs. They actually created a foundation that would be controlled by a board. Today, the Wilson school's funds total $650 million, about 6 percent of the university's $11 billion endowment.

The case was complicated and involved several charges, including that the school wasn't graduating enough people who entered government, that it wasn't living up to its original mission, and that Princeton was cooking its books so that less money could be spent on the school's activities and more could be used for other purposes at the university. A report by Robertson's accountant said that $207 million had been diverted from the Wilson School and used elsewhere.

The university denied the charges. While a few relatively minor accounting changes were to be made, it said the vast majority of what was on the books was legitimate and well within accounting guidelines.

On top of that, the mission was doing just fine, according to the university. Basically, the mission called for men and women to "prepare themselves for careers in government service," with an emphasis "in those areas of the federal government that are concerned with international relations and affairs."

NEITHER THE TULANE nor the Princeton story is about donors whose egos got in the way of a charity's mission. If anything, they're about the opposite.

But the heirs, with an eye on the original gift's purpose, thought the charity went wrong. It's a growing trend, too: charities around the country are facing charges that they aren't spending the money in the manner the donor wanted, and many are looking to their state's attorney general or the court system to resolve the issue.

At the time the research for this book was being conducted, neither the Tulane nor the Princeton suit had been fully resolved. It's quite possible that the courts in both cases will settle in the charities' favor.

This isn't because charities can do no wrong or because donors and their heirs shouldn't be aware of how their money is used, even after a very long time. It's that, in these two cases, the charities—if good faith is to be any guide at all—actually were acting as the donors wanted.

No one can predict the future. No one knows a specific circumstance that may take place a century from now.

Who could have known in the late 1800s that a hurricane would wipe out a town 120 years later? If anything, Tulane acted more than admirably by keeping the spirit of the Newcomb gift alive while facing the need for many changes.

How could the original Mr. Robertson know how the world would change after he died? The son, whose complaints of wrongdoing cover a long time, had been sitting on the board since 1978, and only in 2002 chose to publicly challenge the foundation's policies.

Donors need to be flexible, and charities need to be sure the gifts they accept are going to be used for the purposes outlined in the gift agreement. In the past, the donor-charity relationship has been cozy. It generally is still, filled with warm hearts all around, but the last several years have seen an increase in donor dissatisfaction and an increase among those willing to fight it out in court.

IN 2000, I spent several months on the travel circuit representing one company to present charitable concepts before young and newly rich entrepreneurs. Their wealth was mostly created during the dotcom era.

The audience was interested in charity and wanted to know all the techniques they could use to give, including establishing their own foundations so they could control how their money was spent.

These were good people, hard-working in their professions, and they found themselves in a position few of their parents could have imagined. At the age of thirty-something they were told they could retire, and part of what they wanted to do—since retirement does not, for most people in their thirties, mean they stop working—was involve themselves in charitable pursuits. Almost to a person, each wanted to make his or her personal imprint on a charity.

Many of those in the audiences are no longer retired, having rediscovered work. That's the way it goes, both in life and in the stock market. But even though we can't predict the future or our legacy to it, we can take a page from the modesty of Walter Annenberg—and many others less celebrated—and view a gift, no matter its size, as a way to reward the society that gave us our roots and later gave us our wings.

In other words, sometimes large donors should put aside their ego and celebrate the charity's work. And let the charity—the people who run it today and those who will run it several generations from now—do their work as they see fit.

That's not always a welcome message. Those who have succeeded in working society's most universal commodity—money—to their favor, especially at a young age, tend to feel they can do anything. Bless them for that, and if their interests lie in the world of philanthropy, those who work in philanthropy owe them the time required for money to be given wisely.

Imagine the pressure on most charities when given a chance for big money that comes with strings attached. Of course, the trustees will discuss whether or not to accept it, and probably even view such a gift as a way to keep the organization afloat. But the real test is staying on the road that the charity must travel to reach its goals.

The state of Michigan, through its Natural Resource Trust Fund, rejected a $1 million gift in 2006. Fred Meijer, the owner of chain and merchandise stores who had established a private foundation from which the gift was to be made, stipulated that his name be added to the White Pine Trail State Park. The administrator of the trust fund, Jim Wood, told the *Grand Rapids Press* that "It would go against state policy to rename the trail the Fred Meijer Pine Trail State Park." Putting one person's name on such a public place just didn't sit right.

Accepting a gift with the wrong strings attached may open a Pandora's box of problems.

If Yale University and the Smithsonian Institution are susceptible to that box, certainly any charity is. The Michigan trust is the exception. And even though that was only a name change, not an ongoing meddling in the decisions about the way the trail should be operated, the idea still didn't work.

Making an imprint doesn't equal taking control. But since the world is imperfect, we will always have an ongoing list of people who try to control too much. And we will always have people who, marketing-oriented as they are, stretch the definitions of words like "perpetuity" to secure a gift.

The key is for donors to respect a charity's mission and for charities not to be greedy.

There is no "new philanthropy," as *Business Week* put it, and there never will be. There can only be new energies brought to concepts that have lost nothing in either their appeal or their impact on society.

SOME PEOPLE WERE wondering when Bill Gates would give some of his billions to charity. He and his wife established the Bill and Melinda Gates Foundation in 1997. After all, the richest man in America couldn't possibly spend everything in his bank account. As it turned out, Gates was waiting for the right time to make the right impact. Today it is by far the largest foundation in the world.

Before anyone knew Bill Gates's name, though, there was Warren Buffett. No one knew him as a philanthropist; they all knew that he was the nation's savviest investor, the genius who grew Berkshire Hathaway into one of the world's wealthiest holding companies. After Microsoft got going, it didn't take long for the upstart Gates to overtake Buffett's personal wealth. As far as charity was concerned, Buffett said he preferred to give his wealth away when he died.

So it came as a surprise—as well as a major media event—when Buffett announced in June 2006 that he would donate most of his $44 billion fortune to the Gates Foundation and that he would do so immediately.

With a few strings attached—but not many—Buffett said he would give the Gates Foundation about $31 billion over the years, and several million to four other foundations established by Buffett in the name of his family members.

The pledge promised to double—from $1.3 billion annually to approximately $2.8 billion—for many years what the Gates Foundation could spend on its work, primarily on health and education around the world, especially in poor countries.

Each year's gift was to be used entirely. It was not to be invested so that five percent—a foundation's minimum legal distribution—could be spent. In his letter to Gates, Buffett, as one of his conditions, said that his annual gift "must be fully additive to the spending of at least five percent of the foundation's net assets." In effect, Buffett, unlike the other well-known philanthropists in American history, directed that his money be used up over a period of time. This was because he felt that the money could do the most good if it was used quickly.

Even more impressive, given how ego can direct the charitable impulse, is that Buffett, this man of gargantuan wealth and success, gave his money to a foundation that did not have his name on it.

SOME PHILANTHROPISTS CAN be something, though.

Tom Monaghan, who earned $1 billion by making Domino's pizza, decided that Catholic education in America was far too liberal, so he started a new university. With 235 Catholic colleges and universities in the United States, Monaghan felt the compelling need for one more.

Thus began Ave Maria University in Florida where students are taught the right way to "get to heaven." Monaghan's university is the result of twenty-five years of searching for a "school with more spirituality." If you have $200 million and are so inclined, you too can start your own university.

Some are old concepts with new twists. Leon Levy, the hedge fund pioneer who died in the spring of 2003, was a dedicated philanthropist who gave $140 million to charities during his lifetime, and most of that was with no strings attached. There were occasional exceptions, and one gift to the Metropolitan Museum of Art did carry a string.

It happened when Philippe de Montebello, the museum's director, offered to name the museum's new wing of Greek and Roman antiquities for Levy and his wife, in perpetuity.

Levy asked, "And how long is perpetuity?"

"For you, fifty years," de Montebello replied.

Levy thought about that for all of a minute and then asked for seventy-five. He explained that his daughter's feelings might be hurt if the name change took place during her lifetime.

The director agreed, and the Metropolitan Museum was funded for the new wing.

17

HOW CHARITIES RAISE
THEIR MONEY

"Don't worry. You can still give, even if you're dead."
A FUNDRAISING APPEAL

THE PROCESS BY which charitable donations are sought and made has become increasingly sophisticated. Long the province of the friendly fundraiser in a small windowless office, the way donors are solicited these days is as much a part of sophisticated planning teams from financial giants like Merrill Lynch Wells Fargo Bank, State Street Bank, and Fidelity as it is the result of an appeal based solely on the charity's mission.

The mailboxes of prospective donors are constantly packed with letters explaining how they can make annual gifts, and how employers might match those gifts. They learn how the stock of publicly held corporations can be cheaper to give away than cash. They are told that they can easily leave estate assets to charity in their wills.

The charity fundraiser is likely to wear clothing that befits those successful in business, and often travels to resorts for conferences and to meet with wealthy donors.

Fundraisers also earn respectable incomes.

Many chief fundraisers at large nonprofits now earn more than $200,000 a year. Executive directors earn even more. Indeed, a hot topic these days for those who scrutinize charities is the issue of salaries. Cynics might conclude that it is no wonder charities need to raise a lot of money.

Most charities have problems raising enough money. We hear about the big charities and the large gifts, but we rarely read about the charities that live on the constant edge of economic disaster.

An exhaustive examination of charity reports would show that perhaps 5 percent of charities raise what they need to keep their infrastructure and their ability to provide services at a healthy level. This means that 95 percent struggle.

In 2001, Dartmouth College, in Hanover, New Hampshire, reported that it raised $200 million, lived on a budget of $500 million, and sat on an endowment valued at almost $2 billion. In the following years, it cut back some services and delayed some raises.

The president of Dartmouth, James Wright, reported a salary of nearly $500,000 that year.

In the town of Lebanon, five miles down the road and a universe away from Hanover, ACoRN, the AIDS Community Resource Network, would have enjoyed some of Dartmouth's problems. Toward the end of 2002, the *Valley News*, the area's local paper, reported that ACoRN's co-executive director, Tom Mock, said the organization was facing a $20,000 deficit.

He hoped that one fundraising appeal would bring in $9,500, but "after checking with the bank account and factoring in a new $1,000 check," ACoRN had raised only $3,200 and had spent half of that on the mailing.

ACoRN was a charity living on the edge. Its $300,000 annual budget fell short because the contributions it hoped for did not materialize. A benefit concert failed to produce enough revenues.

It seemed the organization would have to cut services. But Mock, whose salary was just over $20,000 that year, said, "People living with AIDS who get services from us will be the last to be affected. We can't cut services to people living with the virus." To ACoRN, which raised $25,000 from donors the previous year, a $9,500 shortfall was a big deal.

A few years later, although the place was still struggling, things were a little better. The budget was $309,000, not much higher than in 2002, but government contributions had increased, donors contributed $70,000, assets totaled $46,000, and Mock reported a salary of $54,000.

FUNDRAISING IS THE lifeblood of most charities. Without money from the public, they would not be in business. Some exist solely on endowment income or on fees they charge for their services. But the majority must figure out how to supplement their other revenues to balance the budget each year with gifts from the public, foundations, corporations, or the government.

In a sense, asking for a charitable contribution and selling something are not all that different. In either situation, one entity is wrenching money from another. Instead of appealing to a person's material benefit, however, as is the case with selling a product or service, charities make an emotional appeal.

The appeal might try to instill guilt.

I regret to inform you that we are faced with a severe crisis here at Amnesty International. In plain English: Our lifesaving Urgent Action Network to help prisoners of conscience and others threatened with torture or death is literally staggering under the weight of heavy new emergencies.

Amnesty International USA, Virginia

It may call for an act of faith.

After leaving the White House, Rosalynn and I searched our hearts for ways to use our unique position to help those less fortunate here in America and around the world. In an "act of faith," we founded The Carter Center.

The Carter Center, Georgia

Or it may be heart-rending.

Mr. Barbour was in the hospital for several months after he fell and broke his hip. He had no family to see that his rent was paid. By the time he left the hospital, he had been evicted. There's something about Edgar Barbour that people gravitate toward. It's a little hard to put your finger on, but the

simplest word is charisma. He's got bright active eyes and an engaging
manner that captivates everyone who meets him.
Emmaus Services for the Aging, Washington, D.C.

Each of these appeals was mailed to hundreds of thousands of potential
donors. The names were very likely purchased. Each appeal cited here—
as are most others—was accompanied by a card and a self-addressed
postage-paid envelope.

ONE OF THE hottest pitches in the fundraising world is the appeal for
used cars. This is the stuff of letters, telephone calls, the Internet, and
billboards—even truck banners and paper bags.

The appeal goes something like this: "Donate your old car and receive
a great tax deduction." This may sound marvelous, assuming you have a
used car that you no longer want and don't need its trade-in value to get
a new car.

If the car cost $20,000, new, ten years ago, you know it's not worth that
today. Its beat-up value is far less; a few thousand or maybe just a few hundred dollars. That "great" deduction, therefore, may not be so great.

The rules on car donations changed recently, the result of too much fraud.

The problem was that donors placed too high a value on their cars.
Because non-cash donations of $5,000 or more have to be valued by an
independent appraiser, a lot of donated cars were "valued" at something
less than $5,000.

Making a good-faith effort to determine the value of a car is tricky,
and the blue book or trade-in values aren't reliable for deduction purposes. Taking into account all the things that are wrong with the car (not
very many people give away nice cars), it's probably not a coincidence
that the average claimed value for a car donation is something less than
what would trigger a legitimate appraisal.

In fact, in 2004 the average claimed value was $3,400. We know this
because the General Accounting Office conducted a study on the issue
in 2003. The study concluded that in 2000 (IRS statistics take a long time
to compile and analyze), 733,000 taxpayers reported that they donated
cars worth a total of $2.5 billion. The deductions for those donations
reduced each donor's tax bill by an average of $892.

Congress, thinking there might be something amiss with all those deductions, held a hearing on the matter. In testimony before the Senate Finance Committee, Cathleen Berrick, a financial expert for the GAO, provided an example of what was amiss.

A donor of a well-used 1983 truck, which was seventeen years old at the time, claimed a $2,400 deduction when he gave the vehicle to a charity. After selling the truck at auction, the charity received $375—15 percent of what the donor said the truck was worth. The charity paid $312 for advertising, cleaning, and repairs. That left $63. Then it split that amount with its fundraiser (not an employee, but a company contracted with the charity). The value of a gift that the government recognized as $2,400 provided $31.50 for charity—a little over 1 percent of what the donor said was the truck's value.

If the donor was in the 25 percent tax-bracket (the average bracket in the GOA report was a little higher), the Treasury gave away $600 in return for $31.50 of social good—which is totally backwards. The government paid nineteen times that $31.50. The cost should never be a multiple, let alone so high a multiple; it should be a fraction, one that equals the donor's tax bracket—in this case, 25 percent.

Some charities, according to the GAO report, actually lost money on the auto donation deals. They explained to auditors that the program was nevertheless worthwhile because accepting junkers generates "good will for future donations."

In business this would be called a loss-leader. But businesses that use loss-leaders are usually good at making sure the loss is made up.

Charities are not always so business-minded. One of the expenses often associated with disposing of a car is the towing bill, which charities usually pay. In fact, many of them tout it as a major benefit for donors.

You have to wonder, though. If the car is in such bad shape that the driver can't use the ignition switch to get it going, how much can it be worth?

Of course, charities must spend money to raise money, but this example—and it was hardly unique—showed Congress that the used car contribution process was a farce.

The car donation business is at the lower end of legitimate fundraising. Even though donors have a mix of legitimate motives for making charitable gifts, when charities appeal primarily to greed—which, with few exceptions, is really what's going on with car donations—the result is going to be fraud.

So the rules were changed. Now you can deduct only the amount a charity receives for the car when it's sold. If the charity keeps the car—and charities sell cars far, far more often than they keep them, because they need the money—your deduction is based on a tightly defined evaluation of the car.

Because of the change, these days, using the GAO example, the donor with the 1983 truck would be entitled to a deduction of $31.50. The donor's tax savings: $7.88.

Many charities complained about the change.

By the way, this same rule applies to gifts of boats and planes, too.

Some in Congress think that's the way it should be for all non-cash gifts. They want to get rid of appraisals, except when the charity keeps the asset and there is no sales price, because they're so imprecise.

Charities and donors vigorously opposed that idea.

The New York Times Magazine carried an interesting question in "The Ethicist" column on January 5, 2003.

When I donated some old clothes to charity, I was given a tax form to itemize them but am unsure how to do so. Considering a dress shirt, for example, I could list the value of a used shirt, under $10; its original price, $30; the current market value, $45; or its price at a chic vintage store, maybe $50. What is the ethical price to list?

This was the ethicist's answer.

List the value of a used shirt. Its original purchase price, while of historical interest, is not germane. But it is fair enough: it has already given you years of happy wear. And besides, I hear that the minute you drive a shirt off the lot, its value plummets.

Nor should you put in for the current cost of a similar new shirt: that's not what you donated, and you're not filing a claim with the Shirt Insurance Company for its replacement cost.

The shirt's value in a chichi shop is no more relevant than its value at a boutique on Neptune: neither place is where it will be sold. It is its value at the Salvation Army, or someplace Salvationish, that you must calculate.

The used-shirt value is not only the ethical deduction but the legal one as well. The key idea here is that, whether it's a car, a shirt, or anything else, Congress wants your deduction to be as close as possible to the value the charity receives.

ALTHOUGH APPEALS BY mail are popular, few of us have been lucky enough to avoid the intrusive and often irritating phone call, most often during the dinner hour, that asks for our support of this or that charity. Charities are exempt from the rule that permits you to ban calls from telemarketers.

It won't take much, you are told, to help the very survival of a child in Bosnia or a whale in the North Atlantic. Twenty-five dollars would be much appreciated. Even ten dollars would be helpful. Anything.

Then you wonder: if that's the case, is the charity actually raising any money? After the fundraising expenses, is anything left for the child or the whale?

The answer may very likely be no. Usually, mail and phone appeals to people unknown to the charity result in only small gifts. These range between five and a few hundred dollars. The appeal is designed not to raise a lot of money—although some people send in surprisingly large gifts—but to acquire names for future contacts.

Once a person responds to the mailing or the phone call with a contribution, even if the money doesn't provide any actual gain to the charity, the charity hopes that the donor will give again. Next time, the cost involved in snaring the gift will be less and it will provide the charity with more funds.

If the irritation of a cluttered mailbox or the nuisance of getting phone calls from strangers isn't overwhelming, you might find yourself reading or listening carefully to the appeal. After all, charities are raising money for good causes.

Whether a particular cause matches your passion is for you to decide. If you are not familiar with the charity and think you might be interested in supporting it, you should ask to see some promotional information from the charity, including its most recent annual report. You should also check out the information it files with the IRS (more on that in the next chapter).

If the charity is not forthcoming, don't support the organization.

Just don't.

WITH REGARD TO the telephone solicitation, how can you know if the person on the other end is telling you the truth?

In the spring of 2003, the state of Illinois took a charity's telemarketing firm to court. The firm was raising money on behalf of VietNow, a charity that assists veterans of the Vietnam War.

Illinois went to court because the telemarketing firm charged VietNow 85 percent of the donated money. The charity was also responsible for expenses associated with the solicitations, such as office space, rent, and telephone charges.

This is a growing concern in the world of charities, as more and more people wonder about fundraising efficiency. A 15 percent efficiency rate—where the charity spends eighty-five cents to raise a dollar—is extremely poor. The total amount wasn't trivial. The telemarketing firm raised $7 million and kept $6 million for itself.

But when the case was argued before the U.S. Supreme Court, the justices were skeptical about the problem of fundraising costs. Charity efficiency isn't the domain of the courts.

Eric Copilevitz, who presented the telemarketer's case, argued that small, new, or unpopular charities often had to pay more to get their messages across. "High fundraising costs along with a failure to disclose cannot be the basis for fraud charges." He added, "I don't believe you can measure the worth of an organization by economic efficiency."

Illinois's assistant attorney general argued that there was "fraudulent misrepresentation" if donors could be expected to infer that more than 15 percent of their gifts would go to the charity. "There is no constitutional value," he said, "in artificially contrived half-truths."

Then the justices asked their questions.

Justice Antonin Scalia asked, "Who's to say how much is too much" for a fundraiser to keep? He said he wasn't comfortable with the idea that there's a defined limit for fundraising costs, past which fraud can be identified.

Justice Sandra Day O'Connor asked' "How would anyone know when the attorney general was going to charge them?"

Justice David Souter commented, "I don't see where any charitable fundraiser could draw a line in advance."

Justice Stephen Bryer simply wondered, "I don't know how you can possibly prosecute people for fraud when there is no fraud."

It didn't look good for Illinois. And keep in mind that one of the reasons the Supreme Court decided to hear the case was that forty-five other states supported Illinois's position.

The reason the case was appealed was that the Illinois Supreme Court dismissed the charges against the telemarketing firm. And that was because the U.S. Supreme Court in the past had ruled that states can't limit fundraising costs or require charities to inform prospective donors what they're paying their fundraisers. These matters are a form of protected free speech.

A few months later, the Court ruled against the telemarketers, but not because of the high cost of fundraising. The problem for the telemarketers wasn't the percentage they took, but what they told donors the charity would receive. When someone asked—and it's crucial that someone asked—the telemarketer responded with, as the court put it, "misleading affirmative representations."

The fundraiser lied.

Justice Ruth Bader Ginsberg summed up the central idea in the unanimous opinion: "The First Amendment does not shield fraud. States may maintain fraud actions when fundraisers make false or misleading representations designed to deceive donors about how their donations will be used."

Illinois and the other forty-five states didn't get all they wanted, but they still got something important: a protection of truth for donors. Although telemarketers aren't required to voluntarily disclose the amount of their cut, if they are asked they must tell the truth. It may seem amazing that it took the highest court in the land to declare that lying is wrong, but it did.

So, ask.

If you're inclined to help, you should at least know what the person on the other end of the phone is getting and what the charity is getting. With luck you'll get the truth.

By the way, if the charity is using its own staff to make the calls, which is highly unusual, the response you should hear is that no percentage is taken by the fundraisers, as they are on salary.

* * *

EVEN A TRUTHFUL response, however, leaves a large gray area. A charity may have several appeals during the year, the first of which may be inefficient, the later ones more efficient. At the end of the year it's possible to see what the results are, but day by day the calculation is incomplete. This means that whatever the telemarketer says, even if the answer is honest, he or she may be conveying something that does not reflect the charity's overall fundraising efficiency for the year.

Unfortunately, not all good charities are well established with efficient fundraising ratios. (Conversely, not all well-established charities with efficient fundraising ratios are all that good.) In fact, many good and financially healthy charities hire outside firms to call people for donations. Inefficiency or the use of an outside telemarketing firm shouldn't be an automatic scarlet letter.

A story a few years ago on KITV, a commercial television station in Hawaii, highlights the problem of the perception plaguing charities.

From the station's online site on June 23, 2003, came this assertion: "*KITV 4 News* Investigates found out how little of your money goes to national charities that use telemarketing companies to raise funds in Hawaii. When you respond to their call for help, most of your donation goes to the telemarketing company, and not to the cause you intended to support."

Local charities, those in the viewing range of KITV, were okay in the station's snapshot. "Most Hawaii-based charities that fundraise over the phone, use their own staff along with volunteers so all the money raised goes to their organization. However, it's a different story with national charities."

The television station reported, "The worst example *KITV 4 News* found was the Wilderness Society, which works to protect and restore America's wilderness areas." In fact, the Wilderness Society is one of the nation's premier and most highly regarded environmental organizations. Its headquarters is in Washington, D.C.

KITV noted that the Wilderness Society "actually lost money in its telemarketing efforts last year. If you gave them $100, all of it would have gone to the telemarketing firm, plus the Wilderness Society would have to cough up $4 more."

Clearly, we are to infer, the Wilderness Society is no place to donate. What with tons of money lining the pockets of telemarketers, and nothing left to save America's wilderness, why would anyone donate a dime? Wouldn't this be one of the clearer examples of things gone wrong in charitable fundraising?

Actually, no.

One problem is that the slice of the telemarketing action that KITV sampled was not representative. The Wilderness Society used the telemarketing firm in question for a test run to increase members in a long-term membership program. I know this because, following the story, I reviewed and analyzed the raw telemarketing data at the Wilderness Society.

The goal was to break even on a short-term basis and to acquire supporters for the long term. It would be a little like someone criticizing your financial prowess because you spent more on one day of the year than you earned on that same day.

The other issue, slightly skewed in almost all reporting, involves the percentage of fees going to the telemarketer. KITV said, "The contracts reveal that the charities pay the telemarketers for each phone call that results in a conversation whether the people donate or not. The fees range from $3.70 to $5.25 per successful contact."

Whether the people donate or not. One of the bigger problems, the one the Illinois attorney general fought before the Supreme Court, is the contractual basis upon which telemarketers do their job. Even though the court said that attacking percentages would be to attack the right of free speech, the idea of so much going to a telemarketer still doesn't sit well with most people.

To the degree that the perception is a problem, the solution—aside from not using a telemarketer at all—is to pay the firm on a flat-fee basis. This is what the Wilderness Society did. The telemarketer wasn't hired on a percentage basis.

The fee was based on the number of calls made with no consideration of the number of positive responses. The absence of percentage-based fundraising fees is actually a good thing for many critics, and in line with what KITV and the rest of the public would seem to want.

The problem arises when the effort doesn't bring in a lot of money and the telemarketer is paid anyway.

But that is the conundrum: pay a flat fee to avoid paying a high commission, or pay a commission to ensure the charity will get at least something.

We can't have it both ways.

HOW DOES THE telemarketing firm get your name to begin with? The charity probably bought it, perhaps even from another charity. In fact, selling (or renting) the names of donors is itself a form of fundraising. It sounds strange, but it's legal and often done.

Even though a Better Business Bureau survey recently showed that most Americans feel that charities have a responsibility to respect and protect donors' privacy, it doesn't always work that way. If you get a phone solicitation for a group you've never heard of, it's likely that another charity to which you've donated sold your name.

You may want to ask a charity you're supporting about its policy on selling the names of its donors. You can request that your name not be sold, and if the charity doesn't respect your request, you can stop donating. And you can tell that to the charity.

Actually, when you get a telemarketing call on behalf of a charity, just say no. No matter what, just say no.

Please understand: saying no to the telemarketer is not the same as not supporting the charity. The Wilderness Society and many other charities do good work and they do it efficiently.

If you might want to support the charity, get the information you want independently. Visit the charity's Web site and follow up with a call or a request for information. Then, if you're still interested, write a check.

The only downside is that you may be partly responsible for putting some telemarketers out of work.

Okay, some good charities would also be hurt. But on the scale of things, it's a price worth paying. If their mission is really all that compelling, the good charities, while they'll have to fight harder, will find a way to identify donors.

THE REAL MONEY per donor is derived from what is called the "major gift," a much larger gift than usually results from an annual appeal, even from already-identified donors. Different charities define the lower limit of a major gift differently, but depending on the size of a charity's fundraising program, think of a gift of between $1,000 and $25,000 as the minimum amount to reach major gift status. No upper limit exists.

There are stories, almost daily, of those who make gifts valued in the millions of dollars.

Charities spend a lot of time catering to wealthy individuals. Fundraisers develop proposals describing how the gift can be made and how the money will be used. If the gift is to fund a scholarship at a university, for example, the terms of the scholarship are spelled out.

This may include a description of the type of person eligible to receive it. While the tax laws do not allow donors to choose particular individuals to receive the scholarship—the donor's grandson or neighbor cannot be specified as a condition of the gift—donors are allowed latitude in determining the kind of student who will be eligible. For example, a donor may specify only students who live in a certain town, or only those who earn a certain grade point-average in high school.

Some donors may want a room or a building named after them. A donor to a hospital might want the emergency room named after him or her, in which case the hospital needs to work out a cost for that privilege.

These two examples—a gift to establish a scholarship and one to help pay the cost of a building—are fundamentally different. The first gift is placed into the university's endowment with the expectation that the gift's income (not the principal, which is placed into the endowment) will be used. With the second gift, the principal is spent right away to build or refurbish the room or building.

Usually, charities spend approximately 4 to 5 percent of the value of their endowment each year. This means that if a university's tuition, room, and board add up to $50,000 annually (a number always rising), and the school's policy calls for spending 5 percent of the endowment's value, the amount needed to fully fund the scholarship is $1 million.

AN INTERESTING CULTIVATION technique is the invitation to what is euphemistically called the "estate planning seminar." If you've ever been to one, you'll recognize it.

Charities invite people likely to donate large sums of money to attend a seminar, the topic of which might be "Effective Estate Planning," "Charitable Estate Planning," or "How the New Tax Law Affects You." Something like that.

To this gathering, which is often held in Florida or Arizona in the wintertime, people pegged to be likely donors are invited for free cookies and coffee (maybe wine, but nothing more spirited) as well as to hear information about how to avoid or reduce taxes. The speaker explains how the income and estate tax laws work and what changes are being considered in Congress.

Planned gifts (the type discussed in the Texas lawsuit and Ohio State chapters) are usually covered at the seminar.

A person of high local, sometimes national, repute conducts the discussion. While the ploy is to gather people who believe they will learn something about estate planning and taxes—establishing this trust or writing that will provision—the real purpose is to tell people how they can include charity in their estate plans.

Attorneys and financial planners are often in the audience, because combining estate planning and charitable planning is complex. They may be well-schooled on many other aspects of their profession, but since their own clientele may include charitably inclined people, they can always pick up a tidbit or two, even if the presenter isn't an attorney or a financial planner. The charity welcomes their presence, even though they are unlikely to donate anything, because one of their clients could very well become one of the charity's donors.

Although the steak on the seminar platter contains a lot of sizzle, the gatherings are often helpful for both the audience and the charity that sponsors the seminar. By all means, if you are invited and you are curious, you should attend.

WOVEN THROUGHOUT EVERY aspect of fundraising, particularly planned giving, should be ethical considerations, which are getting as complex as the gift transactions themselves. This is an issue that the fundraising profession is trying to grasp, and its results have not been entirely successful. After all, getting the gift is important. The means are often less so.

All the consequences of a gift should be disclosed so that both the donor and the charity take into account the appropriateness of the gift. Proper disclosure—what the donor should know before making the donation—requires an engaged ethical process.

For example, an elderly widow who has a close emotional bond to a charity may want to simply donate all her money to the organization. Or a donor may not have told his children about his charitable intentions at death, and the charity is surprised to learn later that the children are contesting the will, perhaps claiming that the charity coerced the gift from their unsuspecting father.

These things have happened, and charities are foolish, both legally and ethically, to ignore the personal circumstances of a donor. The goal for the fundraiser is to balance the privacy of the donor and the need to know enough about the gift to make sure it's in the donor's interests.

The wise fundraiser makes sure the donor sees his or her attorney before making a large gift.

The donor doesn't like attorneys and trusts the fundraiser implicitly? That's why they're called ethical dilemmas.

For people in the right circumstances, large and sometimes complex gifts are just what the doctor ordered. But the important first ingredient in all of them is a desire to help charity, just the same as it should be when a person writes a check for ten dollars in response to a mailing.

Regardless of how a charity raises its money or what its fundraising message is, donors need to be aware that the most important consideration of all is whether the charity is worth supporting and whether their gift will actually help the charity's mission.

18

WHAT CHARITIES TELL THE IRS

"You are prohibited from posting on the internet any portion of our 990 . . .
If it is not removed by the end of the business day today, I will be forced to
take action with the appropriate Attorneys General."
FROM A CHARITY THAT WAS ASKED FOR THE INFORMATION IT IS REQUIRED TO
MAKE AVAILABLE TO THE PUBLIC

BECAUSE A CHARITY'S activities are largely subsidized by the public, the IRS and the public have a right to know what charities do with their money. The legal requirement that expresses this idea is found in IRS Form 990.

The 990 is not a tax form; with rare exceptions, charities do not pay taxes. The form is an "Information Return," and thousands of charities file it each year.

Form 990 has been around since World War II. Back then, it was two pages long and asked few questions. Today, the form is five pages, but what with schedules, appendices, attachments, and supplementary information, it is long and complex. Some charities' 990 filings are over one hundred pages long; a filing of fifty pages is typical.

Although a charity's financial picture has always been public, far too many organizations have treated it as a closely guarded secret. In any case, the public didn't much know how to go about getting the information. The 990 initially was available only through the IRS or from a state's attorney general's office.

But when that proved cumbersome and not in keeping with the idea of disclosure, the law was changed so that people could go directly to a charity and ask for the form. Sometimes, however, when a charity did not want to release the information, it simply didn't.

In 1999, the IRS clarified its rules, reiterating how all charities must make information relating to their financial activities easily available to the public. A charity must disclose its application for tax exemption and any documents associated with the application, as well as its three most recently filed 990s. This means that anyone can walk into a charity and demand to be shown its filings for the past three years.

The charity must produce that information in full on the same business day that the person arrives. The charity cannot refuse this request without violating the law. Except for the portion of the form that identifies the names and addresses of contributors, the charity is required to provide every page of Form 990 plus any attachments.

You can also ask for copies to take home. This request, too, must be honored on the same business day. If no one is around that day, or if the copier is broken or the charity has any other unusual circumstances that prevent copies from being made, the charity must make copies available on the day after the staff returns or the copier is fixed. Under no circumstance can the delay exceed five business days. Depending on the charity's policy, the person asking for the information may have to pay a modest amount for the copies.

A person does not actually have to go to the charity's office to get a copy of its tax form. Anyone can write to ask for the information. In that case, the charity has thirty days from the day it receives the request to provide copies by mail.

A charity that fails to comply with these rules faces penalties. The cost for not adhering to the disclosure law is $20 per day up to a maximum of $10,000 for each return. It is the same for a charity's application, although the $10,000 maximum does not apply.

In addition, any person who willfully fails to comply with the public inspection requirements is subject to a penalty of $5,000.

ALL OF THIS, though, while still the law, is basically history. The Internet has changed everything. Charities can avoid providing hard copies of their 990s if they make the documents "widely available," as the IRS puts it. This term essentially means "on the Internet."

The rules require the forms to be posted "in a format that, when accessed, downloaded, viewed and printed in hard copy, reproduces the image exactly as it was originally filed." Furthermore, charities must tell inquiring individuals the Internet address where they can view the 990.

Not many charities have done this yet on their own Web sites, but as time passes more and more probably will. Then again, maybe not. Charities have had a difficult time over the years getting used to the idea that their information is public.

So, if not at the charity's Web site, where?

Currently, the most comprehensive service that provides 990s for almost all charities in the United States required to file the form is Philanthropic Research, Incorporated. This is the group, itself a charity, that runs GuideStar, the online site where hundreds of thousands of 990s can be found.

Even though their tax returns are available on the Internet, charities are still obligated to make the documents available for on-site inspection. Furthermore, if all three of the most recent returns are not on the Internet, the charity must physically provide them upon request.

Incidentally, not all charities must file Form 990 (or its simplified counterpart 990 EZ). Only charities that receive revenues of over $25,000 during the year need to file—the 990 EZ for those whose assets are less than $250,000 and whose revenues are less than $100,000 (and more than $25,000); the full 990 for charities with over $100,000 of revenues.

This excludes some hundreds of thousands of small charities. Also excluded, as we saw earlier, are religious charities. To learn of the financial affairs of any of the exceptions—the small and the religious organizations—people must rely on the willingness of the charities themselves to open their financial records to the public. No law requires them to do so.

UNHAPPY CHARITY OFFICIALS have expressed their objections to the idea that their work is public. Here are a few of the most frequent complaints that I have received in my work over the years, and my responses to them.

Q: I don't believe my organization's financial information, particularly the salaries of its employees, is anyone's business but ours. Don't employees have a right to privacy concerning their personal compensation? Doesn't my organization have a right to control the uses made of its own financial information?

A: The answer to the second question first: No. Tax-exempt organizations operate for the public benefit and enjoy a variety of privileges, starting with exemption from the requirement to pay taxes on their income and real property. Tax-exempt organizations operate as public trusts and have certain legal, ethical, and moral requirements for openness in their operations that may not apply to for-profit corporations.

The federal government, as well as many state governments, treats the information returns, corporate organizational records, and other records of tax-exempt organizations as public documents. These records may be demanded by anyone without that person giving any reason for wishing to see them. This situation is completely appropriate, given the public-trust environment in which tax-exempt organizations operate.

Now to the first question: no again. Even though some executive directors wish it were otherwise, charities are required to disclose the compensation levels of their highest-paid employees. This is a less restrictive standard than what applies to government employees, who have long been accustomed to their salaries—at any level—being treated as part of routine public records.

To know if a tax-exempt entity is conducting its affairs in accord with the public trust, everyone is entitled to have a great deal of information about the organization, including the salaries of its highest-paid workers.

Q: I understand that the law requires my organization to make its tax return available for public inspection in our office and that IRS regulations may require us to provide immediate photocopies to anyone who asks for them. But that's very different from advertising our private financial information by placing our tax returns on an Internet Web site. Why should we do that?

A: There is no such thing as a public record that is not entirely public. Accordingly, a tax-exempt organization—especially one that is confident of the integrity of its operations—should recognize that there is no difference between a record available for public inspection at the front counter of its offices and a record widely available on the Internet.

An organization that makes its tax returns freely available on its own Web site—and several (although not enough) now do—is making a strong statement that it invites and welcomes public scrutiny of its operations.

Enlightened tax-exempt organizations recognize that their privileged tax status obliges them legally and ethically to operate both in the public interest and in the public view.

They should be happy to make financial information available to the public. Many organizations recognize that the integrity of their operations can have a positive effect on their public images and lead to greater support from donors.

A tax-exempt organization that makes a name for itself as one that recognizes and aggressively cultivates the image of operating in the open can expect to find heightened public sympathy for its causes and increased public support for its operation.

Q: What about our contributors' identities? We don't want people who give us money to find that their names have been disclosed without their permission. It just isn't right.

A: You're correct. And the IRS and Congress agree with this view. That's why lists of contributors that must be filed with a charity's 990 are not deemed part of the public record.

A charity can comply fully with the letter of the law, as well as the spirit of openness, and still keep confidential the identities of people who support it financially.

The IRS needs to know, but the public does not. Therefore, you should conceal that information when photocopying it for physical or electronic distribution. Of course, if Congress wants to know, as it did when The Nature Conservancy came under scrutiny, the charity must hand that information over.

Q: People unfamiliar with nonprofit financial affairs will simply not understand what the numbers in our 990 mean. Putting them on the Internet will create confusion and misimpressions about our operations.

A: Did you work for Enron in a prior life? It's not your job to make decisions for the public. Internet accessibility of 990s offers nonprofit organizations a valuable public-education opportunity and a challenge. These inquiries provide excellent opportunities for conveying a nonprofit's messages.

It doesn't matter whether you think the public will understand the information.

I'm convinced that if GuideStar, which automatically and electronically collects its information on charities, did not publish 990s on the Internet, some charities would delay as long as they could.

A FEW YEARS ago, I was putting information about charities on my own Web site.

Of the approximately twenty-thousand 990s I requested at the time, less than 40 percent responded within one month, the legal time frame. Before sending a reminder letter, I added another ten days for the mails and then another few weeks for good measure.

I got the distinct impression that, contrary to what I had believed, having worked in the charitable sector for over twenty years at that point, charities were reluctant to share this information.

Many charities, it turned out, didn't want their public information to become public. One group wanted to sue me. Another group, which claimed to know professional "hackers" and "virus originators," threatened to sabotage my Web site.

More benign, but as irritating, one person wrote to say that "my firm" had no authority to make the request, but that if I wrote back as an "individual," not on the company's letterhead—and if I promised not to put the information on the Internet—he would be happy to comply.

Of course, his organization's information was put on the Internet. Also, the rules don't make a distinction between an individual and another entity; the interpretation of the word "public," which is in bold letters at the top of Form 990, has little room for error. He wasn't happy, but he eventually complied.

As a matter of practice, that kind of request is not as relevant now that GuideStar posts 990s on the Internet, and the law does say that charities do not have to comply with written requests if the 990s are on the Web.

Anyone who wants to can go to GuideStar to find the information, which is good, because, based on the reactions I've had from far too many charities, they would much prefer to fight the request.

WHAT DOES THE 990 tell us? It offers information about the amount of money charities raise, how their revenues are spent, and about their fiscal health as measured in net assets.

We also learn who the trustees are. Trustees of charities in the United States currently do not typically earn any money for serving on a board. Acting as a trustee is usually a voluntary job, so much so that even a trustee's out-of-pocket expenses are rarely reimbursed by the charity. The practice of paying a trustee is highly unusual.

The exceptions to this standard are increasing, and some charities, as for-profit entities do, pay people to serve on their boards. It would be convenient to say that the legitimate ones do not do this, but some charities find that the only way they can attract good people is by paying them an honorarium.

But only *some* charities, and then for highly unusual and specific reasons. Hospitals, for example, require a high degree of technical expertise on their boards, and so a few feel they must reward trustees with a monetary stipend.

Because it is still so rare, if you see that a board member, other than a person who is also an employee of the charity, is paid (it is typical for some senior employees to also serve on the board), you should ask the charity why. It does not necessarily mean that the charity is doing anything wrong, but it may be a sign of a charity spending money badly.

THE QUESTION OF most interest to people is: "How much does a charity spend raising money?" Some agencies that rate charities look at the ratio of fundraising to overall expenses as the most revealing of all. That isn't true, but the curiosity makes sense: a charity that spends too much money to raise money doesn't have much left for its programs.

On the other hand, a charity starting a capital campaign—a concentrated fundraising effort for specific purposes—typically spends a considerable amount of money preparing for the campaign before it actually raises anything at all. The process often takes more than a year. This hardly makes it a bad charity; it is simply investing money, preparing to raise more than it otherwise would.

Young charities can also have legitimately high fundraising ratios. Charities that don't have a large group of followers must spend money to let the public know they exist, and then they must cultivate prospective donors, a process that can consume many years.

Charities without a built-in constituency, such as environmental organizations and homeless shelters, generally have a more difficult time identifying prospective donors—and keeping them—than those with an established base of prospects, such as colleges with lists of alumni.

Evaluations that do not take such relevant facts into account perform a disservice to the public.

That said, the average healthy charity will spend somewhere between 10 and 20 percent of what it raises. A charity that spends $1 million on fundraising and raises between $5 and $10 million is in the right ballpark. Less of a percentage is more efficient, of course, but the number should not be seen as an absolute determinant of a charity's efficiency or, certainly, of its worthiness.

The public should also be interested in the relationship among the amounts spent on all three major categories of a charity's budget: programming, management, and fundraising.

SOMETIMES CHARITIES ARE not forthright on the 990 and claim no costs for fundraising. This may look laudable but it is hardly realistic, and the motives to create such a result—looking good on the fundraising ratio and getting high marks at the ratings agencies—are not laudable.

Charities that raise money spend money to do so. They must.

A charity that raises, say, $1 million, but claims no fundraising costs, should make a person pause. This is almost impossible. The common response to a query about how this can be reported is that the very act of fundraising—asking people for money—is so intertwined with disseminating information about the work of the agency that it is considered a program expense. The IRS has revised its instructions to make certain that charity accountants don't do this, that the charity take care to distinguish between education and fundraising, even within the same appeal. Nonetheless, as long as people and ratings agencies look at this number with the expectation of low numbers, charities will have an incentive to keep the reported, if not the actual, fundraising costs low.

Is this deceitful? Of course. And it doesn't square with the spirit of the law behind disclosure.

Another response is that a different, related organization actually pays the salaries and fundraising costs. While this might be legitimate from an accounting perspective, it does nothing to enhance a person's understanding of what is really happening at a charity.

In that situation, the charity should also provide the 990 for the other organization so the public has access to all the relevant information, convoluted though it may be.

In fact, a charity is very much like a for-profit business. A woefully slow computer system, not upgraded because of cost, can slow down the work much faster than the payment needed for a faster computer system. Just because a charity is not a for-profit entity does not mean it has to be inefficient. Nor does it have to be oblivious to how things best work.

Of course, donors want their money to be used to further the aims of the charity, to do the work necessary to help society, but only the most naïve could possibly think that the actual work can be accomplished without an adequate infrastructure. Administrative costs, including salaries, and fundraising costs are part—a welcome part—of the picture.

Donors are not wise to demand that their money be used only on program costs. Make no mistake: a healthy infrastructure *promotes* programs. Similarly, while a charity's commitment to funding its programs is crucial, donors who huff and puff about money going only for programs are simply whining; worse, they are parroting the simplistic message that an uninformed media has itself been parroting from equally uninformed critics. When donors don't fully understand how a charity operates, they don't fully appreciate what they're really asking a charity to do.

A CHARITY IS also very much like a business when it comes to having enough cash and other assets around to do its work. While charities are exempt from paying taxes, they are not exempt from fulfilling their financial obligations. The 990 also tells us what surplus, if any, the charity has, how much of it is liquid, and what the charity's debts are.

The amount of a charity's debts is not by itself a warning sign; many charities issue bonds or take out loans for all kinds of legitimate purposes, often with an enviable ability to service the debt. Here, too, however, the 990 can reveal problem areas.

A charity where debts exceed assets is in trouble. Both numbers are clearly stated on the 990 and anyone can do the math just by looking at those two numbers.

A more complex evaluation would include the number of years a charity can hold on without receiving any income. Less than a few months, for example, might be pretty devastating, although an evaluation must take into account the realities of the charity's revenues. More than three or four years, though, represents ample resources.

The 990 also tells us of other enterprises that the charity may be involved in (yes, charities are allowed to own businesses) and other information pertinent to the taxpayer whose dollars are subsidizing the charity's activities.

DESPITE THE EXPLANATION of how important a charity's non-program budget is, the 990 can reveal some real problems, problems where the fundraising costs—some of which are slyly placed—should make a potential supporter wary.

Just for fun, let's look at the Children's Wish Foundation International in Atlanta. On the 990 for its fiscal year that ended on June 30, 2004, we see on the first page that the organization raised $14,789,798. To learn how the money was spent, you would have to dig deep, to the page of the form in the "notes" section, where we learn that all expenses of the charity are:

> incurred to fulfill the wishes of seriously ill children and their families. This is a once-in-a-lifetime experience for a child facing the most devastating circumstances, therefore care is taken to ensure that the quality of each wish far exceeds the expectations of the child.

On a past 990, the organization said that

> since CWFI's inception in 1985, the foundation has created thousands of once-in-a-lifetime opportunities for these children, providing them and their families with memories to cherish forever.

Well, who could finish reading that with a dry eye? Such a worthy charity must deserve a lot of support. Hence, the almost $15 million in donations.

Now, returning to the second page, we learn how much is spent on fundraising. Here we see that $8,324,077 was spent to raise that $15 million. The Children's Wish Foundation spent a little more than fifty-six cents to raise one dollar in 2004. That's not very efficient.

What is worse, the charity's budget for that year was $14, 909,479, almost the exact amount that was raised. That left less than half to be used to fulfill all those wishes. The amount spent on programs was $5,988,309. Just 40 percent of the budget went to fulfill those wishes. That's not very good either.

Since healthy charities generally spend between 10 and 20 percent of their budget on fundraising, program expenditures are generally no less than 70 percent of the budget.

Then it was off to Schedule A, where I noted that almost $2 million was spent on an item called "Telemarketing." As we know from the Viet-Now Supreme Court case, telemarketing costs can be very high. A breakdown of those costs, on another page deep inside, showed that just under $3 million was spent on telemarketing and another $2.2 million on the "Vehicle Donation Program." That's a lot, but a deeper look revealed that an additional $122,000 for the car program, and over $800,000 more for telemarketing, were placed into the program side of the equation.

Not good.

Believe it or not, this is a better picture than the organization's 990 showed in 2000. Back then, although the fundraising and program ratios were about the same as they were in 2004, three firms were paid over $10 million for "telemarketing" services. While those numbers are astronomical, the really weird thing back then was that Children's Wish reported fundraising costs to be $8.47 million. The charity spent $1.5 million less on fundraising than it paid its fundraising telemarketers.

How could that be?

A little sleuthing showed that it was in—*viola!*—programming.

Things looked better in 2004 than they did in 2000, but they still weren't good. In fact, Children's Wish reported, deep into its 2004 990, costs of $2.58 million on children's wishes. About 17 percent of the budget went toward the charity's stated goal.

WHAT MAY ACTUALLY outrank fundraising costs as the most interesting number a charity can provide the public is the salary of the person who runs the place. The 990 tells us that, as well as the salaries of other high-paid employees.

Earlier, we saw how, in the mid-1990s, the president of Adelphi University, Peter Diamandopoulos, went amok with a salary hopelessly in excess of what would have been fitting under the circumstances of the school's poor economic state and decreasing enrollment.

A decade later, in late 2005, the trustees of American University in Washington, D.C., fired its president, Benjamin Ladner, for "inappropriately" spending $125,000 of the school's money. This was on top of his $633,000 salary in 2004 and an additional $181,000 in benefits. An audit showed that he had spent over $500,000 during the prior three years, including $44,000 for private parties and over $22,000 for a first-class trip to Nigeria. All that being apparently too modest, according to one of the trustees Ladner asked for a bonus that year of $1.12 million and $5 million in retirement benefits. He didn't get the bonus and received "only" a $3.7 million severance package.

It was enough, though, to pique the curiosity of Senator Charles Grassley, the chairman of the Senate Finance Committee, who announced an investigation into whether the board had acted properly in giving him so much money and why it did such a lousy job of overseeing his spending sprees with the university's money.

In late 2005, *The Chronicle of Higher Education* reported that five college and university presidents earned more than $1 million in 2004. Lynn University, a two-year Catholic college in Florida, which was once almost bankrupt, led the list. Its president, Donald Ross, took in a little more than $5 million.

The other four colleges were Wilmington College in Delaware, Vanderbilt University, Boston University, and Middlebury College in Vermont.

It's not surprising to see that John Silber, the president of Boston University, made the list with a salary of $1.25 million. Silber was Peter Diamandopoulos's close pal on Adelphi's compensation committee. But if anything, you'd expect the best universities to pay the best. How in the world, you might wonder, did a place like Lynn University make that list?

And that's just universities. Many hospitals and other charities pay their top executives well. Barry Munitz, the former president of the J. Paul

Getty Trust in California, which runs the Getty Museum, resigned in 2006 after all sorts of acrimony. A large salary and excessive personal expenses paid by the charity—including a $72,000 Porsche Cayenne and trips with first-class airfare and $1,000-a-night hotels—were part of the problem. He even made his assistants express-mail umbrellas when he traveled.

Then there's the Smithsonian Institution. The salaries don't involve malfeasance, but the story is interesting nonetheless. Congress wanted to reduce Lawrence Small's salary as secretary from a base of $574,000 to $400,000. The Smithsonian, you'll recall from the earlier discussion on large gifts, is financed in large part by the government, and the thinking was that no salary at an organization with such close ties to the federal government should be higher than the $400,000 salary of the President of the United States.

An article in the *Washington Post* on May 11, 2006, noted "There are 28 people at the Smithsonian who are paid more than Cabinet secretaries," and that 22 people were paid more than the vice president, who currently receives $212.000. Six were paid more than the president. Small's total compensation package in 2003 was $813,000.

The chair of the board committee that sets the executive's salaries at the Smithsonian was quoted as saying, "Who can argue that someone should be paid more than the President of the United States? But in fact there are 40 museum directors around the world that are."

The argument wasn't specious. There's only one place to go if you want to be the President of the United States, but there are many high-quality museums around the world, and all of them compete for the best talent. Besides, a plane designated as Air Force One isn't a perk of any museum director.

Representative Mike Simpson from Idaho, who sits on the House Appropriations Committee, the committee that reduced the salaries, didn't see it that way. He said, "I can't go back to Idaho and justify this. I can barely justify my own salary. For a farm boy the salaries look pretty big."

WHILE YOU MIGHT be thinking that no charity executive should make a million dollars, it's also important to keep in mind that large charities are a lot like large for-profit corporations. True, a charity's goal isn't to make money for shareholders, but the responsibilities are many: overseeing the budget, resolving personnel issues, ensuring revenue streams, maintaining the integrity of the mission, and looking toward the future to ensure the survival of the organization. All of these tasks are shared by the CEOs of both for-profit and nonprofit organizations.

Also, the head of a charity needs the same qualities—the work habits, intelligence, stamina, experience, and attitude necessary for success—as the head of a major for-profit corporation.

Taking that into account, and considering the exceptions for what they are—exceptions—the salary situation at charities is, for the most part, the opposite of what many people think: executive directors of charities are too often *under*paid, not overpaid. Heads of for-profit organizations often earn millions of dollars. Charity heads are not in that league.

Take the retired leaders of, for example, Harvard University and General Electric. In 2000, the president of Harvard, Neil Rudenstine, earned $380,272 in salary and benefits. According to the watchdog group United for a Fair Economy, the head of General Electric, Jack Welch, earned more than $93 million in 1999. A startling difference. And Harvard doesn't even offer stock options.

Both men retired in 2001. Which one had the tougher job? Which one worked harder? Which one was more dedicated? Which organization has a more meaningful impact on society?

Let's assume that each was hard-working and performed magnificently on the job. Why the salary discrepancy, aside from stock options, of $92.6 million? At the end of 2001, Harvard's endowment was $25 billion while General Electric's market value was roughly $400 billion.

A simple straight-line equivalency measurement on the basis of those asset values would show that the CEO of General Electric might have made sixteen times the president of Harvard. Instead, the differential is closer to 232 times. The skills of Mr. Rudenstine, who retired at a fairly young age in large part because of the exhaustion associated with the job, were certainly no less valuable than those of Mr. Welch.

The answer to the discrepancy is that General Electric is a for-profit company with many shareholders. Make them money, and the return to the person responsible is leveraged geometrically. A leader in the nonprofit world with a similar skill set, an equally positive—although different—impact on society (some would argue a far better impact), and generally more education earns a salary of less than one-half of one percent of his or her for-profit counterpart.

The choices we make.

WHERE, BEYOND THE sterile numbers on an IRS document, can people go to determine what they should support? The 990 is all we have when we want to request information about a charity, a request that has the force of law. Yet, despite what it does tell us—and, as you've seen, the numbers can tell a story—you would know no more about a charity from its 990 than you would about your neighbors and friends from their tax returns.

The form does not explain anything meaningful about the actual accomplishments of the organization, nothing about its trustees except their names, and certainly nothing about what the charity has done during the year to improve the quality of life for either its employees or the public it serves.

While the public can get a good sense of a charity's fiscal health—its assets, liabilities, expenses, and revenue—a 990 provides none of the context that lure people to a charity: the hungry-looking children that get fed, the pathetic-looking homeless that are given shelter, the manatee or whale that is saved from fishermen, the level of appreciation of having seen a Dégas, the full-time mother who, because of her recently earned degree, can now find better work outside the home. None of this is on a 990.

More, you will never know how committed its board members are or how much actual work the executive director and other employees perform.

In addition, it's human nature to stay away from the deadly dull. Only geeks could find as much joy as I did in perusing the 990 of the Children's Wish Foundation. The average donor has no such interest. The government is tinkering with improving the reporting system, but it probably can't do much more than it is doing now. Besides, more government regulation is probably not going to solve anything.

Much more information should be available.

For the eighty million Americans who give away some of their hard-earned money each year—as well as for the rest of the country, because all taxpayers play a subsidizing role—charities ought to be more responsive, more transparent. They should provide better and more compelling information. And they shouldn't require prodding from the government to do it. The 990 is a good start, but, for donors who care about what they are supporting, that's all it is. It certainly isn't enough to make a heart-felt decision.

We all should have access to more information, and charities should do more to provide it.

19

THE RATINGS GAME

"There is great potential for these ratings to be misinterpreted and misused, which would cause more harm than good."

NATIONAL COUNCIL OF NONPROFIT ASSOCIATIONS AND NATIONAL HUMAN SERVICES ASSEMBLY, "RATING THE RATERS," MAY 2005

SOME CHARITIES ARE not worth your while. But how can you tell? Are you going to take the time to review the documentation charities send to the government, or pore over their annual reports, looking for financial discrepancies?

No. Most of us aren't built that way.

A group of self-appointed watchdogs has decided to fill in the gaps, to help you better understand the worthiness of a charity. In much the same way that Morningstar evaluates mutual funds—a goal of at least one charity watchdog—these organizations use financial criteria to measure charities. They all have access to and, for their principal analyses, use the same data: numbers from the 990. And they put some of the information in what they think is a helpful context. Then they rate or grade charities.

The usual variables for analyzing a charity include its revenues and expenses for the year, the amounts spent on fundraising, administration, and programs. If you are aware, for example, that one charity spends less than another to raise money, you're better off with that information and, as a result, you'll support the charity that spends less.

Other criteria can include the charity's liquid reserves, and its fundraising and revenue trends over a period of time, as well as the annual salary of the executive director or president.

The idea is that, if the public has access to consolidated information, donors will make decisions based on comparative efficiency, which, in principle, will lead to better management and service at the charities. The agencies also claim that their reports are objective. "We only use the information from the 990," the head of one agency once said. "Therefore, the people who use our service will be assured that we have no axe to grind."

ONE OF THESE groups is the American Institute of Philanthropy (AIP), which issues grades from A to F to approximately 500 charities in the United States. As its online literature states, "The American Institute of Philanthropy is a nationally prominent charity watchdog service whose purpose is to help donors make informed giving decisions."

The criteria AIP uses include the annual amount of total revenues spent on a charity's purpose, the cost of raising money, and the number of years a charity could exist solely with its available reserves. AIP, which also employs audited financial reports, believes that charities should spend 60 percent or more on programs, and no more than 35 percent on fundraising.

Another group, Charity Navigator, uses a star rating system—four stars being the best—for a few thousand charities around the country. Charity Navigator does not outwardly impose an ideal percentage for either programming or fundraising costs, but it does calculate its ratings by giving the best scores for program expenses of 75 percent or more and for fundraising costs of 10 percent or less.

A third watchdog firm is the Better Business Bureau's Wise Giving Alliance. It employs a slightly more comprehensive approach to the process than the other two and asks charities to supplement the information on the 990. That group asks twenty questions designed to lay out the organization's board involvement, calculate how efficiently it spends and raises money, determine how truthful the organization is, and measure the charity's willingness to disclose information.

From the Better Business Bureau's Web site:

> The overarching principle . . . is full disclosure to donors and poten-
> tial donors at the time of solicitation and thereafter. However, where indi-
> cated, the standards recommend ethical practices beyond the act of
> disclosure in order to ensure public confidence and encourage giving.

According to the BBB, at least 65 percent of a charity's budget ought
to be spent on programs, and no more than 35 percent of what is raised
should be spent on raising it. Note that the Better Business Bureau is
interested in the amount spent relative to the *amount raised*; often, when
analysts speak of fundraising efficiency, they are talking about the amount
spent on fundraising relative to the whole budget. Each is important, but
they are two different concepts. Distinguishing between the two is a
source of confusion for many people.

While the Better Business Bureau is more comprehensive than other
ratings groups, it evaluates few charities—under 1,000—which means that
the charities you are interested in learning about are probably not listed.

With hundreds of thousands of charities in the United States, however, that's true about any of the watchdogs.

Generally, donors have an idea of what they want to support and are
already doing so. The value of the watchdogs for most people is in
checking on how a familiar charity stacks up. The watchdogs tell you
which charities are good and which are not. They will analyze charities,
some of which might have a few issues you should know about, and present their findings in a supposedly neutral manner. You don't have to dig
into the 990 or other financial information yourself, because the watchdogs will do the work for you.

BUT THE INFORMATION is not as neutral as it is advertised to be. A common mistake is to think that, since numbers are neutral, conclusions
drawn from manipulating them are also neutral. Conclusions are always
the result of a subjective process, so the analyses performed by any charity watchdog group are not objective.

For example, AIP says it "strongly believes that your dollars are most
urgently needed by charities that do not have large reserves of available

assets. AIP therefore reduces the grade of any organization that has available assets equal to three-to-five years of operating expenses."

Charities with assets that are equal to more than five years of operating expenses automatically receive a failing grade from AIP on the basis that they are therefore not needy.

While some people may think that large endowments are a waste, others passionately disagree.

One need look no further than a disaster to see the importance of a healthy financial reserve. After Hurricane Katrina wiped out New Orleans, who would argue that the Red Cross shouldn't have had money in the bank? It's not just the disaster-relief charities that need reserves. Tulane, one of the nation's preeminent universities, had to rely on its financial health to ensure that it could rebuild and continue operations after it lost the better part of an academic year to the hurricane's floods.

And it's not only disasters that bring out the need for healthy reserves. Many charities need resources to implement new programs to further their missions. They should not be expected to be constantly begging and wondering where money will come from.

To fail a charity because it is not needy equates *neediness* with *worthiness*. From there, it's not a large leap to conclude that *financial health* means *worthlessness*, a pattern of thinking which wrongly indicts valuable charities that are not near bankruptcy.

The watchdogs rely almost exclusively on ratios to do their work. As a result, they strongly imply that a charity with less overhead or fewer fundraising costs than another charity is the better one.

While an eye needs to be kept on those percentages, they can be misleading. Charities can in fact get into trouble by *not* spending enough on their infrastructure or fundraising. A charity that pays its employees too little may experience high turnover; a charity that does not invest in technology might not be able to process vital and time-sensitive information, with the result that programming or critical administrative functions are inadequately executed.

In sum, it isn't a question of whether the charity that spends ten cents on the dollar for overhead is worse than the one that spends fifteen or twenty-five or thirty cents. What matters are the resources the charity has available and that it performs its work as it should, while at the same time not wasting money.

Not only are the watchdog's calculations weighted subjectively, the raw numbers used are often the result of a subjective process. That is, the manner by which charities calculate the information on the 990 is not uniform. A 2002 GAO report, in response to concerns raised after the 9/11 tragedies, said, "The Form 990 expense data is not adequate because charities have considerable discretion in recording their expenses in the program services, general management, and fundraising categories."

Some charities, knowing this is a hot topic, refuse to claim *any* expenses for fundraising, even though they raise a lot of money. Or they fudge it, labeling some fundraising activities and their associated costs as program expenditures.

The IRS has not been interested in pressing the matter. Except for receiving a memorandum and updated instructions on how to properly fill out a 990, charities are free to categorize expenses pretty much as they wish.

Besides, for lack of staff, the IRS is able to review, let alone evaluate, far too few 990s each year. Who knows whether the information is accurate?

All those numbers—and the resulting rankings—have attained a status well beyond their value in what passes for evaluations. When it comes to learning about a charity's worthiness—which, at best, involves the study of a complex interaction of activity and mission, and where finances play only a supporting role—the public cannot afford to rely only on numbers and ratings.

The Nature Conservancy, by the way, came up clean as a whistle, receiving four stars on the Charity Navigator watchdog site. The site used information from The Nature Conservancy's 2001 Information Return, even though much of what the *Post* uncovered took place at that time. The American Institute of Philanthropy rated the environmental group among its best, with a grade of A-. It can be argued that the newspaper's coverage was not complete, fair, or accurate, but legitimate issues did emerge, and none of them could be found on any watchdog site.

In his Congressional testimony in December 2005, the head of AIP talked about the response by charities to hurricanes Katrina and Rita.

"The Red Cross continues to be a financially efficient organization and receives an A-minus grade," he said. A real evaluation would have arrived at a far different conclusion. The one provided by the International Red Cross teams two months earlier, if it had been reduced to a grade, would have been an F.

RANDOMLY, A WHILE back I looked through one watchdog site and came across the Ocean Conservancy in Washington, D.C., an organization with which I was already familiar and knew was dedicated to saving marine life in our seas and oceans. I also came across Florida West Coast Public Broadcasting, which runs public broadcasting station WEDU in the Tampa and St. Petersburg areas of Florida.

The conservation group, as judged by the watchdog, was wonderful and, in fact, deserved your support. Not only was the information in the 990 acceptable by the watchdog's standards, the group had done good work with dedicated staff. To know that, though, a donor needed to do some homework: reading the organization's literature and science reports, and talking to some people there.

The television station, however, flunked badly. The watchdog saw nothing redeeming at WEDU.

On the off-chance that something more than the information on the TV station's 990 might reveal something interesting and even important in determining the value of WEDU to its community, I spoke with Patrick Perkins, the chief financial officer. It turns out that WEDU was in the middle of a capital campaign in response to the federal government's decree to convert to a digital signal, a process that cost approximately $12 million.

Most capital campaigns are determined by the charity, but this one had been forced upon WEDU by a mandatory requirement, and so raising the money was even more difficult than it would have otherwise been.

I learned more. This was the first capital campaign in the station's forty-five year history. Perhaps the people running the place should have done more fundraising during those years, but they had been getting along just fine. The base of community support was strong, and while a good part of the money for the campaign came from the state and federal governments, the larger part came from private donations.

In addition, the auditors, after the station learned of the watchdog's low rating, scoured the information on the 990 and discovered that some of the fundraising costs should have been shown in the program side of the equation. Richard Lobo, the president, asked the auditors if there were any incorrectly placed expenditures that could "legally and ethically" be changed. As it turned out, the costs for the program guide, sent to members each season, were entirely in the fundraising column. As a program guide is not a fundraising expense, the station, with its auditors' encouragement, re-characterized 20 percent of the guide's cost to program expenses. This was a conservative decision—more could have been shifted, perhaps even 100 percent, to programs. But even 20 percent would make the ratios different enough to affect the results of the watchdog's analysis.

On top of all that, the information was about two years old before the watchdogs got it. "If they want to be like Morningstar, they should be as timely as the information on Morningstar," said Patrick Perkins. "Would you make an investment decision on the basis of two-year-old information?"

That's not the fault of the watchdog agencies—they access the IRS information as soon as it's available—but it does highlight a serious flaw in how the 990 information is used.

Charity Navigator, for one, does take into account the higher expense that public television incurs to raise money. Its Web site acknowledges the cost of the airtime used to raise money during telethons and adjusts its standards slightly.

Even so, the real question remains: does this charity serve its community? "Absolutely," said Perkins. "We do a lot of local programming, such as public affairs programs geared to this area. We've had the debates for governor here and we broadcast live performances of the local symphony."

Lacking a serious scandal at WEDU, viewers in the Tampa Bay area should keep sending their money.

One example, of course, does not make a statistically valid argument that the ratings agencies do not tell nearly enough of the relevant story. But it is true that you should be skeptical of ratings. There is a very high probability that there is more to the story.

Indeed, in 2005, two Washington, D.C.-based groups—the National

Council of Nonprofit Associations and the National Human Services Assembly—conducted an assessment of the charity watchdogs and concluded that they have a few problems. The watchdogs, the report says, provide confusing, incomplete, unfair, and misleading information to the public.

The study noted that each watchdog's criteria and approach vary, that the criteria are not apparent and are overly simplistic, and that they focus on financial measures while overlooking program effectiveness.

Most biting of all was the report's assertion that the evaluators themselves were not competent.

IT'S NOT THAT the information on a 990 isn't valuable, or that the ratios derived from that information aren't important. Actually, they are quite important. It's just not the whole story. No one disputes the value of good tires on a car, but who buys a car after examining only the tires?

It has been said often that charities, traditionally almost the opposite of business in their efforts to show results, could use a dose of corporate culture to be more efficient. While it is true that far too many charity employees think of their jobs as eternal and inviolate, paid for by who-knows-what bottomless pit of permanent funding, it is also true that charities are less efficient than business. A for-profit firm can analyze results relatively quickly because its results—sales and profits—are, if not always easy to obtain, easy to measure. A nonprofit's results are far more abstract. How do you objectively measure a better classroom experience? Or a better painting? Or a more content parishioner?

Is a food shelter to be judged by the number of people it serves? By that measure, perhaps more should be encouraged to come for dinner. If cost is an issue and efficiency a goal, then half the normal portions should be served to twice as many people. But would doing that make the food shelter a better charity?

The watchdogs, mired in and restricted by the process of simple math, cannot convey the human role that charities play in society, and the intricacies and nuances involved in the process of making the world a better place—important considerations in any calculation of a charity's worthiness.

Small minds create false drama from the mundane, all the while oblivious to the real drama. Although the watchdogs have made fundraising and other financial ratios front and center, very few real problems at charities show up as warning signs. It's like the police officer who lets the thief get away with all the jewels while he tickets the jay walker: in part because he doesn't notice, in part because he doesn't understand the relative seriousness of the crimes.

You can rest assured that the charity watchdogs have their trained eye on that which is largely inconsequential.

When you think about it, though, what could we have expected? In an era of increasing public scrutiny, and in the absence of legitimate discourse and forthrightness on the part of charities, it's rather natural that someone would fill the void. With no credible measures in place, with no discussion about the perils of rating charities on the basis of inadequate and misleading information, and with charities shirking their responsibility to inform the public, the ratings game has flourished, and the raters are free to impose their false, unearned credibility.

IN A PERFECT WORLD

"Donors, more than ever before, want and are demanding accountability for their philanthropy."

THE WALL STREET JOURNAL, MAY 14, 2003

WHAT CAN WE expect from charities? A lot more than we're getting.

As we've seen, the 990 as an evaluative tool is called upon to do too much work, and the analyses resulting from it are unhelpful. The laws aren't going to do the job.

Most charities do as little as they can to satisfy their obligations to the public. When the answer to the question "Why don't you do this good thing?" is "The law doesn't require us to do it," something is wrong. At least at a charity.

Laws can rise to the challenge when something egregious becomes public, such as at the United Way of America or the Baptist Foundation of Arizona. But those scandals came to light not because of any routine filings—and certainly not because anyone at the charity informed the state authorities—but because the media got their hands on it. It's safe to say that, had it not been for the *Washington Post*, William Aramony would still have his job today. The United Way board was that unconcerned.

Even though Congress has shown more interest than ever in charities, except for a few minor statutory changes, not much is likely to happen. The IRS and the states' attorneys general are overwhelmed. We're actually fortunate when they're able to muster up enough resources to follow up the scandals that show up in the newspaper headlines.

So, aside from ramping up the enforcement of what's on the books now (and a few other things), don't look for many legal changes. (By the way, one of those other things is making the process of valuing non-cash gifts more precise. Congress and the IRS are concerned that too many donors deduct too much.) Tightening appraisals, however, would only help the IRS enforce what's already on the books.

The public needs charities to provide more and better information about their work.

Knowing what to tell people about the job isn't easy, of course. The job of a charity itself isn't easy. Compared to what a charity must accomplish and how it must define its priorities, a for-profit business has a rather easy time of it. It has no need to adhere to any mission more grand than legally making a profit for its stockholders.

But you would think that charities, being what they are—in essence, ethical organizations—would take more interest in being more forthright.

Charities have the inherent obligation to work at high moral standards, and one of those standards is accountability. It's a moral standard because it is an elusive and subjective term, and because those who demand it must rely on the values of those providing it.

Accountability is paramount because charities use the public's money and because the essential purpose of a charity is to serve the public good.

Public skepticism about charities has intensified over the years, and not just because of the problems that arose after 9/11. People want to know, more than they did a generation ago, how their money is used. Far too many charities, however, take the position that how they spend their money doesn't much concern the public.

No wonder watchdogs have risen up, albeit in their awkward and superficial way, to demand a better accounting from charities. The question is: why don't charities demand such accountability and transparency of themselves?

Because of their unique position and mission in society, nonprofits cannot view ethical behavior as merely a bonus. Ethical behavior needs to be embedded in a charity's mission. It cannot be an aside.

The secrecy on the part of charities has left the public wondering what they're all about. And if we really don't know what they're all about, then it doesn't take much imagination to wonder why they exist at all.

Judges and juries, Congress and the IRS—they don't go to that land beyond the law's reach.

But you can. You can enforce the unenforceable.

No one forces you to donate to charity. Instead of waiting for legislative bodies to catch up, or for boards to behave better on their own, a far simpler and more effective approach lies within you: your ability to withhold your money—until *you* are satisfied.

Nobody else will do the job for you.

The good news is that you have a great deal of power. The bad news is that you need to be more engaged and educated than you ever thought necessary. But that can actually be good news, too.

A CHARITY NEEDS to be clear about its mission and what it does for its community. It should ask and answer what would happen if it closed its doors tomorrow. Who would be hurt? What difference would it make? Who would care?

Each year the board ought to be required—by you—to answer this question. The board ought to evaluate honestly the charity's impact on society. Then it ought to share the results of that self-evaluation with its public, no matter what it uncovers

One charity official told me that this vision is "far too Utopian," but it isn't. Such an honest, regular self-examination is essential to ensuring that the charity is doing what it should and meeting the needs of its constituents. Donors can ask that question and demand an honest answer.

This exercise would reveal whether the charity has what has come to be called a "convincing rationale." As Lester Salamon writes in *The State of Nonprofit America,* "Ultimately, the lack of a compelling vision may threaten the future of the nonprofit sector as a vehicle for socially beneficial change."

This statement makes an assumption about vision at the nation's charities, and some charities will be quick to dispute it. But most of them will do so at their own peril because Salamon is right: too many charities do in fact flounder and wallow in their own existence, rather than move forth to new goals, or to new strategies to accomplish traditional goals.

It's possible that a charity really doesn't actually serve any useful purpose. Or that it does the same thing as several other charities but not as well.

Do we really need hundreds of charities devoted to the cure for cancer? When the financier and ex-con Michael Milken came down with cancer, he did not support a program at one or more of the several established charities devoted to its cure. Instead, he started his own charity—the Prostate Cancer Foundation—whose goals might have been better and more quickly accomplished if his money had been combined with that of others.

Think of the confusion you have endured trying to keep the missions of charities distinct.

Some charities should go out of business. We simply have too many. The IRS approves tens of thousands each year, and most of them—plus a lot of the charities that have been around for a while—don't elevate society very much.

Of the several hundred thousand charities that ask for donations from the public, the world would not suffer very much if perhaps a hundred thousand or so closed their doors tomorrow. I say this not on the basis of their economic inefficiency, although that surely is part of the idea, but because of their lack of impact.

It's not related to size; many small charities know exactly who they are, what they're doing, and what they want to do. Conversely, many large charities don't have any idea what they're doing. The task of publicly and annually answering what would happen if the charity stopped doing business tomorrow is important. If leaders of charities take their responsibilities so blithely that their boards and executive directors practically run the place into the ground, or just don't do much good, then what's the point? If the only reason they exist is to raise money, then they don't deserve donations.

The public is in a position to determine whether the board's answer is valid. As a member of the public, and particularly if you are a donor, you ought to demand the answer.

A charity should also not be shy about telling the public about its accomplishments.

How many patients did the hospital care for during the prior year? How many of them lived?

How many Cézanne showings did the local art gallery have? How many visitors stopped by to see them? How many women who lived at the rehab residence are now out and working again?

This report doesn't have to be laden with statistics. As to the question of how many patients lived after receiving care at a hospital, the numerical answer may not necessarily be a sign of excellence, or of its opposite. A hospital that advertises no deaths during the year might have cared for very few patients, or perhaps few with anything seriously wrong would ever go to that hospital. On the other hand, plenty of kids die every year at Children's Hospital Boston, but that's a last stop for some kids who, other than in the experienced hands of some of the best doctors in the world, just have no chance.

All charities can tell you what they have accomplished and put it into context so you understand. Thoughtful narrative, even in this instant-information society, can play a vital role.

CHARITIES OUGHT TO come clean on their fundraising results. Far too often, the number reported in the fundraising materials is not quite what it seems. These days charities raise money in a variety of ways and they reach their goals, whether in a capital campaign or not, by using creative math.

A normal person would think that, if a charity says it raised $1 million during the prior year, then it raised . . . $1 million. Some of it may have been used during the year to help cover expenses, a portion for overhead, and the rest for programs, or some of it may have been put into an endowment. But all of it, most people would believe, was received. Or pledged to be received within a short period of time. After all, isn't that what the term "fundraising results" means?

No. Not by a long shot. In today's world, as we have seen, charities use a variety of methods to raise money, and not all the money comes in during the counting period. That is, not all the money that was counted actually arrived. This goes well beyond the automobile-donation problem, where the donor took a deduction of one amount and the charity received a much smaller amount; many gifts are established to be available to the charity only at the donor's death.

To be fair, charities have long discussed how to report gifts that have a future interest. Their concerns, however, have been primarily directed to others in the fundraising profession.

Accounting standards can make it difficult to convey accurately what a charity has raised, but nothing in any of the variations on valuing future gifts precludes a little honesty. That is, the charity ought to have two categories of gifts: current and deferred. Current gifts, actual money or assets, are those that have come in during the year. A subset of this might be pledges that are due in within a period of time, such as five years.

Deferred gifts are those that are committed but don't affect the charity's current budget. If a charity raised $400,000 in outright gifts and obtained bequest commitments of another $600,000, it should say that. That the total is $1 million is a good thing and something to tell the public, but it is not the entire story.

Thus, every charity needs to show:

- what it raised—what it actually took in during that one year;
- the pledges it obtained that will be collected during the next few years; and
- the gift commitments it obtained for the distant future and their value.

By the way, in the category that shows what the charity actually collected, delineation should be made for gifts that came in as part of a prior pledge or part of a prior, longer-term commitment. With just a few lines, a charity could go a long way toward being honest to the public about what it raises.

The pressure to report bloated fundraising results, you'll recall, is what prompted the chief financial officer of the District of Columbia chapter of the United Way to resign in 2006.

MOST PUBLIC UNIVERSITIES should be ashamed. As a result of one of the weird corners of charity law, they are government entities and thus not required to file the IRS Form 990. While this means that donors can make tax-deductible gifts to these organizations, supported in large part by their state governments, it also means, ironically, that the public does not have access to their finances.

Many public universities, such as Ohio State, have created supporting foundations. (Note that, in Chapter 11, it was the Ohio State Foundation and not the university that was named in the lawsuit.) One of the original ideas behind supporting foundations at a public university was to protect assets from hungry state legislators who look everywhere imaginable for funds and, since their future is defined by the date of the next election, too often see little need for large endowments.

This is one reason why some public universities show ridiculously inconsequential fundraising expenses or none at all. The money comes into the foundation, and the expenses are allocated to the university. In addition to the resulting misinformation on the foundation's 990, there is no reason for such sleight of hand. The only reason for this practice is an intention to deceive. Laziness may be at play, too.

Any donor to a public university ought to demand the same sort of financial information that is found in the supporting organization's 990. Better yet, the university should willingly provide it on its Web site before being asked.

Donors should demand 990s from religious organizations as well.

All charities should provide audited annual reports to anyone who asks. Again, though, that should also be on a charity's Web site.

BUT, AS WE know, the 990 communicates almost nothing of comprehensive value, nothing that anybody other than an accountant understands. Donors should know what really happens to their money, and they shouldn't have to ask to find out. Reporting out that a certain percentage of the budget went for programs doesn't cut it.

This is not to say that every dollar needs to be reconciled with every donor. In fact, few donors, at least those who make modest gifts annually, care much about the details. A broad reconciliation should suffice.

In part because of the watchdogs, and in part because of media stories that focus on fundraising costs, charities have been taught to fear acknowledging any expenditure that is not intended for programs. They need to get over this and get real. Donors have to get over it, too, and come to grips with the reality that, unless the charity is fully endowed for all its administrative expenses—and I'm unfamiliar with any fundraising charity so flush—only by accounting legerdemain can it be shown that all of the public's support funds programs.

Endowment gifts require more communication. The income used each year is determined by the charity's policy to spend money from the endowment. A $1 million gift might generate $50,000 of income in the first year, which is usually intended to fund a specific program, such as a scholarship for a student attending a university.

Does that money, however, actually get used for that purpose? That may seem like an odd question, but think of it this way: The total scholarship budget might be $2 million at an educational organization, but if the $1 million gift does not increase that budget by $50,000 (or thereabouts), then the donor is simply adding money to pay other bills. That is, the school is shifting money around. While your name might now be assigned to the scholarship, it's quite possible that the scholarship budget— and the offerings of the school in this vital area—hasn't been increased at all. Perhaps it is not true that students who otherwise could not enroll will now attend.

Budgets at all charities are fungible, and it is almost impossible to track and identify every dollar that goes through the system. But people should know if they are making an impact in the area where they want to make an impact. Charities should explain their policies on this point.

That annual fund gift designated for a particular program? Probably nothing more than a marketing gimmick. If money is designated for one program, the charity can simply shift an amount it had allocated from its general fund to something else. That doesn't make it the worst fundraising message, but that is probably what's going on.

Perhaps the scholarship budget is increased, but by only $45,000, because the school allocates 10 percent to pay for any expenses associated with executing the gift. Would this be wrong? No, as long as the school is clear and communicates that fact to the donor before the gift is made. If the donor does not like that policy, he or she does not have to make the gift.

But policy or not, the reality is that there are expenses associated with the gift, and those expenses come from somewhere. If it comes out of the school's general fund, then that fund is diminished by the amount going to the scholarship fund.

No wonder donors were upset with the Red Cross after 9/11 when they discovered that their money was initially put aside for future emergencies and not used for the needs at the time. The irritating part is not the policy to use funds in the way the charity decides, but that charities don't tell anybody what's going on or, worse, they lie. All charities need to be able to run their shop the best way they see fit, but they also need to explain what is going on. And they should do this before, not after, a gift is made.

IN A DIFFERENT era, people would simply give because they felt close to a charity's mission. Today, even though far too many people still do not care, many more than ever are asking tougher questions. The public has a right to be fully informed.

"Fully informed," of course, is a subjective term. In the description of planned gifts at Ohio State, the charity did not fully explain all the relevant aspects of the gift. As a result of the Texas lawsuit, the law now requires disclosure for most gifts, but charities should disclose important information about *all* gifts.

The law does not describe what disclosure is, however, and so charities must decide for themselves what to explain. Some charities have hired law firms to write their disclosure statements and they end up reading like legal briefs.

The head of the SEC told me after the Philanthropy Protection Act was passed in 1995 that disclosure can mean many things, especially to attorneys. But—and these are his words—"If a seventy-five-year-old widow doesn't understand what you're talking about, you're not disclosing anything."

John Glaser, the author of the book on the United Way scandal, quotes William Lehrfedl, a former IRS attorney with the exempt organization division: "The damage that can be done by non-disclosure by a charity or a related entity is far more serious than any actual money that could be involved. Lack of disclosure brings distaste, and distaste brings lack of trust, and that could hurt donations to the main charity."

★ ★ ★

DONORS SHOULD BE particularly alert when they receive calls asking for charitable dollars to support victims of a disaster. The Red Cross is a well-known name, but post-disaster days are heydays for the fraudulent types.

In the days following Hurricane Katrina, FEMA noted the prevalence of fraudulent solicitations and put forth some of the more common themes:

- Donate to charities you have given to before;
- Watch out for charities that have sprung up overnight;
- Be wary of charities that sound like familiar organizations, but are not;
- Give directly to the charity and not to solicitors for the charity;
- Do not give out any personal or financial information to anyone who solicits a contribution from you;
- Don't give or send cash;
- If you are approached on the street, ask for the identification of the person soliciting your gift.

Inexplicably, as it did after 9/11—as if there were too few charities in the United States—the IRS *expedited* charity applications after the Katrina disaster.

The problem isn't that there aren't enough charities; it's having enough money go to the right charities so they can do their work. As opposed to making it easier for charities to be created after a disaster, because of the high potential for fraud, the IRS should instead put a hold on approving applications from people who want to start charities. With dozens of well-established charities to deal with disaster relief, a few more in the heat of battle are unnecessary.

The best advice for donors is not to make a gift at all, unless they are absolutely certain that the charity and its solicitation are legitimate. Under no circumstances give to a stranger over the phone who represents a charity with which you are not familiar. As I mentioned earlier in the chapter that reviewed the Supreme Court telemarketing case, if you are interested in the charity, then you should tell the person on the other end of the line that the charity should forward information to you. Or you can contact the charity yourself.

That may sound draconian, and if everyone always followed this advice many legitimate causes would receive less than they do now. But at least no money would be donated to a fraudulent cover.

The Internet is worse than the telephone, for you are even more unlikely to recognize potential fraud. Within two weeks after Hurricane Katrina, over 4,000 disaster-relief sites were up—four times the number that existed before. After receiving numerous complaints, the FBI estimated that 60 percent of the 2,100 sites it had investigated had domains outside the United States, with connections in Europe, Asia, and elsewhere. Many were thought to be fraudulent. The FBI said that new sites were popping up "faster than we can pound them down."

The Internet site Scambusters said that "whenever there is a major natural or other disaster, scammers begin sending out charity relief scams within just a couple of hours!" Also, Scambusters says that there were four times as many scams after Katrina as there were after the tsunami disaster in Asia at the end of 2004.

One of the more prevalent scams is the type that copies the look of legitimate sites. Some of the fake sites look eerily the same as the Red Cross site. But while they look the same, and the appeal sounds legitimate, they will ask for financial information that can be used to steal financial information and implement identity theft. Any "contributions" you make are of course not contributions at all.

Confirm the Web address of any charity to which you want to donate over the Internet.

Viruses and Trojans are also a problem in fraudulent charity appeals. Scambusters says, "Spam is sent that includes photos of disaster areas or individual survivors, and these attachments contain computer viruses." The Trojan—basically, a false come-on—arrives through an e-mail and then generates access to your hard drive.

And then there's the old Nigerian prototype, the fee-scam. If you've had an e-mail address for any time, you've likely received an appeal from an important-sounding person from Nigeria who is, for a variety of legitimate-sounding reasons, having difficulty transferring some millions of dollars out of the country and now needs your help.

You are told that your help will earn you some significant percentage of the amount transferred. With just a small fee and a few bits of your financial records, you're on your way to millions—just for acting as a conduit and helping the poor soul keep his or her money out of the hands of those local bad guys in Nigeria.

A big lie. Not a dime ever sees a victim's hand. An Internet crime that, to date, cannot be tracked down.

We are not going to change society to the point that we eliminate the con-man in so many people, so we should do what we can: control our donations.

That means ensuring that we give only to those charities we know are not fraudulent.

WHEN THE RED Cross came under fire, Congress got interested.

When the GAO conducted its study on car donations, Congress got interested.

When it was made widely known that certain charities received very little money from fundraisers' efforts conducted by telemarketers, Congress got interested.

When the media reported on The Nature Conservancy's program to allow insiders to buy land and take advantage of the tax laws, Congress got interested.

Clearly, Congress should be interested in how charities conduct their business. Yet, since most members of Congress, with good reason, think highly of charities in their districts, absent a serious and growing list of complaints, strict measures are highly unlikely to be legislated. Some relatively minor changes might be made, but don't hold your breath.

In any case, more government oversight is not the answer.

IT'S UP TO you. You must get engaged in the charities you want to support. Nothing can take the place of your own efforts to learn about a charity's organization, finances, and work in the world. Educated, caring donors will do more to get charities to be more honest and transparent than anything else.

What can you do?

There is no official, comprehensive list. I can only share with you some of my own thoughts as they have developed over a few decades. Some ideas you will want to employ and some you won't. And some of your own might not be on the list at all.

Figure out where your heart is. With so many charities, certainly there are those that work in the areas you want to support. Conversely, a homeless shelter's efficiency won't mean a thing to you if you don't care about homeless people.

Find out what you can before you contact the charity. Go to the charity's Web site and review all the sections. You'll get a feel for what it thinks is important and how sophisticated it is in conveying information. Also, use a search engine to see if the charity has been in the news. The charity may have a press section on its Web site, but it usually won't have any bad news. It's nice to know, for example, if the charity has been sued recently.

By comparing where your heart is with the information on the Internet, you'll get a sense of whether this is the place for you.

Download a copy of the charity's 990 from the charity's site or from GuideStar. If the charity doesn't have a link to its 990s for the past several years, ask why. While you won't be interested in most of the document, you can see for yourself on just a few pages what the watchdogs use: the expenses, salaries of the key people, a list of the board members, and fundraising results. Charities have to provide three years of 990s, but they are not limited in what they can share. Ask for what you want to see.

What will happen to the community if the charity stops operating? I discussed this earlier, but don't forget to ask. It will reveal much.

Ask to see the annual report. Although this can often seem like a glossy, confusing, and self-serving publication, it will often reveal the accomplishments the charity thinks are important. It will also outline its financial picture.

Ask about programs. What does the charity do? The Red Cross's problem after 9/11 wasn't that donated money wasn't used to support programs, but that donors weren't aware of the change in programmatic purpose. The 990 is too broad to give you any idea of how the charity addresses its programs, so you may want to know more than what is provided in the annual report.

Ask how many years the charity has been in business. A young charity may have higher overhead or fundraising expenses as a portion of its budget than older charities. Also, a young charity may not be where you want to invest, if you feel that it is too small or ineffective to do the job you want.

Ask about the trustees and the board. The board, as you now know, is responsible for the big issues at the charity. What is the structure of the board? What committees does the board use? What are its policies about providing meeting minutes?

While it's not necessary to know the reason for every decision, the completeness of what is shared will tell you a lot about how secretive the board is. Find out what kind of time the trustees spend on their jobs and whether they are paid. If they are paid, ask how much and why.

Also, find out how many charities each trustee serves on. A person who is spread too thin on boards—in addition to his or her professional and family commitments—may not be the most effective board member. Conversely, successful people are busy people, and some trustees are able to do many things. You should know, though, and decide for yourself whether the board members spend enough time with your charity's business or not.

Ask about the key staff. Charities experience far too much turnover, and longevity is key to making an impact on the community. In addition to asking about the experience of the executive director, ask about the backgrounds and professional qualifications of the chief financial officer and the top fundraiser.

Ask about transparency policies. In addition to board minutes and decisions, a charity should be willing to explain why it does what it does. If tuition went up last year, what led to the increase? If the board paid a lot of money to a departing executive director, ask why. Most important, ask to see the written policies relating to transparency that the charity has said it will uphold. See if they are adequate for you. Stay away from charities that have no policies on this topic.

Ask why you should give. Charities should have a compelling message when they ask for money.

Ask about the infrastructure. A charity that saves money, but can't do its work efficiently, isn't saving money. Ask the executive director about the charity's mechanical ability to do its work.

Ask about fundraising. If you have any questions about what the fundraising results mean, request a clearer explanation. Be careful, however, not to demand that something complex be made simple at the expense of accuracy or truthfulness. But if a charity says it raised a certain amount of money, ask whether that means it went into the bank or whether it's pledged, or where it is exactly.

Also, ask about the foundations that support the charity. An absence of foundation support isn't the worst thing, but it is true that most foundations carefully investigate the charities they support.

Target your giving. Once you know where your heart is, support the charity that you think will do the best job. One thousand dollars to one charity will do more good for society than ten one-hundred-dollar gifts.

Ask how the charity communicates important news to the public. Whether it issues press releases, or whether it uses physical letters or e-mail, ask to see copies of what was communicated. In particular, if you are aware of any negative publicity, you should want to know how the charity explains itself. This will give you a sense of how clear the charity is—not only of the job it does, but how people learn about its work.

Ask about gift-acceptance policies. If you make a gift for the endowment and it has a specific purpose, will your gift increase the amount going to that purpose, or is money just being shifted around? It's not so bad if it's being shifted around, but you should know. The charity ought to have comprehensive written policies on gift acceptance procedures and should be eager to share them with you.

Ask about ethics policies. Rarer than well-thought-out gift-acceptance policies is the ethics policy. The document needs to be more than a statement of vigorously following the law and should address the way the place runs even though it is not required to. Although the bulk of the Sarbanes Oxley Act applies only to for-profit corporations, charities are not prevented from adopting the spirit of openness the act tries to enforce. For example, charities now are more likely to have a policy where they change their auditors every few years, so that the relationship isn't too cozy. Also, some charities have implemented a whistle-blower policy, making it easier for employees to raise concerns about their superiors.

Charities should also have a conflict-of-interest policy. Despite the scandals and a growing public awareness of the role charities play in society, far too few charities have ethics policies.

You should delay your donation until a charity develops and writes its ethics policies to your satisfaction.

NOW THAT YOU have something to get you started, let loose. Don't be shy. It's your money.

At first, you'll probably have to talk with someone in person. After a while, however, as more people ask more questions, charities will voluntarily become more expansive and put the information on their Web sites.

You'll note that there are very few questions that I think ought to be answered uniformly. I impose no grade or star system. No financial thresholds. Charities are too complex and too filled with their own legitimate nuances to impose a one-size-fits-all mindset. Besides, nobody should tell you what should be important to you. If a charity is in financial trouble, you'll find out. Even if it is, though, it could still deserve your support. It's your call, and no matter what you decide—as long as you know what you're doing—it's not wrong.

Your inquiry should not be—and should not be inferred by the charity to be—a punitive process. Foundations ask detailed questions all the time. So should you.

Start from the premise that the charity is doing quite fine in everything it does. Expect good will from the people who work and volunteer there.

Most charities, even if they're not used to the kind of scrutiny you may now impose, are good places. Give them any benefit of the doubt. Even though most charities could do a far better job of communicating what they do—and many could do a better job of executing what they do—just a tiny fraction are real troublemakers.

But charities that are not open and honest with the public should invoke the ire of donors. A charity needs to take itself seriously enough to examine itself critically.

The public has a right it has never exercised as a group, and it is time to understand that right and its implications. Many charities would have kept themselves out of a lot of hot water had they been proactive about explaining what they do and how they do it. The more charities are transparent, and the more the public demands transparency—a demand that can be backed up by withholding donations—the less the need for legislative action, and the fewer the stories about charity malfeasance.

From a personal perspective, the most important criterion of all is your heart. You must be certain that the charity's mission means something important to you. But if you don't think that donating means engaging yourself beyond where your heart takes you—whether in the aftermath of a disaster, during the calm of an annual solicitation, or whenever else a charity calls upon you for help—then, when you are upset, you will have no one but yourself to blame.

The bad news is that it's up to you.

The good news, also, is that it's up to you.

EPILOGUE

*"Human beings have neither kindness, nor faith, nor charity beyond
what serves to increase the pleasure of the moment."*
Virginia Woolf

I SEE HIM every day. He stands, sometimes sits, on the corner of two major
streets in downtown Washington, D.C.

The streets are full of pedestrians hurrying somewhere. In the immediate background I can hear the cars and trucks rumbling by; in the
deeper background a siren—it seems to be coming this way—will soon
warn the traffic to move aside. The sounds of the city.

It could be any corner of almost any major American city, and the
image would be the same: a man wearing tattered clothes and a cup on
the sidewalk directly in front of him with a scrawled sign. Something like:
"Please. No home. No work. No money. Help."

Every weekday morning, he sits there, repeating his barely audible plea
at each passerby. When I furtively glance down to the ground at his cup—
when I'm not peering into the indeterminate distance in mock
concentration, a sophomoric effort to avoid looking at him—I see a
smattering of hard change; on a rare occasion something that folds.

He is pathetic. He is ugly and smelly and most certainly unaccom-
plished. Worst of all, in one skill he is accomplished; he has the effrontery

to ask me for money. He is not subtle. He simply asks, "Could you spare some change?"

When he says this, he tries to smile, and his mouth widens enough so I see that most of his teeth are missing; the ones that aren't are decayed and sooty. He looks me in the eyes. I avert mine.

This wretched soul was once a boy, a boy who may have, in his distant past, thought of a life that did not include begging on the street. He may have begun his life in the ghetto, but somewhere along the way he might have thought about a life in society as an attorney, a businessman, a teacher. Perhaps he once was.

Now, he's a bum. An elderly white male whom I strongly suspect is an alcoholic.

Chances are he is in desperate need of medical attention. His mind may be gone or, as is the case with many beggars, it may never have been fully present. But here he is, reaching out to people in search of their dreams and reminding them that he is nothing near anyone's idea of a dream. Just a nightmare.

And he is not the only one. They seem to be everywhere, on so many corners and stoops. So many dashed hopes all in one place. It's overwhelming.

Dashed hopes, perhaps, but disgusting nonetheless. The last time I looked, the newspaper was full of job advertisements. But this man wants charity.

THE BUM ON the street is possibly the closest we get to confronting what it means to be purely charitable. The money we transfer, when the guilt overwhelms, as it sometimes does, is used immediately for its purpose. It may go toward a beer or some other drink, and, less often, toward something to eat. But the charity is used by the person to whom it is given.

No overhead. No fundraising costs. No administration.

Still, I am unlikely to give. I have other priorities. Guilt fights with reason, however, and I'm distracted by uncomfortable thoughts.

The beggar takes the same spot each day, as if that spot were his designated place of business. He catches my eye as well as my ear. He is quite popular, actually, as he greets the morning commuters with not-so-bad renditions of melodies produced from an old and battered trumpet. He receives a bit of money each day. He cheerily talks to people as they pass, whether or not they drop some cash into the small cup next to him on the sidewalk; the man is working for his quarters. His approach to it all generates smiles.

Perhaps we think of him not as a beggar, but as a worker. The others, those who don't perform—those who look droopy and sad—are not so popular and I seldom see anyone actually give money to any of them. I suspect that the few quarters in their cups are often just seed money to persuade passersby to give on the basis that others have already done so. A marketing strategy.

They must receive some money, I surmise, or else they would not be there day after day. But maybe not, their work ethic such that this is as strenuous as it gets. Certainly, it is a tough existence.

I normally pass them by. I don't, as a rule, give money to a homeless person. Not any more. I accept that the plunk of a pebble makes almost no difference in the ocean. And even though he's no ocean—any tiny bit helps him—if I continued to follow my conscience, to allow my guilt to take over, my wallet would forever be empty.

There's the conundrum that faces all of us who like to think we have a conscience: what to do when confronted with others who are so much less fortunate?

So Others Might Eat (SOME), a charity that serves the homeless in Washington, D.C., acknowledges that responding to a homeless person's request for money is a personal decision, but suggests that, if we don't give, we at least acknowledge the person with a polite "no" or "not today." This, I am told, is better than simply ignoring the person. SOME also asks that, whatever we do, we leave our judgments aside.

From time to time, I lose the battle with my conscience. The lesson learned early on is not absolute, and a compromise emerges. I will do this, but only this, and only rarely: I will walk up to the person and tell him that I will purchase a sandwich, a bowl of soup, and coffee or a soft drink for him. This I will do in lieu of providing actual cash. I will walk with him the half–block or so to the nearest street vendor, ask the beggar what he would like, and then purchase it. I will then walk away.

I am not interested in his thanks or his feelings. I'm not there to discuss anything with him. I don't care if he'd prefer a stop at the liquor store. Beggars can't be choosers. It is an extremely uncomfortable moment and I want it to pass as soon as possible.

Most of us experience discomfort when confronted with a homeless person, but the experience is made all the more uncomfortable by actually engaging with the person, actually talking to him, actually sending words out that need response. Actually looking at his face. Where does one find meaning in such an exchange? But then, whence the impulse to help at all?

Why the food and not just the money? Why go through the process of enduring the actual transaction? The person is not good company; we don't have a lot to talk about. Won't my self-imposed obligation to help the person end with success only if I drop a dollar or a quarter into the cup? The exchange I choose costs four dollars and seventy-three cents.

I do not know this person. Either way—whether I help or don't—I walk away from the person slightly changed. An uncomfortable confrontation has taken place, and I am forced to examine my role in a great sea of people, many of whom are walking or driving to work to sit at computers all day long, dressed smartly, thinking nothing of spending five dollars for a paper cup full of fancy coffee and another fifty dollars for lunch.

These people will then return home from work to eat meals calibrated to provide the most taste and nourishment, the product of pricey supermarkets, and spend time with their spouses and children. Their idea of a problematic life is not spending enough time with their families, or that they must take their cell phones and their computers with them on vacations. They might worry about which car to take on a day-trip to the country or how they will endure the horror of a child who has earned only a B in her private school English exam. Perhaps the household is short on dog food or toilet paper. Maybe the husband worries about his wife learning of his extra-marital relationship. Many people walk by with serious financial concerns: the late mortgage, an unpaid hospital bill, the IRS.

That people fret over such matters would make the homeless person feel that he lives in a world inhabited by aliens. He must make do without any money at all. His life is incomprehensible to us.

So incomprehensible, a large portion of our population thinks very little about this. The idea of community or home does not include the

vagabonds who—even if the fault is not entirely theirs (and how convenient to rationalize that it is)—stoop so low as to ask for money on
the street.

And in exchange for nothing at all!

When there are jobs to be had, work to be done, one's self-respect to
re-acquire—how can these people muster the gumption to beg? While
it's possible that the beggar had no education beyond fifth grade, or that
his mental capacities are rivaled by those celebrating their seventh birthday, is that any fault of mine? Is it, even, of society's?

Success stories are littered with erstwhile poverty. Effrontery, indeed.

If you react this way, some would say you are privileged. The minister and philosopher Reinhold Niebuhr in his book *Moral Man and
Immoral Society* said harshly, "It has always been the habit of privileged
groups to deny the oppressed classes every opportunity for the cultivation of innate capacities and then to accuse them of lacking what they
have been denied the right to acquire."

But of course, that's nothing but naïve balderdash. The beggar is inferior to me. I look at him in disgust as the world passes. The sound of the
sirens—I can discern more than one now—gets closer.

ALTRUISM: "DEVOTION TO the welfare of others, regard for others, as a
principle of action; opposed to egoism or selfishness." The paradox of
altruism is that its ideal is impossible for humans to attain.

Sure, we can be devoted to the welfare of others. We are devoted to
the welfare of our children or our parents—we want to see no harm
come to them. But at what point do we stop? Where do we decide that
doing something on behalf of someone else conflicts with our own sense
of well-being?

If a deed is performed with a total lack of selfishness—the core idea
of altruism—then even satisfaction, the good feeling of helping another,
must be absent. Nikolay Levin, a character in Tolstoy's *Anna Karenina*
reflects: "If goodness has a cause, it is no longer goodness; if it has
consequences—a reward—it is not goodness either."

The seed of altruism may never fully blossom—not in humans anyway. But we often want to do good, and good can be expressed by
helping others.

We don't deny the beggar our quarter because we need the quarter. Something else is at play. Conversely, charitable donations are often not the stuff of sacrifice. Even after making his stunning gift to the Gates Foundation, Warren Buffett still had billions to spare. His charity did not affect his ability to buy a hamburger or a cup of coffee.

News accounts of charitable gifts do not speak of sacrifice. They report of generosity, but not of what must be denied as a result.

As the result of a wealthy man's charitable bequest, the widow perhaps received less than she would have otherwise. But who can believe she has been forced to alter her lifestyle?

Besides, what sacrifices can one make, really, after death? As someone who once raised money for Dartmouth College said, he often explained to alumni that they couldn't take their possessions with them and that, if they could, their possessions would probably burn anyway.

The Christian tradition calls for tithing. So do the Jewish and Muslim religious teachings.

Muslims traditionally give during the holy month of Ramadan, the ninth month of the Islamic calendar, which falls late in the year on the Gregorian calendar. Muslims are obligated to donate at least 2-1/2 percent of their net worth each year as part of *zakat*, a tenet of Islam similar to Christian tithing. Muslims often fulfill *zakat* by supporting a charity or giving money to a needy relative, neighbor, or friend. And Jews are told, as are Christians, to donate 10 percent of their savings.

Doesn't sacrifice play a role in generosity or in what we think of as charity? Do the religions have a clause in the small print providing an out if a sacrifice must be made, if that 10 percent would interfere with an outing at the movies or with needed clothing or food? Or does that obligation apply only when it does not cut away from what is needed?

What is generosity without sacrifice?

SOME YEARS BACK, at a twenty-fifth alumni reunion at Phillips Exeter Academy, three ministers spoke at a seminar about religion. Those in the audience had once thought, as they came of age in the relatively cynical late 1960s and early 1970s, the topic to be irrelevant. They vividly remembered the April 8, 1966, cover of *Time* magazine, which boldly, starkly—and, by some standards, offensively—asked the Nietzschian question, "Is God Dead?"

The room was packed.

Deep into the discussion, one member of the audience—his name was Graf—rose to ask a remarkable question. In recalling the difficult time of the Vietnam War, he noted that, for him, the choice had been to fight or avoid the military draft. He commented on how that choice was philosophically small compared to the choices so many others have had to make in truly difficult times.

Would he, he wondered, have been able to choose not identifying a Jew in Nazi Germany in order to save his soul, if not his life? Would he have served patriotically in World War II, which, in his view, threatened the security of the United States in a way that the Vietnam conflict never did, and face possible death fighting for a cause to save others?

These were choices of import.

Graf wondered if there was a way he could have been taught to know if he possessed untested courage or none at all. How could he have known if he was equal to a real challenge? How could he know whether there was a cause somewhere out there for which he would be willing to die, and whether the concept of religion could help him find the answer?

The question was awesome, revealing a vulnerability most people would not dare acknowledge.

After a period of awkward and fascinating silence, one of the ministers said, "You say you want to know if there are any causes for which you would die. Let me ask this: are there any causes for which you would live?"

After some thought, Graf said that yes, he would live for his partner, that he found great daily joy in living for him.

Then, the minister asked, "Would you die for him?"

A longer pause, a tentative smile quickly erased, a creased forehead in an effort to deal with a wholly unexpected question, a show of discomfort, another smile—all this while standing alone in a room full of people intensely curious about the moment's drama and its main actor. And then, finally, a response: "I don't know."

From the heart, his answer bared him in front of the audience. Not satisfied with his own response, one for which he could not have prepared, Graf steeled his resolve. With a nod of finality, he repeated, "I don't know."

The ball's in your court now. You're the expert, the man of God. You tell me how I should answer.

"Think about it," the minister insisted. "Would you die for him?" An expert whose life's work takes him between the lines and inside heads to unspoken words and fears, the minister would have none of it. If you're going to bring up such a profound idea, the minister seemed to be saying, you're going to have to think on your own just a tad more.

A truly long silence then followed. The seriousness was now sinking in. In situations such as that, more than a few seconds seems like a long time. Anything longer, and an audience of over one hundred people can get uncomfortable.

On this day this crowd was uncomfortable, for sure, but not impatient. No one could be heard breathing. Still, people noticed the pressure. This was a reunion, after all, not confession.

Finally, after slightly more than one full minute, with over one hundred people practically holding their breaths, Graf said with resolve, "I've never thought about that before, but, yes, now that you ask the question, I'd have to say that I would die for my partner."

Although no one spoke, after a few moments the room was awakening to a growing comprehension: that at least one person among them had acknowledged he was willing to sacrifice a great deal.

Graf could not know that for certain, of course; the setting was not a true test, nor even a laboratory. He was engaged in a discussion of the mind at a forum, hardly on the brink of making any decisions or doing anything that would actually test his courage in the world beyond. Still, it was more of an examination than he had ever allowed himself, and during it he told himself and others that he would make a great sacrifice.

WE LAUD STORIES of sacrifice. The words "Let's roll" evoke the chaotic efforts of Todd Beamer aboard United Flight #93 on September 11, 2001, as the plane was overtaken by terrorists. Due in large part to his efforts—after he told his wife, in the last words he would ever speak to her, that he and the others would try to stop the hijacking—the plane was flown into the ground, killing all aboard. A death trip to save others.

Altruism should be reserved for describing this type of moment. Not for insisting that a building have your name on it.

If we think that giving away a dollar is contrary to human nature, then how can we explain the willingness to risk one's own life on behalf of someone else?

It is a love of humankind. For our lives to be meaningful, we must encompass the lives of others. And not just the ones we love, either. A strand of something connects all of us. We are not islands.

The definition of philanthropy is the love of humankind. If not with sacrifice, then with generosity.

Certainly, then, can't a quarter be found?

THE IMAGE EVOKED by the phrase "charity begins at home" is of taking care of one's family before venturing out to tackle the unknown. While it's noble to give of yourself and your means to your friends, community members, and others, it is foolhardy to do so at the expense of your own family. If you have difficulty putting bread on your table or are strained to pay your children's college tuition, by all means, and without apology, be charitable toward your family first.

But that's not charity. Taking care of family is an obligation. What does charity have to do with it? Don't we reserve the idea of charity for those not nearby? Think of it. Do you go to the grocery store after a hard day's work to buy food for your family because you are *charitable*? Purchasing food—or clothes or soccer lessons or school trips—for your children comes under the category of parental obligation, not charity.

Charity is most often offered to people we don't know, and it often means suspending our cynicism about what another person or organization will do with the money. It means that we must be more than ourselves, that we and our families are not the only *us* on the planet, that others are also part of this world and to some degree our responsibility, even though we impose that responsibility voluntarily.

Tens of millions of people in the United States think of those who receive charity as a whole community of unknowns in need. And they find no paradox in defining *home* in this far broader way. Indeed, the idea goes well past that, to future generations, to animals, to the earth itself. Many of us want to help, want to give. Charity, guided by where the heart goes, can go anywhere and be anyplace and help anyone.

REINHOLD NIEBUHR SAID that philanthropy is a form of paternalism, that the privileged class tries to preserve its status by doling out funds to the needy. In *Moral Man and Immoral Society*, he says, "the generosities of the privileged" are "efforts to incite the envy of their fellowmen by a display of their resources." He also says that "philanthropy combines genuine pity with the display of power and that latter element explains why the powerful are more inclined to be generous than to grant social justice."

After reading that you might think generosity a form of injustice, a form of judgment. Is that where critical thinking on the roots of charity takes us?

The Jewish tradition, in fact, talks of this very divide and asserts that the whole point is justice. The beggar on the street may be looking for charity, but he—or we on his behalf—cannot help but think how unjust his circumstances are.

Charity should be the stones with which the road to justice is paved.

If it just weren't so awkward. How can we take charity to better places, beyond the feelings of superiority, beyond the irony that we care about society even though our ability to care is derived from our sense of privilege?

The Jewish word *Tzedakah* is about a more complex act than merely giving to the needy. It is really an expression of justice, with charity as the vehicle. The obligation to perform *Tzedakah* can be fulfilled by giving money to the poor, to health–care institutions, to synagogues, educational institutions. It can also be fulfilled by supporting children beyond the age when parents are legally required to, or supporting parents in their old age. To the learned Jew the familiar concept of donating goes well beyond satisfying one's ego with mere numbers, claiming that this or that amount was given in any one year. In fact, according to Jewish tradition, the donor's spiritual benefit when giving to the poor is so great that a beggar actually does the donor a favor by giving the donor the opportunity to perform *Tzedakah*. Think of that: the beggar does the *donor* a favor. Accepting charity is good.

When someone offers you something, the person wants you to accept the offer. Refusing is akin to saying that the offer isn't good enough. Accepting the offer honors the donor.

Acknowledging that charity involves two points of satisfaction may be the intellectual escape route from the awkwardness. It may be the explanation that serves both donors and recipients of gifts.

By the way, Judaism acknowledges an otherwise unspoken truth when it comes to helping the poor: that many people who ask for charity have no genuine need. In fact, the Talmud suggests that this is a good thing. If all people who asked for charity were in genuine need, we would be subject to punishment from God for refusing anyone who asked. The existence of fraud diminishes our liability for failing to give to all who ask because we have some legitimate basis for doubting the beggar's sincerity. That is, it is permissible to investigate the legitimacy of a beggar—or a charity—before donating.

We can doubt the beggar's sincerity, even while recognizing the act of giving to the beggar as an act of justice. We can also question his attentiveness to employment opportunities. A person has an obligation to avoid becoming in need of *Tzedakah* and should take any work that is available, even if he thinks it is beneath his dignity, to avoid becoming a public charge.

Yet if a person is truly in need and has no way to obtain money on his own, he should not feel embarrassed to accept *Tzedakah*. No person should feel too proud to take money from others. In fact, it is considered a transgression to refuse *Tzedakah*. Some say that to make yourself suffer by refusing to accept *Tzedakah* is equivalent to shedding your own blood.

Perhaps, because the idea of charity is fraught with awkwardness or contradiction, true charity may be larger than we all think. The idea of helping others, because it is so ingrained in a vague religious understanding, and because our everyday lives are filled with so many reasons to give that have nothing to do with generosity, may be confused with merely parting from money.

Tzedakah, however, gets past that. It means justice and, according to some, it is the highest of all the commandments, indeed equal to all the others combined. In Judaism, giving to the poor is not viewed as a generous, magnanimous act; it is simply an act of justice and righteousness, the performance of a duty: giving the poor their due.

Giving to the poor is an obligation in Judaism, a duty even of those who are themselves in need. Furthermore, those who are dependent on public assistance or living on the edge of subsistence may give less; no person should give so much that he or she would become a public burden.

Certain kinds of *Tzedakah* are better than others. From the merely good to the best, there are giving begrudgingly; giving less than you should, but giving it cheerfully; giving after being asked; giving before being asked; giving when you do not know the recipient's identity but the recipient knows your identity; giving when you know the recipient's identity but the recipient doesn't know your identity; giving when neither party knows the other's identity; and finally, enabling the recipient to become self-reliant.

How can tossing a quarter or a dollar into a can make a beggar self-reliant? It doesn't, of course, but not doing so doesn't do much for us either.

On the other hand, I can't give him money all the time.

THE SIRENS ARE upon me now, and I now recognize what is going on. But for my absorption, I would have recognized in this capital city of the United States, the most charitable country on earth, the difference between the sirens of an ambulance and those of a motorcade.

I look up, as even the most calloused Washingtonians do, if only briefly, as the motorcycles and the police cars and the vans and the luxury limousines (an ambulance just in case) quickly pass by. As I look toward the moving, darkened window of one of the limousines (there is always a decoy), I imagine the President on the other side.

I wonder what it takes to move this one man from one place to another in this city, to say nothing of what it costs to transport him to another city or another country. It's mind-boggling when you think of the approximately $75 required to fill the tank of each of the many vehicles, to say nothing of an airplane that requires $15,000 worth of fuel for each hour it flies

Then I think about the tiny, infinitesimal fraction of that which would feed and clothe and shelter this man—and so many others—for a very long time. Although we quickly deny it—our consciences loathe going there—some lives are clearly more valuable than others.

Tzedakah and charity are for people. Government—the public purse—does not, and never will, provide enough.

AS I BEGIN to move on along the street I again look into his eyes. The question has troubled me long enough, and I want to know, even though I never will: what has society done to create this terrible inequity? What can I do to correct it? How can I give money, no matter how modest, without feeling superior, and how can a person who feels superior dispense charity or justice?

Yet my refusal to give must be allowable, for I am in charge of what charity—or is it merely money?—that I wish to dispense. It is at this moment that I am grateful to the middleman, the structured organization whose purpose is to take my money while keeping from me the awkward exposure to its real work.

To demand that he use whatever I give him for food or something else that I deem worthy accomplishes nothing; it mocks charity. In so doing I would belittle the idea of equality, and after all, although my clothes are expensive and I can choose where I eat and sleep, I am, I can only hope, his equal.

When I give something, I no longer demand that he forego his liquor and buy a sandwich.

In his humble pity, he reflects perfectly the values of our society, of my neighbors. Me. And so I live each day in the anguish, only slightly tempered by repetition, of not knowing what to do. Some questions cannot be answered, at least for the ages. So each day, confronted with the same question, I answer anew and often differently.

One observation, when I do dare to look, is the same no matter what I do: in his eyes, as clearly as if reflected in a mirror, through the sadness and the want, I see myself. He is not, in fact, inferior to me. If a life can be the measure of sacrifice, and if this man's life means anything to my idea of community and therefore to me, surely a quarter must be within reach.

While I fear that my charity encourages me to act like God, I realize it does much more: my charity brings me closer to Him.

INDEX

Second Harvest 101
Secrities and Exchange Commission 39, 46, 47, 124, 125, 265
Self-dealing 30
Senate Finance Committee 145, 149–151, 153, 154, 171, 219, 242
Shanahan, Maribeth 74
Silber, John 16, 18, 20, 242
Simmons, Terry 123, 124, 128, 129
Simon, William 43, 46
Simpson, Mike 243
Small, Lawrence 199, 243
Smithson, James 199
Smithsonian Institution 193, 199–201, 211, 243
Smithsonian Institution - Museum of American History 193, 200
So Others Might Eat 277
Solferino, Italy 157, 158
Souter, David 223
Southern Baptist 23, 24, 27, 30, 32, 36, 175
Spring Arbor College 45
Stanford University 18, 72, 112
Stanford University School of Medicine 45
"State of Nonprofit America, The" (Salamon, Lester) 259
Stengel, Beverly 167
Stupak, Bart 164
Suer, Oral 11
Supreme Court, U.S. 85–87, 114, 223, 225, 266
Sycuan Band of the Kumeyaay Nation 167

T

Tauzin, Bill 165
Telemarketers 221–226, 267, 268
Telemarketing 222, 224–226, 241
Templeton, John 43
Terrorism 97, 100, 104, 106, 107, 155, 165
Terrorists 99–103, 106, 282
Thompson & Knight 123
Tocqueville, Alexis de 59–62, 87
Towey, Jim 84
Tran, Kim 11, 12
Transylvania University 181
Tresson, W. Kyle 33

Trumbull, John 112
Tulane University 207–209, 250
Turner, Ted 194, 202–204
Tyco 50, 52
Tzedakah 284–286

U

United Arab Emirates 173
United for a Fair Economy 244
United Jewish Appeal 122
United Nations 194, 202–204
United Nations Foundation 194
United Negro College Fund 205
United Way
  of America 3–6, 9, 10, 19, 52, 56, 257
  of Central New Mexico 3, 8, 9
  of the National Capital Area 11
  "United Way Scandal, The" (Glaser, John) 5–7, 55, 265
University
  of North Carolina at Chapel Hill 77
  of Pennsylvania 43, 45, 80, 81, 205
  of Richmond 125
  of Southern California 205
  of Wisconsin - Milwaukee 105
  of Wyoming 172, 173

V

Vanderbilt University 242
VietNow 222

W

Watchdogs 249–255, 258, 263
Watkins, Thayer 38
Webb, Igor 17
Webster, Daniel 87
WEDU 252, 253
Welch, Jack 244
Whack-A-Mole 131, 132
White, Douglas 125–128
White Pine Trail State Park 211
White, Rick 125, 127, 128
Whitehead, John 43
Whitworth College 45
"Why Charity?" (Douglas, James) 69